LIGHTHOUSE
DISPATCHES

LIGHTHOUSE DISPATCHES

Ramblings of a Modern-Day Lightkeeper

Paul Morralee

ONTARIO HISTORY PRESS

2024

© Copyright 2024 Paul Morralee

All rights reserved. No part of this publication may be reproduced, stored in a retrieval system, or transmitted in any form or by any means, electronic, mechanical, photocopying, recording, or otherwise, without the prior written permission of the author.

The dynamic nature of the Internet and the World Wide Web can cause web addresses or links contained in this book to change, and they may no longer be valid after publication.

The views expressed in this work are solely those of the author and do not necessarily reflect the views of the publisher, and the publisher hereby disclaims any responsibility for them.

The author has claimed all responsibility for securing the rights to any photographs, images, quotations or other material which appear in this publication, and the publisher acknowledges the author's responsibility to secure all rights.

ISBN paperback: 978-1-7387801-2-9
ISBN hard cover: 978-1-7387801-3-6

Ontario History Press
Prince Edward County, Ontario, Canada
2024

Comments and inquiries can be sent to the author at
press@ontariohistory.ca

This book is available from local booksellers and from major online retailers.

Front cover photo, *Paul Painting the No.10 Lighthouse*, by Lissi Ranta, 2016
Back cover photo, *Porphyry Island, c.1935*, courtesy of the Mckay Family Collection
Cover design by Rita Visser

Table of Contents

Preface	1
Editor's Note	3
Chart Showing CLLS Lighthouses	4
Introduction	7
2015 – The Rookie Lightkeeper	9
2016 – All of Us Working Together	25
2017 – Unexpected Visitors	49
2018 – A Sense of Peace and Tranquility	71
2019 – Monarch Butterflies and Crashing Waves	103
2020 – Self-Isolating... Since 1873	127
2021 – Pandemic Restrictions Relaxed	165
2022 – Visitors From Around the World	201
2023 – 150 Years of Lightkeeping	241
2024 – Now, a Veteran Lightkeeper	289
2025 and Beyond	335
Index	339

Vignettes

Steamship *Thordoc*	14
The Point Porphyry Lighthouse	23
The Shaganash (No.10) Lighthouse	28
The McKays — A Family of Lightkeepers	36
Lightkeeper Andrew Dick	48
Porphyry Harbour	52
The Graham Family	59
CLLS and the Ontario Historical Society	80
Porphyry Island's New Light Tower	99
Canadian Coast Guard Supply Ships	119
The Wooden Boat *Nina*	130
Lightkeeper Charles Merritt	135
The Silver Islet Mine	151
The Heritage Lighthouse Protection Act	168
Porphyry Island Provincial Park Nature Reserve	179
Lighthouse Automation	196
The Porphyry Helipad	218
The Trowbridge Island Lighthouse	235
Lake Superior Islands	252
The Boreal Forest	265
Lake Superior National Marine Conservation Area	279
The Lake Superior Water Trail	297

Preface

As a little explorer splashing around in the River Thame, a charming tributary to England's famous Thames River, history was my playmate. In the picturesque Cotswold village of Dorchester-on-Thames where my family resided, every stone whispered tales of the past.

Fast-forward, moving to Canada at age five, and water and history continued to weave through my life, introducing me to the majestic Ottawa River surrounded by Algonquin tribes, lumber tycoons, and nuclear science wizards. My father's adventures at the Chalk River Nuclear Labs sparked my curiosity for engineering, while my mother was a household hero keeping us kids in line, as I have two brothers and a sister. Inspired by my mother's dedication, I dove into volunteer work when I was just eleven, teaming up with Oxfam to provide famine-relief in Africa.

Embarking on a filmmaking career for thirty years led me to a whirlwind of adventures across the globe, satisfying my curiosity and unveiling the intricate web of connections in the world. Then, settling into the industrial city of Thunder Bay, my current home, I felt an irresistible pull towards majestic Lake Superior. I acquired a charming old wooden boat named *Nina*, transforming her into my cozy, summer retreat for idyllic lake explorations. Immersed in various marine-related roles with a number of non-profit organizations, I savoured the great outdoors away from the city buzz.

My life changed considerably when I started volunteering to help fulfill the mandate of Canadian Lighthouses of Lake Superior and then taking on the role of managing director. For me, the only option was to go forward by investing time to develop these lighthouses for visitors to further explore and enjoy.

Based on the remote Porphyry Island and armed with an enormous "to-do" list, it took some determination and persistence for me to establish a weekly routine of sending a "Lighthouse Dispatch" to the local newspaper. This process began with reviewing my notes from the daily lighthouse log, sorting through my photographs, conversing with volunteers, and compiling a list of topics to write about. Then, like a machine-gun, "tatta-tat-tat", I would rapidly convey the facts of the week's happenings, always striving for precision in my choice of words. In each sentence, I aimed to paint a vivid picture through language; hopefully igniting the reader's imagination and engagement. My objective was to share the sights, sounds, tastes, and smells of the lighthouse islands to entice people to visit.

Sharing my experiences on this Lake Superior island has been truly rewarding, especially when witnessing the reactions of visitors. Over the past decade, as the *de facto* lightkeeper welcoming guests to the lighthouse, I've found joy in observing how people cherish the moments that create lasting memories. Visitors, volunteers, and boaters alike are captivated by the island's ecology, geology, the pristine waters of Lake Superior, the breathtaking views and, of course, the enchanting lighthouse stories.

The traditional role of lightkeepers has begun to fade now since most light stations across Canada have been fully automated. Reviving parts of this history today invites readers to reflect on the significance of safely transporting people and goods across this vast inland sea we call Lake Superior. The accounts of the hardships faced by keepers offer valuable insights into and appreciation of the conveniences of modern life. This retrospective encourages us to pause and reconsider our role within the environment.

Having lived for the past thirty years in Thunder Bay, Ontario, an industrial hub known for trans-shipment and blue-collar jobs, I find excitement in sharing with residents what lays just beyond the harbour breakwater. Comforted by the hum of this industrial city, Lake Superior constantly calls me to explore further. I have recognized the value of being on these islands, and my desire has become clear: to share this experience with others.

I would like to sincerely thank Marc Seguin from Ontario History Press for his invaluable guidance and editing of *Lighthouse Dispatches: Ramblings of a Modern-Day Lightkeeper*, and for the captivating design and presentation of this book. I also wish to express my gratitude to those who reviewed the draft, including Andrew Ehn, Susan Wade, Marjorie Seguin, and John Morralee; your insights were incredibly helpful. A special thanks goes to Chen Chekki, the news editor of *The Chronicle-Journal* newspaper, who played a crucial role in the early development of the "Lighthouse Dispatches" column by reviewing and editing the work.

I am grateful to Donny Wabasse, my collaborator at Porphyry until last year, for his creativity, dedication, and breathtaking photography that brought our journey to life. His wisdom, spirit, and support significantly enhanced the visitor experience.

I would like to acknowledge the founding board of directors of the Canadian Lighthouses of Lake Superior, some of whom have sadly passed away. Your support and guidance have been vital over the years. I also appreciate the hard work of the many volunteers, supporters, and sponsors whose names are mentioned throughout the book. Your contributions have been essential.

Finally, I want to thank all the readers who followed the "Lighthouse Dispatches" adventure in *The Chronicle-Journal* over the years. Your feedback and comments made my time on the isolated island a truly rewarding experience.

Paul Morralee
Managing Director
Canadian Lighthouses of Lake Superior
November, 2024

Editor's Note

As the editor and publisher of *Lighthouse Dispatches: Ramblings of a Modern-Day Lightkeeper*, it has been my great pleasure to devote much of my time and energy over the last year to produce this book for Paul Morralee and Canadian Lighthouses of Lake Superior (CLLS). For many years now, I've been a passionate heritage lighthouse preservationist and, as founder of the lighthouse protection group, Save Our Lighthouses, as well as principal of the publishing house, Ontario History Press, I knew it would be a labour of love for me to bring this book to print and introduce others to Paul's amazing accomplishments on Lake Superior.

Paul has spent every summer of the past ten years working to preserve and promote lighthouses while also writing a weekly newspaper column for Thunder Bay's *Chronicle-Journal*. When he first told me of this decade-long series of articles highlighting the happenings and events at Point Porphyry and the other lighthouses maintained by CLLS, I immediately offered to volunteer my services to compile his articles along with the related photographs and explanatory vignettes into a book that would form a complete record of the amazing work that he and many, many volunteers have done to conserve these iconic structures. This was to be my own, minor contribution to these efforts to preserve the lighthouses and their stories.

While many of the original newspaper articles have been carefully edited, they all remain true to Paul's straightforward style and his ability to tease out the essence of the activities at the lighthouses while downplaying his own enormous contribution to the cause. His work over the past ten years can serve as a model for other lighthouse preservation organizations across Canada. Paul's high energy level combined with his ability to establish connections with people, coordinate volunteers and manage day-to-day operations on a remote island in Lake Superior is truly remarkable.

Thank you Paul, for all of your efforts as a modern-day lightkeeper, helping to preserve an important part of Canada's built heritage and our country's history.

Marc Seguin
Editor and Publisher
Ontario History Press
November, 2024.

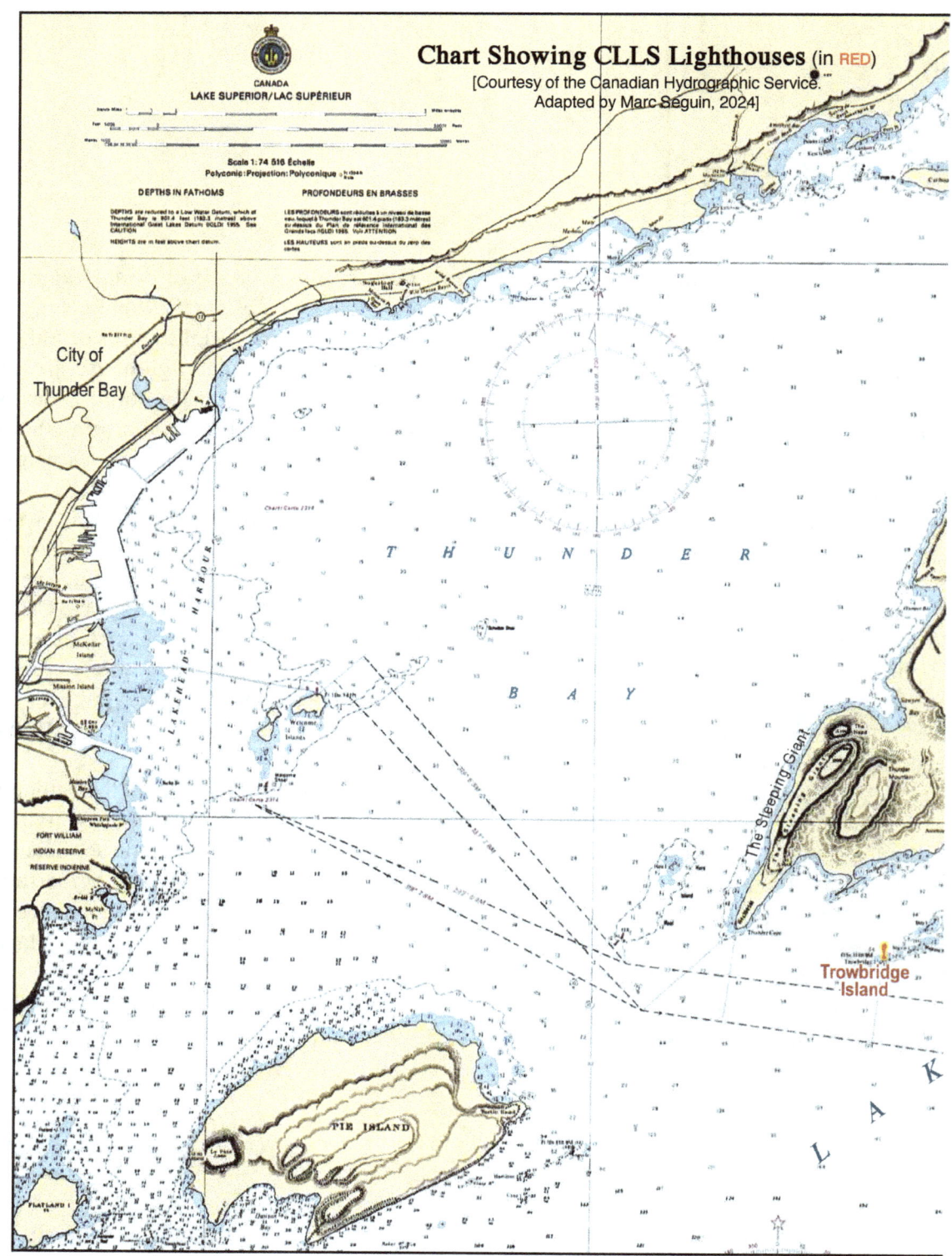

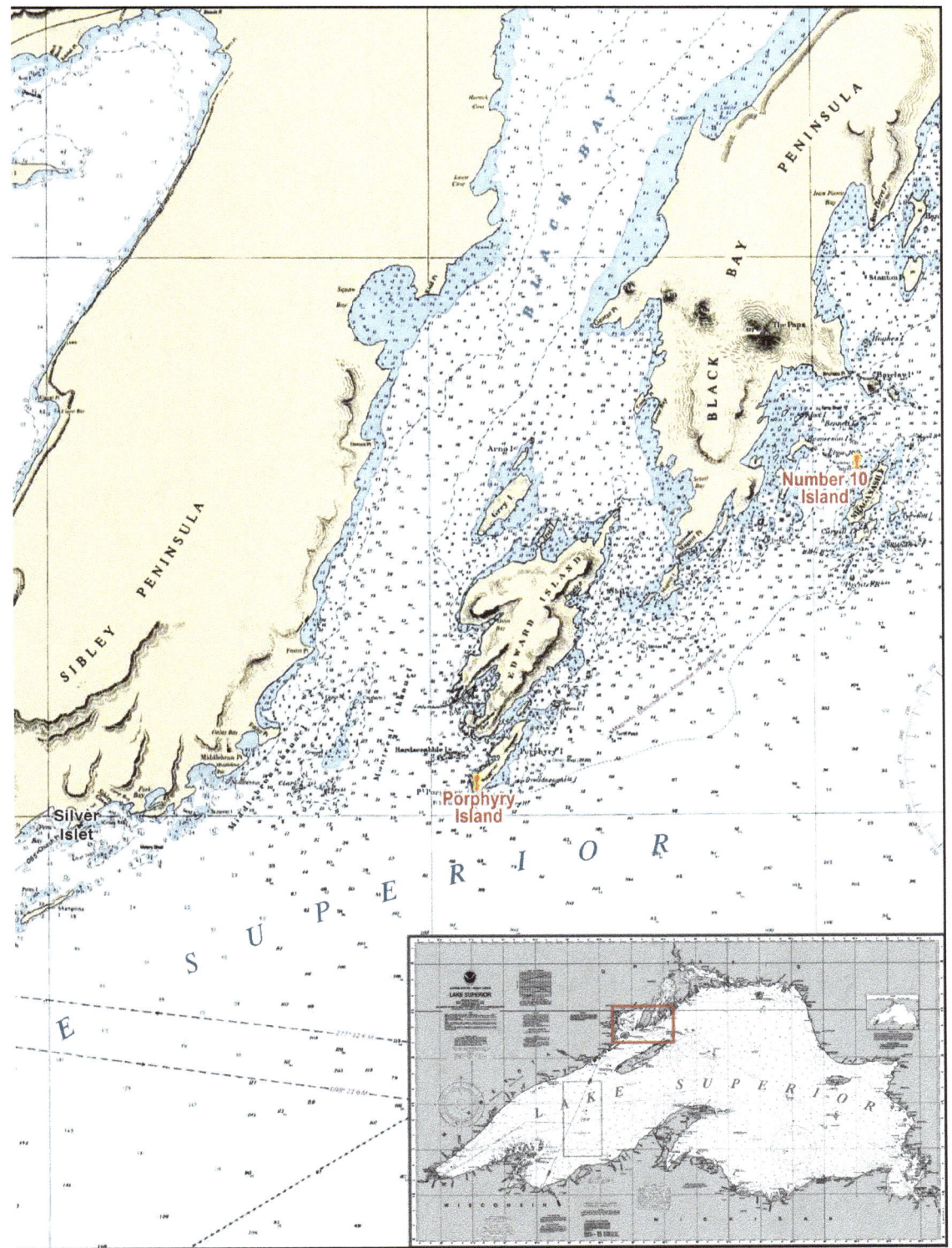

LIGHTHOUSE DISPATCHES

Introduction

A decade's worth of articles that appeared in Thunder Bay's *Chronicle-Journal* newspaper under the banner "Lighthouse Dispatches" have been collected together in this book to highlight the latest chapter in the story of three lighthouses on Lake Superior and the work that has been put into restoring and maintaining these iconic heritage structures. Reviving lighthouse history is a captivating journey that reveals the progress we have made as a society—or perhaps how far we still have to go!

Historically, the movement of people and goods relied heavily on waterways. As Canada expanded and commerce grew, lighthouses were established to aid marine navigation, ensuring safe arrival of ships with their crew, passengers and cargo. Due to its immense size, Lake Superior is often referred to as an inland sea, and it can evoke a sense of the Ice Age having just passed. Its clear, cold waters demand respect; displaying various moods that have contributed to numerous shipwrecks.

From the late 1800s, lightkeepers and their families led challenging lives maintaining these beacons that provide safe passage across Lake Superior. In 2008, Canada's Heritage Lighthouse Protection Act (HLPA) was passed by Parliament, allowing community groups, municipalities, and other levels of government to take ownership of and preserve lighthouses which were then controlled and maintained by the Canadian Coast Guard as part of the Department of Fisheries and Oceans Canada (DFO). Many community groups discovered that acquiring ownership of one of the surplus lighthouses could take a decade or more.

After petitioning the government to designate 12 lighthouses along Lake Superior's north shore, Canadian Lighthouses of Lake Superior (CLLS) was incorporated as a non-profit charity under the Ontario Historical Society. Operating on a membership-based model, a CLLS board of directors was elected to define a mission and vision for the organization: to promote, protect and preserve lighthouses on Lake Superior for the public benefit. Membership opportunities were created to engage volunteers in restoration efforts and fundraising for several lighthouses along the North Shore.

In 2014, DFO granted ten-year leases to CLLS for the Point Porphyry Lighthouse, the Shaganash Lighthouse (locally known as the No.10 Lighthouse), and later the Trowbridge Island Lighthouse. Now, CLLS is responsible for maintaining these three light stations. In 2023, the Shaganash Lighthouse was designated as a heritage lighthouse under the HLPA and the building, along with Number 10 Island, were transferred to CLLS to be conserved according to the terms of the Act.

Several years earlier, the public dock at Silver Islet had fallen into disrepair and was condemned. Tourists who wanted to visit Porphyry Island were then forced to travel 30 kilometres by boat from the city of Thunder Bay, rather than the 15 kilometres from Silver Islet. CLLS, in collaboration with the Silver Islet Camper's Association and the Silver Islet Yacht Club, gained ownership of the dock under the newly formed Silver Islet Harbour Association which is now committed to maintaining public access to the marine facilities. This change has allowed commercial charter boat operators to provide tourists with lighthouse tours by significantly reducing travel time to Porphyry Island.

Programming at Porphyry Island, the main base of CLLS lighthouse operations, now gives visitors learning opportunities in aspects of ecology, art, geology, and history, and it also enables host-keepers and artists-in-residence to stay at the light station for a week at a time. These initiatives have raised the organization's profile while enhancing the facilities to allow for additional uses, such as a wood-fired sauna, that visitors can enjoy. The annual fundraising carnival also draws local boaters who volunteer their time and energy to make improvements.

Since 2015, Paul Morralee, has been the CLLS managing director responsible for all lighthouse operations. In effect, he has become a modern-day lightkeeper. Although the essential aids to navigation (the lights) continue to be maintained by the Canadian Coast Guard, the upkeep and improvement of the buildings and the grounds at the three light stations have fallen to Paul along with the summer students and volunteers that he is able to recruit every season.

Lighthouse Dispatches: Ramblings of a Modern-Day Lightkeeper documents the daily operations at the Point Porphyry light station and the other lighthouses over a ten year period; highlighting the challenges faced while operating on an remote island. The primary goal of these dispatches is to maintain a record of progress, allowing CLLS, the public, and supporters to understand the ongoing process and to build interest in the region, which is vital for the organization's sustainability into the future.

Informational vignettes have been interspersed throughout the book to provide the reader with more detail on a number of subjects related to the lighthouse dispatches.

LIGHTHOUSE
DISPATCHES

2015

The Rookie Lightkeeper

July 28, 2015

Visitor stories add to lighthouse legacy

It's mid-afternoon and I find myself in a bit of a dreamy state after only my second day on the job. I ask myself... "What am I doing here on Porphyry Island?"

The fog is rolling in off Lake Superior and it can also be seen playing some distance away with the Sleeping Giant. There is a misty atmosphere surrounding this island while a gentle rain is falling on the boreal forest. Maybe this is what is creating the dreamy atmosphere?

This island will be my home base for the next five weeks, and I am already in awe of the ever-changing beauty of Superior and the surrounding islands.

Joining me at the Point Porphyry light station is Pete McIntosh, a fourth-year student at Lakehead University's School of Tourism and Outdoor Recreation. He is here working under a Canada Summer Jobs program to help with a long list of lighthouse chores. I wonder... "Did early lighthouse keepers have as many lists as we do?"

My job is to continue the work undertaken by local lighthouse volunteers by guiding the restoration based on the needs of our visitors and the goals of our heritage organization, Canadian Lighthouses of Lake Superior (CLLS), which was founded just last year.

Pete tends to a bonfire, burning some brush cleared last year, and he'll also be surveying visitors to learn more about their experience. I'll try to stay out of the smoke and the fog and greet our visitors.

As I reminisce about the life of lightkeepers at this location 142 years ago, I am constantly bombarded by just how many things need to be attended to — from cutting grass, to getting water, to powering up the lights. I can only imagine what the hardships would have been back then.

Our summer plans are to provide visitors and guests with a comfortable, informative and enjoyable visit. On our first day alone, we had 30 visitors. With cameras and cellphones snapping up images of the freshly painted buildings, I can see how people are enjoying the opportunity to share this beautiful spot on Lake Superior.

As visitors gain a stronger foothold into the knowledge of our nautical history, it's going to be our challenge to build up a repertoire of stories to share.

Many visitors who came out for the day were visiting from Silver Islet. It was a family reunion of sorts and they had their own history and stories to share about visiting the place 50 and 60 years ago.

Together, we can all be part of the lighthouse legacy and provide guests, visitors, and tourists with an experience of a life-time.

That's, I guess, how I feel right now — living an experience of a lifetime. Now, I'm waiting for the Sleeping Giant to reappear from the fog and awake.

Next week, I'll share the adventures of the SUNORA group of 15 vessels from the Thunder Bay Yacht Club and details of their visit.

It's a family reunion for some of the visitors to the Point Porphyry Lighthouse.
[Photo: Pete McIntosh]

August 4, 2015

A sense of discovery

As a sense of discovery captures our mood here on Porphyry Island, we are excited by the experiences our visitors are sharing with us; ever more filling in the pieces of our storied nautical past.

Our experience here at the lighthouse starts with a question, or some local knowledge, and then we work to reconstruct as many details as available for our ongoing interpretive programming, signage and displays.

This week on the island, we are preparing for a visit from 15 watercraft — sailboats and powerboats from the Thunder Bay Yacht Club's SUNORA (SUperior NOrth-shore RegattA) group.

Our objective this week is to provide a solid walking tour backed up with facts and interesting tidbits. Peter McIntosh, the lighthouse's summer student, and the first paid employee on the island since the light was automated in 1979, relishes the facts presented in a guidebook written in 1905 for lighthouse keepers. Titled *Rules and Instructions for the Guidance of Light Keepers and of Engineers in Charge of Steam Fog Alarms in the Dominion of Canada 1905*, the book is jammed with tantalizing information, perfect for visitors.

The sixty page guide provides information on keeping the light functioning, managing the fog alarm along with twenty pages on medical directions if you become ill.

Assembled together in a small work party, way-finding signage is developed to greet the visitor, with poles constructed from driftwood, and ample background information provided to start a discussion.

The SUNORA group arrives on the last day of July, having been cruising for several days to Nipigon and Red Rock, exploring the local culture, food, and taking in the full moon glistening over the water.

Arriving on Porphyry's shores in a blinding rainstorm, guests took cover in the boathouse where they were given a tour of some historical pictures and artifacts in the harbour; giving a sense of both time and place.

Gently guided up the manicured trail to the lighthouse, many were surprised to find a little graveyard near the main site. For years, visitors had silently been walking past, unknowingly, the final resting place of some unfortunate souls.

Reaching the light tower, and following safety instruction, visitors were taken up for an outstanding view of the Sleeping Giant and surrounding islands, and to hear about local shipwrecks that occurred right at this location.

In 1928, for example, the steamer *Thordoc*, loaded with flour, went aground. Afterwards, apparently, the lightkeeper, Ed McKay, and locals had enough Robin Hood flour for two years' worth of baking!

After the tower, the sailors took a tour through the freshly-painted guest dwelling, with its three bedrooms, living room, and a working kitchen.

As part of our summer, data is collected for Tourism Ontario in survey form to gain a better understanding of visitor needs, wants and desires.

Alberta Davis and Mike Fabius write the following in the guest book, "Great job, and we're thankful for the care and the energy spent to preserve our history." This only gives lighthouse volunteers added energy to continue their work to restore, preserve and promote our regional lighthouses.

Next week's installment — weather dependent — features a family expedition, arriving in high style at Point Porphyry's newly painted helipad!

August 2, 2015 — Boats from the Thunder Bay Yacht Club moored at Edward Island harbour near Porphyry Island.
[Photo: CLLS]

Steamship *Thordoc*

The only recorded incident of a ship running aground at Porphyry Island involved the steel bulk freighter *Thordoc*, in November, 1929. The newspaper, the *Daily Times Journal*, featured the headline "Crew Reaches Shore But Ship and Cargo Battered on Rocks." Owned and operated by Paterson Steamship Lines based in Fort William (now Thunder Bay), the vessel was heading downbound to deliver 2,000 tons of flour for overseas shipment.

After departing from Port Arthur and rounding Thunder Cape, the ship was set to navigate along the north shore toward the Battle Island lighthouse. With winds coming from the southwest, the first mate assumed command when the captain went off duty for the night.

Unfortunately, the vessel veered six kilometres off course and grounded on the reef off of Porphyry Island, with the lighthouse only 180 meters away.

When the lifeboat was lowered, it capsized in the shallow waters of the reef. The crew and passengers, soaked and chilled by the frigid waters of Lake Superior, managed to get ashore and they were taken in by lighthouse keeper Ed McKay to warm up overnight. The following day, they were rescued by a local fishing tug operated by Frank Gerow, whose family continues to run fishing tugs today in Black Bay and beyond.

In the aftermath of the accident, the ship was refloated and repaired at Thunder Bay. An official inquiry was held and the captain was found to have failed to exercise due diligence to ensure the vessel was seaworthy by not confirming the accuracy of the ship's compass. Additionally, it was determined that, since the vessel had unreasonably deviated from its course, damages of more than $146,000 were awarded to Robin Hood Mills Ltd. on whose behalf the flour was being shipped.

Thordoc had been built in Great Britain in 1908 and originally named *J.A McKee.* The ship was acquired by the J.M. Paterson Co. in 1927 and renamed *Thordoc*. The name was partly derived from the town of Thorold on the Welland Canal, while the suffix "doc" was shorthand for Dominion of Canada, a designation used for all Paterson vessels.

Steamship *Thordoc* aground on Porphyry Reef, 1929.
[Photo: McKay Family Collection]

August 11, 2015

Flying in for a mission

It was the clack ... clack ... clack ... in the air that alerted us that our visitors would soon arrive. A Canadian Lighthouses of Lake Superior (CLLS) staff member and myself were on hand to greet ten visitors at the Canadian Coast Guard's helipad.

On this volcanic Lake Superior island with its bending trees, the Point Porphyry Lighthouse grounds are manicured with some added features for our fresh arrivals. New interpretive signage had been put up, grass cut, and everything is in position to entertain guests who have just arrived by air.

Mark Wiskemann of Wisk Air Helicopters gently settled his craft on the heliport target, painted appropriately red and white, and which playfully sits with the Sleeping Giant in the background.

The Post family had come for a 45th wedding anniversary, and people had flown in from all over Canada for the celebration. Whether arriving by air or water, there is much to explore on the island, from trees, plants and rocks to our nautical history that built this country.

Of those who have been to Porphyry before, some have been surprised to find that there is a graveyard on-site; now adorned with four simple crosses. It's thanks in part to CLLS board director, Senator Bob McKay, who showed us where this final resting place is.

Other guests have also travelled in from many other places this past week including England, Brazil, Finland and four boats came in from Wisconsin, invited by Alexander Paterson of Thunder Bay.

Tourism is on the upswing here as peoples' curiosity has been piqued by a new sense of discovery. In the past week, we have seen over 70 visitors, each bringing a different set of questions and perspectives to the "picture." Comments have been positive and constructive. There's a sense here that this place is for sharing and not entitled just to boaters. A group of nine Voyageur Outward Bound USA kayakers arrived to say, "This is the best manicured woodlands trail..." they have encountered in their 50-day trip.

Later on in the week, another set of kayakers appear — this time from the east — to share a recipe of vegetables cooked in coconut curry sauce; "...mmm... tasty!"

Not only are we seeing repeat visitors this season, but we are seeing people come for different reasons. One person came to take pictures for a website he is building; another came to look for monarch butterflies.

LIGHTHOUSE DISPATCHES

Our lives managing and maintaining the lighthouse site gives us a great appreciation for the beautiful location in which we are passing the summer.

Lighthouses are built in locations where you can see in many directions. From the tip of Porphyry Island, we can see a stunning 275 degree portrait of Lake Superior.

As the day moves on, many mini snapshots are taken in our mind's-eye, and we think to ourselves how lucky we are to live here in Northwestern Ontario.

A cup of tea arrives as I wind up this week's dispatch. Now to focus back on the journey of restoring, promoting and protecting the lighthouses for future generations!

In next week's Lighthouse Dispatch, I'm excited to share with you a pan-Superior boaters' rendezvous.

A Wisk Air helicopter arrives at Point Porphyry light station. [Photo: Pete McIntosh]

August 18, 2015

Surprising discoveries

The flag fluttered ever so slightly as guests arrived at the Porphyry boathouse. This was not a foreshadowing of what was to come.

As the fire pit was readied for the evening festivities and the table and chairs around the harbour yard were set, the calm, tranquil moments of island life passed us by, lulling us by the serenity. People were arriving from the big city for a resurrection of sorts — a boaters' rendezvous.

One family came and shared their lake experiences as many sat at the picnic tables, ready for dinner. Others spoke of a previous rendezvous held by the Thunder Bay Yacht Club while some shared their views on the increased boater traffic, a resurgence of sorts from years past.

Hot chicken curry over rice, salad, smokies and s'mores were followed by a wonderful sunset, catching the final moments of the day.

Next came the weather overnight, with wind followed by wave action; holding boats tethered to the dock. But not to worry, there are many things for people to investigate on the island as work progresses to preserve the light station.

Around the fire pits, for example, coarse, black beach sand complimented the circumference, which accompanied a bench made of driftwood.

The grass had been trimmed too... back to the old days of a lightkeeper's duties. Gordon Graham had been the last keeper of the light for a 10-year stretch ending in 1988.

Guests who have been coming out to Porphyry Island for years are surprised by the many small discoveries made on-site as brush is cleared away. Famously, the two old cars parked at the lighthouse always get a second look, and some people are reminded of the cars in Havana, Cuba.

Magda and Peter, our first canoeists, visiting from Toronto, wrote in the guest book, "It's an inspiration (Point Porphyry Lighthouse) for other historical landmarks, especially lighthouses, which remain beacons of insight into history and the geography of the place." Wayne, Lee, Dean and Jan, while they were on course kayaking towards Battle Island Lighthouse, wrote, "Nice surprise to find all the great volunteer work going on fix up this historic site."

Visitors will be interested to find that the site also has been designated as a Lake Superior Water Trail location. New, temporary signage has been added to promote this as one of 17 locations around Superior. The water trail, financed in part by the TransCanada Trail organization, will be launching nationally in 2017.

Three more volunteers also came to work on final touch-ups on the houses this week. Paul Capon, the Chair of Canadian Lighthouses of Lake Superior, and two friends, Will and Bill, happily stayed an extra day due to the windy conditions, and they explored the island.

Finally, the wind died down in the morning and our guests and volunteers left pushing wheelbarrows full of luggage to the lighthouse harbour. Others had also departed back home towards the west.

Pete, the summer student, and I made up another to-do list over a cup of tea; dreaming, unrealistically, that we will, someday, be done, but happy that work brings people, saying "thank you" and smiling.

Next week's Lighthouse Dispatch will focus on a weekend odyssey with some radio-contest winners, who will sail Superior to the Point Porphyry Lighthouse, go on a fishing charter, tour the lighthouse grounds, and fly away home by float plane.

Two old cars parked near the Point Porphyry Lighthouse always get a second look by visitors.
[Photo: Pete McIntosh]

August 25, 2015

"Spectacular" views

Charging up the wood-burning furnace with birch in the lightkeeper's dwelling was a welcoming gesture to our guests. A slight drizzle was in the air, and a fresh wind made the interior inviting with hot water at the ready on the stove for tea. No biscuits were available, as the rations had been devoured days earlier.

Sailing, fishing, sightseeing and flying, were all part of the experience for four winners from "The Great Getaway" radio contest on Magic 99.9 and Country 105. The guests were here for two days to enjoy the lighthouse experience.

For most of their first day, they happily sailed on their inaugural journey from Thunder Bay, past the feet of the Sleeping Giant, to the Point Porphyry Light Station on Porphyry Island, 43 kilometres east of the city (as the crow flies).

Pete McIntosh, Canadian Lighthouses of Lake Superior's summer student, was doing double-duty as he welcomed guests and tourism officials to the island. On a guided tour of the new interpretive panels in the boathouse, the new arrivals were oriented to some of the lighthouse's history; giving them a sense of time and place.

It was interesting to talk to the guests later to find that they had not been on a sailboat before, nor flown in a float plane.

I guess this experience was going to be one to remember for many years to come.

Other challenges have filled our weekly roster prior to the visitors arriving, with water pumps being repaired and primed and some other creature comforts added to the dwellings.

We have a volunteer, Josue Passos from Brazil, who has been painting our administrative office and staff accommodations, which we call the bunkhouse. His observation of living at the light station is that he felt constantly bathed in sound, with the lapping of the waves upon the shore and the wind in the trees together with the awesome panoramic view.

Being a tourist in your own backyard is something that locals are also discovering — no need to travel far when the attraction is right on your doorstep.

A middle-aged couple moored their boat in the Porphyry Harbour this past week, and spent the night at the lightkeeper's dwelling. In our guest book, Lori and Bob Vanderploeg wrote, "The views are spectacular from every window in the house, and it is much more spacious than the sailboat!"

Just because we live in the area doesn't mean we can't explore it in more detail over and over again.

The Merritt family visited this week to relive past experiences and to fill us in about their grandfather, Charles, who worked the light as a keeper from 1946 to 1959. It was interesting to learn about how things used to be, and also to discover that a bench that is used at the sunset fire pit used to belong to the ship *Welcome*.

Each day, there is a sense of discovery that takes place, and as the clock ticks down on the summer, it's a pleasure to see the smiles on people's faces as they learn details of our past and develop a stronger sense of belonging.

Next week will be the season's final installment of Lighthouse Dispatches, summarizing observations of the summer.

Archie Hoogsteen of Archie's Fishing Charters, and the Great Getaway winners Karen and Bill Mitchell, and Betty and Lorne Blaikie from the Magic 99.9 and Country 105 contest, share their catch.

[Photo: Pete McIntosh]

September 1, 2015

Journey is part of the ritual

Whether catching rainbows or chasing the Northern Lights, the summer at the lighthouse on Porphyry Island was one to remember.

Seasons roll on from one to the next, and the summer is a time to reconnect with our natural surroundings, and this summer's Point Porphyry Lighthouse saw an influx of visitors from many places.

After entertaining 266 guests, contest-winners, families, sailors, boaters, kayakers and canoeists, the summer had its surprises.

Like the laws of energy — energy in, equals energy out — as I watched many volunteers clean, paint and restore, I was pleasantly surprised at how this work was reflected.

Reviewing visitor comments, keeping Porphyry Island "as is" was a prevailing theme, while others suggested ideas ranging from an adventure travel destination to an art gallery.

There's a sense of freedom when communing with nature, that's deep in one's psyche; bringing us full circle.

When I reflect on my summer, I find that many people visited the lighthouse as an annual pilgrimage; some came for family reunions, some were part of the lighthouse family, and for others, it's the beginning of a ritual.

In 1872, through an act of parliament, the Point Porphyry Lighthouse was conceived to safely guide a growing shipping industry. Now 143 years later, this gift is being delivered back, new and improved, to the hands of locals, visitors and tourists.

Even with comments like, "Wonderful spot to enjoy along the way," and "Fantastic monument for everyone," there is still work to be done.

At every moment this summer there was always something to do.

When you poll people as to what they want, there is a wide range to contend with. How do you make improvements without changing anything? It's a delicate balancing act which we considered daily in our summer journey. As the group of volunteers from Canadian Lighthouses of Lake Superior manages, maintains, restores and improves the current light station surroundings, more challenges will be faced.

We owe it to the former lighthouse families, Ross, Dick, Bosquet, McKay, McLean, Merritt and Graham, to celebrate their role in history.

As a volunteer, sharing a moment in time while moving forward performing many of the duties of a lightkeeper is, to me, an honour. Our work this summer pales in comparison with the past challenges faced by the keepers of the light.

As the ice forms around Porphyry Island and a blanket of snow covers the ground, I can assure you, people will return again next season.

Living with our history is an opportunity I am thankful to have engaged in, and I thank everyone who supported the lighthouse, and for the feedback.

Lori captures one end of the rainbow at Point Porphyry Lighthouse. [Photo: CLLS]

The Point Porphyry Lighthouse [Courtesy of Kraig Anderson, https://www.lighthousefriends.com]

In 1872, Parliament allocated funds for the construction of three new lighthouses on Lake Superior to support the rapidly expanding trade on the Great Lakes. The following description of the new aid to navigation on Porphyry Island was published by the Canadian Department of Marine in 1873:

> Another very superior lighthouse was recently erected at Point Porphyry, Lake Superior, which has already been of much service to the steamboat trade on the lake. Mr. Donald Ross was appointed keeper of this light on the 10th April last, at a salary of $400 per annum. The tower is a square wooden building, painted white, and the light is a fixed white catoptric, and can be seen at a distance of 16 miles. The lighting apparatus consists of five No.1 circular burner lamps and 20-inch reflectors. It was lighted for the first time on the 1st of July, 1873.

The lighthouse was an octagonal wooden tower protruding from the roof of a square keeper's dwelling. Overall, the tower measured 36 feet from the ground and supported an octagonal lantern surrounded by a gallery. The fixed white light shone from the lantern at a height of 56 feet above the water.

The first keeper, Donald Ross, passed away in 1880 and was replaced by Andrew Dick, who had earlier served as a temporary keeper at Battle Island

In 1907, a wooden fog alarm building was constructed next to the lighthouse. It contained dual, six-horsepower kerosene engines used to power the foghorn which went into operation the following year.

Joseph Bosquet took over lightkeeping duties in 1910. He was followed by Edward McKay (1922-1945), Roy McLean (1945-1946), Charles Merritt (1946-1959), Clifford McKay (1959-1979) and, the last lightkeeper, Gordon Graham (1979-1988).

The light's reflectors were replaced in 1911 with a more powerful 4th-order Fresnel lens, and the fixed light was eventually changed to a flashing light.

The original lighthouse was demolished after the current tower was constructed in 1960.

The original Point Porphyry Lighthouse in 1907. The fog alarm building is under construction in the background.
[Photo: Library and Archives Canada. R184, RG12,]

LIGHTHOUSE
DISPATCHES

2016

All of Us Working Together

LIGHTHOUSE DISPATCHES

July 5, 2016

Lighthouse group takes on first mission

This year's lighthouse dispatch begins aboard *Nina*, a 26-ft wooden vessel on course for the Shaganash Lighthouse on Number 10 Island, 54 kilometres due east of Thunder Bay on Lake Superior. Canadian Lighthouses of Lake Superior's first mission this season is to meet up with some young kayakers who will be volunteering and are from the Voyageur Outward Bound School in Ely, Minnesota. They have come to donate their energy doing some conservation work at two of the organization's lighthouses, while also learning more about the area.

This summer, the lighthouse group earned a grant from the Great Lakes Guardian Community Fund to create further access to the islands, build a new nature trail, move existing outhouses, and clean any trash along Number 10 Island's waterline.

As I arrived at the island, the Outward Bound students were doing a water safety dunk test to experience a short exposure to the frigid waters of Superior. They successfully passed the test and got back into their kayaks.

After slipping out of their wet clothes, they learned more about the lighthouse group's ambitions, goals and milestones.

Originally built in 1910 as part of Lake Superior's navigation system, the Shaganash Lighthouse (also known as No.10 Lighthouse) was rebuilt in 1922 as an aid to mariners to provide safe passage shielded from the south-westerly winds between Nipigon Bay and Black Bay. The Lake Superior archipelago that is now part of the Parks Canada Lake Superior National Marine Conservation Area has seen many fishermen, loggers, and passenger boat services in the past, but today it serves mostly pleasure boaters.

Upon completing their work duties, the group headed out to the Point Porphyry Lighthouse — another 15 kilometres to the west — where this year alone has already seen 350 hours of volunteer labour.

Members of the Thunder Bay Yacht Club constructed and helped to provide 39 feet of new docking for visiting boaters, and an outdoors group arrived by freighter canoe and worked on updating the tenting area. Two other crews attended to the guesthouse and grounds.

Several activities are planned at Porphyry Island this summer, with three gatherings scheduled and a new artist-in-residence program beginning with visual artist Gayle Buzzi.

We have other people attending the lighthouse including a writer, a photographer and a filmmaker; all capturing the beauty of the area and sharing their experience.

With two summer students hired as part of the Canada Summer Jobs program, Point Porphyry is ready to accept visitors. This season will see the opening of a new gallery, the introduction of more interpretive information and several new amenities for visitors to experience in the National Marine Conservation Area.

Through volunteerism, community supporters and sponsors, CLLS is providing access for members and the general public alike to come and experience an island on Lake Superior.

As the summer rolls on, I hope to bring you more news, happenings, and events from Canadian Lighthouses of Lake Superior. The next installment will focus on our summer staff and observations as the season begins.

Students from the Outward Bound School practice dunking in Lake Superior near the Shaganash Lighthouse on Number 10 Island. [Photo: CLLS]

The Shaganash (No.10) Lighthouse   [Courtesy of Marc Seguin, with notes from Kraig Anderson.]

Why does this lighthouse have two names? The tiny Number 10 Island, barely three acres (1.2 hectares) in size, is on the edge of the Shaganash Channel, east of the Black Bay Peninsula and 16 kilometres northeast of Point Porphyry. The lighthouse built on this remote island in 1910 was officially called the Shaganash Lighthouse, but mariners familiar with the area usually referred to it as the No.10 Lighthouse. The island's name, "Number 10," was assigned as the official name in 1969, even though the name of the lighthouse and the island is still often written as "No.10".

The original lighthouse was a two-storey, hip-roofed keeper's dwelling topped by a short, square tower supporting a square lantern. The fixed white light from a 5th-order Fresnel lens shone from a height of 36 feet above the water. A hand-operated foghorn was added in 1912.

Near the end of the shipping season, in November 1921, the lighthouse burned down, and almost two years passed before a replacement lighthouse was built on Number 10 Island. During the 1922 shipping season, a temporary light was shown from a hand lantern hanging on a pole. The new lighthouse, built the following year, was a standard-pattern pyramidal tower with a square lantern, the most common form of lighthouse now found all across Canada. A separate keeper's dwelling was constructed nearby. Like the original lighthouse, the lantern in the second Shaganash Lighthouse held a 5th-order Fresnel lens.

A lightkeeper was kept on the island until the light was automated in 1954. At that time the characteristic of the light was changed from fixed to flashing.

The Shaganash Lighthouse was one of a dozen lighthouses along Lake Superior's north shore that were petitioned between 2010 and 2015 to be included in the list of lighthouses eligible for designation under Canada's Heritage Lighthouse Protection Act. After the Department of Fisheries and Oceans Canada (DFO) declared the lighthouse surplus to government requirements, it was transferred to the ownership of Canadian Lighthouses of Lake Superior and designated as a heritage lighthouse in 2023.

A grant from DFO will help CLLS maintain the lighthouse and improve the facilities on Number 10 Island.

The Shaganash Lighthouse (detail) on Number 10 Island, c.1920.   [Photo: Library and Archives Canada, R184/ RG12, NPC 1975-387/24045]

July 12, 2016

Lighthouse coming alive at Point Porphyry

The wind and the waves splash upon Point Porphyry as I write to you about our first week in operation this season at the lighthouse.

Our Canada Summer Jobs grant came through again this year, so this means we are able to hire two students to help us make everyone's visit more enjoyable and informative.

We are happy to introduce Lissi Ranta and Stephanie Cressman to the Porphyry Island staff experience. For them, it's a way to extend their education in the summer and to quench a thirst for knowledge in all things lighthouse-related and beyond.

Ranta studies environmental design at the University of Manitoba, and Cressman, from Lakehead University, studies Environmental Management. Both bring a sense of excitement to be part of the developing lighthouse visitor experience.

Taking notes on their inaugural tour, the girls suggested that a booklet on indigenous, arctic-alpine disjunct plant species be created for visitors to comprehend fully the many interesting plants that populate the island.

Thanks to a former lighthouse keeper's wife, rhubarb can still be seen in the garden, but won't make it into the guide. Maybe the non-indigenous flowers such as *myosotis scorpioides* (forget-me-nots), might get a mention as they spread gently down the trail.

I'm sure that, as these young ladies develop their narratives on what it is like to live on an island as assistant keepers of the light, they will come to experience more than books could ever express.

The past week has been a busy one preparing things for the summer months, and now that most of the hard work is done, the girls can enjoy more free time to explore and develop their once-in-a-lifetime experience. Whether it is the peaceful call of the loon or viewing the many moods of Lake Superior, hopefully it will provide a time for them to reflect on the experience of working at the lighthouse and guide their future studies.

With the on-site picture gallery now painted and the mini-museum being primed for painting, the lighthouse is coming alive.

Slowly the boaters, kayakers, and sailors are starting to appear for tours of the well-manicured grounds and to learn more about historic facts that have been discovered during the winter months.

Next week, we are hoping to see more interpretive work being completed by the Lake Superior National Marine Conservation Area to help capture the true essence of the splendor of this small dot on a big lake.

The Canadian Lighthouses of Lake Superior board of directors and volunteers will be doing work at the Trowbridge Island Lighthouse site near Silver Islet on the upcoming weekend, to start planning for future visitors.

Starting this week, we have our first visiting artist-in-residence for a two-week stint. Gayle Buzzi is excited to be on the island, and next week we will find out more about her story and how she is adjusting to lighthouse life.

As a fishing trawler pushes on through Walkers Channel, followed by a flock of seagulls, I can hear a slight whistle... better go now, my tea's ready.

Lissi Ranta and Stephanie Cressman take notes on a point of interest on Porphyry Island.
[Photo: CLLS]

July 19, 2016

Art helps view role of lighthouse

With summer well underway, the atmosphere on the island is buoyant as the majority of the heavy lifting has been done. The staff are falling nicely into their roles as they welcome newcomers for tours of the lighthouse and share some newly-discovered historical tidbits.

Canadian Lighthouses of Lake Superior artist-in-residence, Gayle Buzzi, has also taken to her new reality. When she arrived she said, "It reminds me of my summer camp some years ago, on Oliver Lake." During her first week, Buzzi met many other visitors and showcased several works of art depicting images of lake and land. Her art is mixed-media acrylic-on-canvas, which offers another texture and take on the surroundings.

As you go into the artist's studio, temporarily set up in one of the dwellings, your image of lighthouse living changes and you see the island through the artist's eye. Buzzi's art draws in the viewer with a textured presentation using natural found objects to complement her work.

Visitor's feedback about the program includes a comment from a kayaker who said, "This is awesome but crazy." I'm sure others might say that kayaking on Superior is crazy too!

Art helps people view the role of a lighthouse in the landscape and its duty to protect boaters' lives from danger. Buzzi said, "It took me a couple of days to acclimatize, and after some frustration and a walk to the black sand beach, I was able to hit my stride."

Later on Porphyry Island, we will be hosting three more creative people who will try to sample the experience and feed back in their works what the island is really like. A photographer, cinematographer and writer will all try their hand at expressing the lighthouse experience.

Further to the artist-in-residence program, work is being undertaken to prepare the on-site photo gallery for works by former lighthouse keeper Gordon Graham. The gallery will host 15 images of the light station in summer, winter, and fall conditions taken 35 years ago.

There is also a mini-museum of lighthouse artifacts that are arriving from around the region. A potbelly stove and ladder from the first lighthouse built in 1873 are currently being featured. It's exciting to activate your imagination when you think of what conversations were previously held around the fire, or who has climbed that ladder?

Finally, some Red Chairs — which are placed in National Parks across Canada — were delivered, assembled and put in place to showcase the water, rocks and the Sleeping Giant. With our on-site wireless network for the youngsters to Tweet, Instagram and Facebook, it allows them to share their experience with family, friends, and the world.

It looks like some nice weather is approaching us for the next couple of days, and with it we are looking forward to sharing more Porphyry Island lighthouse moments.

Artist-in-residence, Gayle Buzzi, features one of her creations. [Photo: CLLS]

July 26, 2016

People rush in for film about lighthouse family

The lineup outside the fog alarm building for the 7 P.M. screening surprised me at first. Where did all these people come from?

With the lighthouse on Porphyry Island open now for the past few weeks, I guess it should not come as a surprise that visitors were excited to attend the soft opening of the Gordon Graham Gallery & Theatre. When the door swung open, people rushed in with their deck chairs to find a place to sit and screen a film about the Graham family maintaining the Point Porphyry Lighthouse almost 37 years ago. This was at a time when the dialogue was about change; the Graham family would be the last family to live, work and stay at the lighthouse in its 120-year history. The Canadian Coast Guard could now operate unmanned stations because the technology required needed only a solar panel, battery and a blinking light.

As the visitors settled in, they were given a brief introduction to Gordon & Eve Graham and how Gordon's passion as a photographer later put him on the national stage. After the screening, there were several questions about the family's lives and how they managed to survive in the harsh November environment when the film was taken. Huge waves and a light blanket of snow could be seen surrounding the light station in the film, but things did warm up when the visitors left as it was a nice summer's night. Some returned to the guest house, some to tents, and others to a boat moored in the cove.

During the day, the Northern Focus Photography Club under the guidance of president and founder John Ongaro, took over the site to capture images of the landscape, flora and fauna, and even chasing after butterflies.

This week also saw the anniversary of a couple that had visited last year, and a group of four seniors from Ottawa who are kayaking from Silver Islet to Rossport.

Everyone's stories of why they love this area becomes clear in moments of the unexpected; for example, as Lake Superior goes quiet. You see, everyone has this picture that Lake Superior is a beast of a lake, but also at times it's as tame as a lamb.

There was perfect weather to install a new floating dock in the cove. This week, a small crew headed by Jim Massey worked to install docks donated by the Thunder Bay Yacht Club. Now, deeper-draft boats can be accommodated for the first time in years.

Departing from our dock this weekend was our first ever artist-in-residence, Gayle Buzzi.

As we move into our fourth week, we can focus on some other projects, such as publishing our self-guided plant tour booklet.

Next week we will share with you our visit from the Superior North-Shore Regatta (SUNORA) and tell you how our mini-museum is coming along.

Visitors in the Gordon Graham Gallery & Theatre view a documentary on the experience of light keeping.
[Photo: CLLS]

August 2, 2016

Waterbound travellers celebrated

From the gunwales of a dingy emanated a tune sounding like Silent Night strummed from a bungee cord strapped across the beam. I wondered, "What is this all about?"

As part of an eight-day excursion on Lake Superior, celebrations were well under way by thirty travellers who started in Thunder Bay, went to Rossport and now were stopping in at Porphyry Island for their last night. The annual SUNORA regatta (for power and sail boats) had made use of the Point Porphyry Lighthouse grounds to host a final wrap-up potluck dinner and closing ceremonies with some rather interesting after-dinner musical entertainment.

When I greeted the group (who were ferried by motor launch, as most had their boats moored near by) a sailor was seen carrying a wind chime made of spoons. The mystery unraveled quickly when other nautically-produced instruments appeared, made of driftwood and boat parts. Later, they held a music contest.

After supper, many went up to the lighthouse to view a film about the former lighthouse keeper, Gordon Graham, whose name also appears on the gallery door. Settling in with deck chairs and sawhorses, all enjoyed a retrospective of lighthouse living and survival on the island in the early 1980s. Many commented on how the film gave them a better understanding of lighthouse life, and the experiences the keeper and his family had to endure. After the film, guests toured the mini-museum to see what artifacts had turned up and to learn more about the stories behind them.

Senator Bob McKay, a member of the Métis Nation and an honorary member of Canadian Lighthouses of Lake Superior (CLLS), provided an old ladder from the original 1873 lighthouse.

An old potbelly stove from the lighthouse, recovered in Dryden, sits majestically in one corner of the room, reminding us of times gone by. Blackened by soot, I can only imagine the numbers of cups of tea and conversations, and the meals cooked on the stove while in use at the lighthouse.

It was with the kind donations and money from the Sirkka Creagh Memorial Fund (former Thunder Bay Yacht Club member), that paint and fittings were purchased to provide free admission for everyone.

With daily visitors now, we are constantly considering the visitor experience

The McKays — A Family of Lightkeepers

One family name stands out in the history of the north shore of Lake Superior: McKay. The pioneer, Charles McKay, born in 1835, lived near Pays Plat on Nipigon Bay. The nearby village of Rossport was once known as McKay's Harbour, reflecting the family's significant influence in the commercial fishing industry in the 19th Century.

In 1877, when lighthouses were being built along the North Shore, Charles became the first lightkeeper at Battle Island, and this role was passed down through his descendants—Edward, Clifford, Robert (Bob), and William (Bill)—for the next century.

Edward McKay began his career as the assistant lightkeeper at Battle Island before moving 90 kilometres southwest to Porphyry in 1922. Life at the lighthouse was one of self-sufficiency, with plenty of rabbits, partridge, and fish available. Fifteen years after Edward's tenure ended, his nephew Clifford took over the light, living there with his wife (assistant keeper) Fran and son Bill during the shipping season until they relocated to the mainland at Black Bay each December. Many local boaters still recall their kindness on the lake, as Fran's cooking was legendary.

One notable descendant, Robert (Bob) McKay, Clifford's cousin, not only served as an assistant lightkeeper, but also co-founded Canadian Lighthouses of Lake Superior in 2014. He and his wife, Gloria, experienced a transitional period in 1960 when the old lighthouse was dismantled, a new tower and dwelling were constructed, and a 1.2 kilometre road was cleared through the forest to the harbour.

In 1983, Bob invited archaeology students from Lakehead University to explore the island after uncovering bones of some Indigenous people, later contributing to the understanding and sharing of the island's rich history.

Today, for visitors flying into Thunder Bay, Mount McKay serves as a reminder of the McKay family's pioneering legacy, standing proudly at the edge of Lake Superior.

Charles McKay.
[Photo: McKay Family Collection]

and adapting when necessary. Our summer staff are now meeting and greeting most guests and showcase work accomplished by the efforts of many volunteers.

As the summer rolls along, and with great weather, many visitors are arriving by kayak. An area cleared specifically for kayakers has received much attention this season, with new tents popping up every night.

A kayak group of seven retirees from the U.S. who visited the site were impressed because, when they had visited five years previous, the place was a mess. In fact, one visitor remembers spending the night in the keeper's screened-in porch.

Due to the work done during the spring clean-up by many volunteers, many guests are commenting on the ease with which they can walk the trails or explore the buildings and beaches. With time, the experience gets better.

Next week we will hear about a cinematographer and our next artist-in-residence, Lois Nuttall, and their adventures at the Point Porphyry Lighthouse.

SUNORA group has potluck supper on Porphyry Island. [Photo: CLLS]

LIGHTHOUSE DISPATCHES

August 9, 2016

Eyes of a family light up during tour

The view from the drone as it passes over Porphyry Island towards the lighthouse, from 400 feet up, is spectacular. Another guest is here to challenge people's perspective by creating a video of "a day in the life" of the staff doing their chores and daily upkeep.

As the drone settles back down to earth, the view offered by this new technology provides us with an opportunity to see how tidy the grounds are looking, with fresh-cut grass and straight lines.

Lighthouses are situated in the most prominent positions to warn mariners of the reefs and shelves that dot the lake, and even with good weather one sailboat did go aground off the point.

Traffic from visitors exploring the island has been increasing. Families can be found wandering the grounds taking in the newly finished exhibits with more questions than we have answers for.

Descendants of the family of Andrew Dick — a Scotsman — a former lighthouse keeper from the 1880s, toured the site recently to much delight. To see the family's eyes light up when they experienced something from their ancestor's past was a pleasure to witness. In the guest book they write, "We are honoured to be able to visit this site. Thanks for maintaining it for our generation to see."

Now, the drone has been repositioned further down the island to fly over the cove as the summer staff is seen paddling a canoe along the craggy basalt shore. Turquoise water, green forest, and glistening paddles can be seen from above. This is what summers are made for.

Videographer Victor Chimenti of Costalproductions.com is happy to be back to work on his second documentary about the island and its inhabitants, as it gives him time to explore further. His work will be seen at the end of the summer at the Movie Nights in the Marina.

Our second artist-in-residence has also arrived to do her thing. Lois Nuttall of Nuttallphotos.com is here to capture still images of island scenery and goings-on. With a camera slung around her neck, she is also exploring the island for the best landscapes and portraits. Light is always being assessed from sunrise to sunset, and Lois is there to imprison the image forever in a digital archive.

Nuttall shares her experience: "The island is very accessible with a variety of places to go and things to do; from the black sand beach and nighttime photography to arctic-alpine flora and fauna, there's an abundance of opportunities."

Now that we are well into the summer, we are looking forward to showcasing and sharing part of the summer experience at the Movie Night on the Waterfront, Friday Sept. 9, at sundown.

Next week, we will be telling you about the Thunder Bay Yacht Club's Annual Rendezvous on Porphyry Island hosted by Canadian Lighthouses of Lake Superior, and also be sharing a few observations from our writer in residence.

Videographer Victor Chimenti is in a dinghy at Porphyry Harbour capturing a moment of staff members with Canadian Lighthouses of Lake Superior. [Photo: CLLS]

August 16, 2016

Sharing the energy of Porphyry Island

Adam de Pencier travels with his son and dog, and finally landed at Porphyry Island after a long voyage north from Toronto. He is immediately taken, not by a concrete jungle, but by a cathedral of trees.

He is our writer-in-residence and is crafting a story for *Lake Superior Magazine*. As a contribution to the lighthouse website, he provided us with a daily synopsis of his activities to share with prospective visitors.

He writes, "The walk itself is a botanical treasure-trove, running straight through with trees on either side dripping with "old-man's-beard" moss that makes it look "pre-historic".

Adam's son, Hannibal, is an eager worker and, considering his schooling at Upper Canada College in the Big Smoke (Toronto), he is more than able to pitch in and knows the value of service above self.

Arriving also during this week, the fourth visit by the Voyageur Outward Bound School based in Ely, Minnesota. With us for a couple of days, the work accomplished by the group is astounding. Clearing overgrowth from the point to expose the original footprint of the lighthouse, it took a team effort to complete in the pouring rain.

Lois Nuttall, our photographer-in-residence, is quick to catch the image of beaded sweat from the brow of the kayakers. After convening in the kitchen and hiding from the rain, eight gorged on Lois' banana cake; which was gone in a flash.

Now that the space between the lighthouse dwellings is cleared and thinned down, it opens up an area once used as a vegetable garden.

Puff the dog can be seen wandering the grounds, but is later brought in when a young bear drops in for a visit. Berry season is here!

Our next tasks are to finish anchoring the dock works while another team builds a couple of picnic tables in readiness for the Rendezvous.

The work team arrives by tugboat with tools, hardware and enthusiasm to match. Later, they are ushered to the main house for some lunch and hot tea.

Smiles and laughs are shared as the progress of the site continues to take shape.

Everyone provides their input, their experiences and energy and, in the end, they leave the site better than they found it.

Sending them on their way, our summer staff leave for a break back on the mainland for some much needed rest.

With foul weather moving in, and sopping wet clothing hanging over the vent in the house to dry, it doesn't look promising for this year's Thunder Bay Yacht Club (TBYC) nautical rendezvous.

Later, around the campfire, and with the wet subsiding, the sparks fly high in the air as the night closes in and everyone's content. Next day is much of the same, but in the distance clearing weather is coming.

Although many people didn't come due to inclement weather, we now have two new picnic tables from the TBYC that, in future, will continue to bring people and families together. And that's what this is all about, to bring people together to share in the beauty of Lake Superior and surroundings done with the support of community.

Next week we will share some of the lessons we've learned this summer and how the future is looking as we go into our final weeks at the lighthouse.

Writer-in-residence, Adam de Pencier, and his dog, Puff, share an afternoon on the porch of the lightkeeper's dwelling.
[Photo: CLLS]

August 23, 2016

Tying up loose ends at lighthouse site

As the sun set last night after a few stormy days, I found myself contemplating lighthouse life from Porphyry Harbour, and the happenings of this summer. There were lessons learned and more to come I am sure.

In the distance, I can see the Sleeping Giant and the Turtle Head on Pie Island, and think to myself, "What a magical place that we live in; such beauty."

The last week has been about tying up loose-ends at the Point Porphyry Lighthouse site, plus completing other work on other lighthouses in the immediate area.

This week, the lighthouse summer staff and myself travelled to the lighthouses on Number 10 Island and Trowbridge Island to do some work.

With the sun blazing on us, we painted all four sides of the 1922 cedar-shingled No.10 light tower on the North Channel between the Nipigon Straits and Porphyry Island, 13 kilometres to the west.

Number 10 Island, where the Shaganash Lighthouse is located, has basic facilities for traveling kayakers. This includes a camping area, picnic table, trails, and an adaptation of an outhouse called a thunder box, which sits in the woods without a roof.

Looking back as we cruised towards Porphyry Island, we could see the results of our day's work; the glistening red and white tower slowly disappearing into the background.

As we motored along, we managed to see two sailing craft and a fishing tug also enjoying the afternoon.

Our next day is spent preparing for our visit to the Trowbridge Island Lighthouse. This site, at the feet of the Sleeping Giant, is another gem in the string of lighthouses that stretches across the North Shore and is operated by Canadian Lighthouses of Lake Superior (CLLS).

The CLLS board of directors was consulting with Department of Fisheries and Oceans officials regarding the current state of the Trowbridge facilities. This light station includes a semi-detached dwelling, a reinforced concrete light tower, a fog alarm building, and some outbuildings ideal for day visitors.

After the site review with board members and a member from the Friends of Battle Island Lighthouse, we all settled down to a wonderful lunch aboard the tug *Rugged*, hosted by Vic Miller.

A common denominator with all the groups in the region falls most often on access to these light stations along the coast. Due to the effects of previous decommissioning, some of the facilities need to be repaired, replaced, or resurrected.

Traveling back to Porphyry Island, we are met by Gus & Sandy Schmidt who had a couple of fishing rods to donate and a mountain bike for people who want to ride up to the light station. It's through this kind of support that the group continues to build strength within the nautical community as a destination for everyone.

Later that evening, we are met by Juzer Noman, who is a surveyor. He has come to offer his time to survey our lot lines and help interpret survey work that stretches back to 1872.

One lesson that we learn along the way is never underestimate the power of Superior. Even when you think you know the power of this body of water, it can surprise you. Sometimes it's absolutely flat, while other times it can be a bubbling cauldron of frothing water.

Next week I'll be sharing with you the reactions of the radio contest winners to an all-expense-paid trip to Porphyry Island, including hotel, catered meals, lighthouse tours, sailing and fishing charters, and helicopter ride.

The Shaganash Lighthouse on Number 10 Island gets painted by Paul Morralee and Lissi Ranta.
[Photo: CLLS]

LIGHTHOUSE DISPATCHES

August 30, 2016

Couples experience island adventure

The sailing vessel *Frodo* is providing the first leg of an adventure for two winning couples who arrive at the Porphyry Island dock. As the vessel is tied to the new floating dock, smiles abound and anticipation grows as the passengers come ashore.

For Peggy and Arthur Petersen, and Melissa and Dallas Hrabok, several weeks prior it was only a dream to imagine a trip to the island and the Point Porphyry Lighthouse. Now, with blue skies and favourable temperatures, their island adventure is about to begin.

"We've been on cruises and the scenery is just as beautiful," said Arthur as he pushed his wheelbarrow full of personal effects up the mile-long trail towards the lighthouse. While Melissa said, "I have no expectations as to what to expect about the lighthouse experience."

When the couples had settled in, they were provided a tour of the island amenities and given a couple of safety tips to follow while on-site.

Climbing up the tower was not easy but once up, the view was spectacular.

Friday night's dinner and all meals were provided by the Prince Arthur Hotel's Portside Restaurant, and included award-winning Chef Michael (Hoss) Ellchook's ribs.

On Saturday morning and with favourable weather, the guests go out with Archie's Fishing Charters and catch four "six-pounders" of varying species including a coho salmon, chinook salmon, lake trout, and walleye.

Later, as the sun sets, Dallas said he was, "...surprised at the number of lighthouses that could be seen from Porphyry Island," which included towers on Passage Island and Isle Royale to the south, and Angus Island and Trowbridge Island towards the west.

With a fresh breeze blowing through the upstairs windows, a good night's sleep was had by all; ready for some hiking on the final day. Discovering the black sand beach on the south side of the island, Peggy says, "The scenery is breathtaking and an eye-opening experience."

For the final leg home, the clatter of a helicopter can be heard overhead. A Wisk Air chopper sets down on target and on time to collect the four lucky winners of the Magic 99.9 and Country 105.3 Radio station contests.

Meanwhile, back on the dock down at the cove, a scuba diver is pulling out old tires and logs from the lighthouse's water lot. Ryan Hamlin of Lakehead Technical Diving mentions to me, "There are enough tires for a car," which are wheeled behind the boathouse.

Looking down into the clear water, you see what progress has been achieved which satisfies one of the objectives of the Great Lakes Guardian Community Fund. Canadian Lighthouses of Lake Superior (CLLS) received $24,500 from the Fund to clean up around the waterfront, along with three or four other conservation projects.

Now, as the summer winds down, our seasonal staff have left for school and we are starting to finish up the projects for the year.

Next week, we'll look at the impact CLLS has made, and what the future might hold.

Arthur and Peggy Petersen, Dallas and Melissa Hrabok, and Archie Hoogsteen show off their varied catch of the day from trawling near Edward Island.

[Photo: CLLS]

LIGHTHOUSE DISPATCHES

September 6, 2016

Engage others by 'doing'

With a strong wind advisory and competing wave action from the south and southwest causing Lake Superior water to haystack, I have decided to delay my departure home and wait for calmer waters.

The final moments of the long-weekend are winding down (and so is my summer), I am waiting out the storm of blowing rain and low visibility. I'm inside the keeper's house, watching the effects of the storm. With a fire set in the basement furnace and a cup of tea in hand, I'm ready to write my final Dispatch in an attempt to distill the summer experience.

My first thought is, "Where did the summer go?", for it seemed to have disappeared too quickly. And my second thought was "How do you share the highlights of such a unique experience?"

The Canadian Lighthouses of Lake Superior's lighthouse on Porphyry Island has left 320 registered visitors — kayakers, boaters and sailors — with something to remember, whether it be the wonderful weather, beautiful scenery or that Lake Superior is always in charge.

Taking in the striking geology of the basalt rock formation that makes up the island or watching the lonely monarch butterfly searching for sustenance, I think leaves the visitor with a lasting memory. And sighting a hungry bear visiting the island for wild berries makes you slightly cautious — that's why I always ring my bell when riding the lighthouse trail.

For me, the journey of the summer has been watching the results of... if you do something, you can engage others to do more!

The lighthouse summer staff are examples of this, with Stephanie and Lissi being self-motivated, hard working and tuned into the experience, which made the site even better for visitors. Or the many other people who assisted in installing the new docks, clearing the trails, or donating something. It creates a movement.

It's an amazing feeling when someone donates a mountain bike so visitors can enjoy a bicycle ride through the forest to the lighthouse. And, as time marches on, I believe more people will come forward to help build further access to our regional lights, not just Porphyry Island.

Not only are the passing boaters helping out, but families who have made the North Shore part of their summer existence recognize the lighthouse group's efforts, and are supporting further the work. This gives a real boost to the visitor experience because it's not about one city, one town, one village or hamlet, it's about all of us, working together to provide access to these beautiful sites for everyone.

The Rogalski family writes in the guest book: "We are descendants of Andrew Dick, Lighthouse Keeper (at Point Porphyry), 1880. We are honoured to be able to visit this site. Thank you for maintaining it for our generation to see."

I'd like to thank all volunteers, visitors and especially the Canadian Lighthouses of Lake Superior's board of directors for hiring me on as the managing director for this summer experience. I feel honoured to have had the opportunity to "pay-it-all-forward" for future generations to share.

I know that, as a society, we have a lot of other important things on our plate, but to hold onto this small piece of history that helped build our country is an important custodial action that future generations can come to appreciate.

See you next year.

The Point Porphyry Lighthouse and lightkeeper's dwelling. [Photo: CLLS]

Lightkeeper Andrew Dick

Captain Andrew Dick arrived at Prince Arthur's Landing (now Thunder Bay) on the steamship *Rescue* in 1855. Notably, he had an encounter with the Prince of Wales (later, King Edward VII) while navigating the North Channel of Georgian Bay.

Originally from Edinburgh, Scotland, Dick settled in this unfamiliar land and married Caroline, a First Nations woman from Black Bay. At age forty-seven, he became the lightkeeper at Point Porphyry. With his wife and eight children in tow, the Dick family settled on the island where two more children were born — a total of five sons and five daughters in all. Caroline died in 1901 and is buried in the First Nations cemetery on the island.

Andrew lived on Porphyry Island year-round for 30 years. A later island resident commented that Dick, "...had two suits of long underwear, a heavier suit for the winter. After six months he'd change. He'd hang one suit over the woodpile and it would stay there until he changed again."

In 1907, Dick oversaw the building of a fog alarm system that emitted a horn sound for four seconds every minute, helping to avert accidents during foggy conditions near the Porphyry Reef.

He earned an annual salary of $400 and documented various aspects of his life, including weather patterns, vessel traffic, and daily chicken egg counts in his journals now housed at the Thunder Bay Museum and at Library and Archives Canada. One notable entry recounts a weasel eating 23 of his chickens, followed by a humorous note about a family dinner the next night featuring... weasel.

For his long and dedicated service, he received the Imperial Service Medal from King George V, and is still honoured today as a respected lighthouse keeper along Superior's north shore. His descendants, now in their third and fourth generations, continue to visit the island, seeking a connection to his legacy.

Building the fog alarm building in 1907 took many hands including two women, thirteen men, and two dogs. In the centre of the picture, Andrew Dick can be seen wearing a white apron. [Photo: Library and Archives Canada, R184, RG12, NPC 1975-387 NPC]

2017

Unexpected Visitors

LIGHTHOUSE DISPATCHES

July 11, 2017

Lighthouse opens, hosts curious explorers

We opened the lighthouse this year with a big splash as 30 students from Blyth Academy descended upon the Point Porphyry light station. The water was cool, but that didn't dampen the spirit or enthusiasm of this travelling band of explorers.

The group had come to further investigate the transportation history of the region as part of their studies, and they were greeted by some spectacular historic sites of Northwestern Ontario.

The former Coast Guard icebreaker, *Alexander Henry*, glided across Thunder Bay as the group watched history in the making. With the resurrection of some of Thunder Bay's nautical history, we are now able to share a broader story of the Canadian Coast Guard and its link to lighthouses in the region.

Point Porphyry Lighthouse, situated on the east side of Black Bay, hosted the school group with activities encompassing our human history as well as the area's natural history accompanied by the beautiful panoramic views of the islands and mainland.

The Gordon Graham Gallery features work from last year's artists-in-residence, Lois Nuttall and Gayle Buzzi.

The mini-museum offered lots to see and do with a demonstration of the portable fog alarm frightening some of the students; the loud noise was unexpected.

Nature walks took place to the black sand beach to explore the actions of volcanic activity from millions of years ago. Also, great interest was taken in the exploration of the arctic-alpine disjunct plants on the point. These plants are happily surrounded by the cool weather that Lake Superior brings our way.

This season, our lighthouse group, Canadian Lighthouses of Lake Superior, is looking forward to hosting many more activities and events with five artists-in-residence, two community celebrations, and six group activities from scuba diving to a sailing regatta.

After a couple of hundred hours of volunteer help in June, both the Trowbridge Island Lighthouse, situated at the feet of the Sleeping Giant, and Porphyry Island have had some beautification to the landscape and buildings.

With the "Canada 150" celebrations well underway, the Point Porphyry Lighthouse and the No.10 (Shaganash) Lighthouse will be part of the festivities too, with a date set in August for the

Great Trail network/TransCanada Trail celebration.

Next week we will introduce you to our summer students and share with you reflections from our first resident artist from California as he works to capture the beauty of our area on canvas. 🔅

Porphyry Harbour, located on the north side of the island, hosted a travelling group with a variety of activities. [Photo: CLLS]

Porphyry Harbour

Most visitors today access Porphyry Island via the harbour, which is nestled on the north side and shielded from nearly every wind direction. During the shipping season, lightkeepers would bring in their supplies and dock at one of the two nearby docks. A marine railway operated in between the docks to haul boats up in the fall. In the 19th and 20th centuries, the harbour buzzed with activity as various other ventures utilized the safe docking area.

The original boathouse at the harbour was established early on, situated somewhat closer to the light station on the beach where visitors now gather sea-glass. However, due to the heavy southwest seas, this location was abandoned, leading to the construction of a new boathouse in 1915 at the current site.

This area was appealing to boaters as a haven, but for those who kept the light, it also served as a hub for various activities. In a census of vessels in the area from 1880, there were 19 fishing boats recorded. Many lightkeepers owned their own boats, and two examples still exist today. The boiler of the steamship *Grebe* remains visible in the harbour, serving today as a landmark for sailors to gauge water levels. Later, in the 1960s, the *North Star*, owned by the McKay family, was in service until it was pulled ashore in 1974. The keepers not only fished but they also collected pulp logs, selling these logs for pennies per foot, along with hundreds of pounds of fish, to supplement their income.

In 1960, as part of a government contract, assistant light keeper Robert (Bob) McKay, supervised by his uncle and main keeper, Clifford McKay, constructed a 1.2 kilometre road to the light station. This was essential to transport the machinery and supplies needed for site upgrades, including a new 25-meter light tower, a keeper's dwelling, and several additional outbuildings. Ingeniously, the lightkeeper's family utilized the construction barges to bring two 1950s vehicles to the site for hauling groceries and supplies.

The boathouse at Porphyry Harbour, 1915. Note the fishing nets to the left.
[Photo: Library and Archives Canada, R184-RG12]

In later years, the site grew popular among local sailors and power boaters, although campfires and camping were prohibited. Some lucky visitors might receive an invitation from the keeper to ride on the tractor to the dwelling for a warm slice of pie and some tea. Today, the charter boats arrive a couple of times a week helping to share the history of the area.

July 18, 2017

History, colours of island impress

It was an unexpected sound that broke the tranquility of routine life as our first helicopter "Wine & Cheese" party arrived — and Dennis McGonagle was contemplating his next brush stroke.

Fortunately for the helicopter visitors, there had been a break in the weather — a parting of the clouds you might say — for a landing to take place as the weather has been pretty inclement the last few weeks.

As the group exited the landing pad, smiles could be seen as a sense of discovery took hold. Having guests who are inquisitive always makes the tour around the site go quickly.

We started with a basic outline of the different phases that the lightstation has gone through — from a staffed lighthouse, to a steel tower with solar panels, to a volunteer-run site . This helped acclimatize our guests and put everything into context.

From whale oil lanterns, clock winding mechanisms, solar power and abandonment, the story was told of how Canadian Lighthouses of Lake Superior (CLLS) is restoring, preserving and promoting our transportation heritage.

Iloe Ariss, our enthusiastic and hardworking summer student, is spun into action when any visitor appears on-site; including a chance sometimes to taste some exotic cheese along the way — the wine will have to wait.

Iloe is studying in Halifax and, with her family owning a cottage locally, she has a good connection to the area and some of its stories. Her duties, other than being a tour guide, include a lot of yard work, painting, cleaning and making the site presentable for visitors. She is excited to meet guests to show them the sites and beautiful panoramic views of the area.

Over the weekend, the light station entertained several fishing boats that are part of a fishing derby on Black Bay. Across the horizon we can see many boats bobbing and patiently trawling the reefs; waiting for the big one.

Sometimes the light station staff get to taste the catch as generous fishermen share their day's adventures.

Many visitors also come from the hamlet of Silver Islet to update themselves on changes taking place on Porphyry Island, and there are many. Additional dock works, for example, have been completed thanks to the continued support from the Thunder Bay Yacht Club and provincial and federal sources.

This past week, Archie Hoogsteen from Archie's Fishing Charters helped to install signage for the Great Trail of which the Lake Superior Water Trail is part.

Stretching from Thunder Bay to Sault Ste. Marie in the south, the water trail passes the lighthouses on Porphyry and Number 10 Island on Superior's Canadian shores.

There are 15 signs across the North Shore that provide a wealth of information for paddlers; sharing local history and giving regional orientation along with some pragmatic safety advice. It's thanks to Gary and Joanie McGuffin who helped to craft these wonderful "sentinels of the shore".

Corralling a prodigious collection of canvases, Dennis McGonagle has spent a week now on the island, painting to his heart's content.

From the dry, arid climate of California, where Dennis is from, to our cold and wet climate has been an adjustment. Extra blankets and hot cups of tea have been delivered to him along the trail. He says, "I left in the middle of a heat wave to get here, and my observations are that I am blown away by the history and subtle colours that raise themselves out of the rock."

Next week we will share the adventures of the Save Ontario Shipwrecks–Superior Chapter, as they do some underwater historical documentation and an eco-dive.

Dennis McGonagle paints a car in his "Little Havana on Porphyry Island".
[Photo: CLLS]

July 25, 2017

Hidden gems often near lighthouses

While in the process of flipping backwards over the water, I realized that the rope had given way. Assembled around the dock were the real divers waiting to survey the waters around Porphyry Island... but I was not prepared. Sopping wet and somewhat shocked, I pulled myself back onto the dock to a gathering of curious onlookers and several laughing faces. The real dive would start soon.

Lighthouse life is often interrupted by unexpected events as you are in the wilds and at the mercy of this inland, freshwater sea: Lake Superior. Through perseverance and endurance, you can overcome most challenges, but the lake is unrelenting.

Our visiting artist-in-residence, Dennis McGonagle, understood this as he captured beautiful waterscapes; yet he also had to run for cover on several occasions due to heavy rain. Daily, Dennis gave a review of his perspective on our environment to visitors, and was bursting with superlatives at the stunning beauty he witnessed. It's through the eyes of others that we can collect more of an objective view of our surroundings and realize, as locals, what we have to share.

Iloe, the Canadian Lighthouses of Lake Superior (CLLS) assistant lightkeeper and summer student, is armed with many books to be ready for her fall semester, but there is lots of work to be done during daylight hours.

The lighthouse site is getting a brush up with new red and white paint, and many visitors are remarking for the first time that the site is looking as it had 20 years ago.

Now that the summer season is well upon us, the boating traffic is picking up. A freighter canoe, kayakers, keen sailors and power-boaters are remarking on the tempestuous weather kissed with occasional spots of sunshine and calm waters. They are always happy to reach the island shores and the well-tended facilities.

Members of the Save Ontario Shipwrecks-Superior Chapter zip up their dry suits, and put on masks, fins and tanks for an eco-dive of the Porphyry Harbour. This is where, since 1960, lightkeepers and workers kept their boats and received supplies for the island. The first of many dives was to survey the underwater lake bed for artifacts and, later, to remove any garbage. This is done under a license from the Ontario Government as some members of the group are certified to undertake archaeological work.

Using a grid pattern, four divers and a spotter on the surface methodically scan the lake bottom for items of interest.

These items are then identified for further action with a bright marker put in place for later retrieval.

The spirit of this community group combining forces with CLLS is wonderful because it helps everyone realize what we have in our area, both above and below the water.

As many are aware, lighthouses often have many wrecks around them, so later in the week several more dives will take place. Walkers Channel, Point Porphyry and Pringle Bay will all be surveyed for known wrecks, and who knows what else?

Next week; we will hear about the return of the Graham family to the island 37 years after they left for other lighthouse duties, and about Eileen K. Hennemann, our artist-in-residence from southern Ontario, who will share her observations.

Waves crash upon Point Porphyry, where the lake can sometimes be unrelenting. [Photo: CLLS]

August 1, 2017

Busy times at Porphyry Island

The echoes of excitement bounced between the light tower and keeper's dwelling after another game of bocce ball was completed. This was an interesting week as there was a variety of activities taking place all over the island. Let's start below the waves and work up from there.

Save Ontario Shipwrecks-Superior Chapter (SOS) continued their four-day eco-dive and archaeological expedition around the island. Their search was for artifacts left in the cove from previous lightkeepers, and later, around the point, looking for wreckage. No major finds were reported.

Volunteerism continues to build a destination for nautical visitors as the SOS chapter left Canadian Lighthouses of Lake Superior (CLLS) with a brand new mooring ball for boaters.

The Stewardship Youth Rangers are next to arrive; working with the Ministry of Natural Resources and Forestry to clear brush out of a new coastal nature trail around part of the island. This will provide visitors with a unique view of the forest floor and the Sleeping Giant, 20 kilometres to the west.

Upon the shores arrived a freighter canoe expedition, headed by Darrell Makin. Called Survive and Thrive, it's a company of youth from Calgary who had experienced cancer. The group, who had been weather-bound spending a day in Silver Islet before visiting Porphyry, were excited to explore the volcanic sands and tumbled sea-glass shores of this mystical place.

The Barrie Canoe and Kayak Club also shared the island's panoramic views. They had started their journey from the western entrance to the Lake Superior National Marine Conservation Area and were looking to venture across the archipelago of islands to Rossport. With a well-tended tenting site, and an ample supply of firewood, they shared some stories with the diving crew, creating a night of camaraderie surrounded by Lake Superior.

The clatter of a helicopter caused the craning of the neck skyward to wonder who was visiting. Kevin Graham, son of former light keeper Gordon Graham, had returned to his home 37 years later with his beaming family in tow; for them, this was all new, while to Kevin, it was an awakening. For years, people had told him not to return as the place was in terrible disrepair and vandalized, and to return would be a sorry sight. Beyond any doubt, this homecoming brought unbridled emotions forward and a few laughs too; for down in the basement of the keeper's dwelling a basketball hoop was found that he'd played with as a boy.

CLLS volunteers and members can take pause and be proud of their work and support for, when former residents visit the facilities, it makes it all worthwhile. Families with the name of Ross, Dick, Merritt, McKay and Bosquet can also be proud of history being resurrected on this Lake Superior Island.

The bocce ball tournament continued on the front lawn and was abated by the dinner bell. The Turpin family, who had won a night's rental of the guesthouse at the lighthouse fundraiser in May, were enjoying themselves so much that later, when a bag of marshmallows dropped into the fire, they laughed. Nothing in the moment mattered. They felt at home on this big lake we call Superior.

Next week, we will hear about the SUNORA regatta of 12 boats, and how our summer students and new artist-in-residence are all enjoying the experience.

Bright and early, the Turpin family leaves after a visit to the island. From left; Beverley Turpin, Keli Cristofaro, Keaton Cristofaro, Kain Cristofaro, Brad Adams, Carter Adams, Olivia Adams, Khris Adams and, in the boat, Captain Paul Turpin with Sal Cristofaro.

[Photo: CLLS]

The Graham Family

Starting his career at the Angus Island Lighthouse located on the south side of Thunder Bay near Pie Island, Gordon Graham found his calling. He was, at that time, an assistant lightkeeper but was also recognized nationally as an outstanding amateur photographer.

In 1974, he moved to become the head lightkeeper at Trowbridge Island, located near the feet of the Sleeping Giant. He was accompanied by his wife Eve who acted as his assistant and their two sons, Kevin and Neil.

Constructed in 1924 the Trowbridge Island Lighthouse was challenging to land at, as the island was very rocky, with high cliffs and surrounding reefs. Built because of the shipwreck of the *Theano* in 1906, the station included a fog alarm building, keeper's dwelling, and concrete light tower. Through determination, storms and challenges, Gordon was able to provide for his family and keep the light functioning. In a letter now held in the Thunder Bay Coast Guard base archives, Graham asks for advice on how to dispose of dynamite that had been stored on the island. This shows how the lightkeeper had to be a handy-man and "jack of all trades" in order to live in isolation on a small island. The tower atop the island has a third-order Fresnel lens (still there today), which takes one hundred steps to reach. In the backyard, pressed into the concrete surrounding the washing line post, can still be found handprints from when the family lived at the light station.

Eve Graham and her children with the CBC film crew.
[Photo: Graham Family Collection]

Migrating some twenty kilometres to the east six years later, the Graham family arrived at the Point Porphyry Lighthouse. Porphyry Island accommodated the needs of the family as it had space for a school room for the children in the old keeper's dwelling, and there were abundant walking trails to explore. CBC Toronto was interested in the Graham family's exploits, and in a series called "Heartland" they were showcased in the dying days of lightkeeping before automation on Lake Superior. Their domestic life illustrated in the film was not for everyone. You needed to be able to deal with the isolation, to be a problem-solver and fulfil your duties to help ships navigate the waters and reach port safely.

Today Eve Graham and her son Kevin are active in supporting Canadian Lighthouses of Lake Superior by sharing their experiences in presentations at the Thunder Bay Museum. Both have also served on the board of directors, helping guide the vision of the organization forward. Keeper Gordon Graham and his photography live on today and can be seen in the art gallery named in his honour.

LIGHTHOUSE DISPATCHES

August 8, 2017

Promoting nautical heritage

The routine of lighthouse life continues with plenty of maintenance work, plus welcoming more guests every day, with over 250 visitors already this season.

Iloe Ariss, our summer student and assistant lightkeeper, happily creates lists of things to do to keep the site looking great and operating well.

Our garden is coming along with the tomatoes just now flowering. Things on the island take longer to grow because of the cool winds that often blow off the lake.

We have a new birdhouse painted in the official lighthouse colours and will wait to see if next season we will be able to attract any feathered friends.

This past weekend, the SUNORA group from the Thunder Bay Yacht Club arrived with 12 boats participating. The group uses the lighthouse facilities to have their final awards dinner and to tour the site. This past week, they travelled across the North Shore and participated in many races and trivia challenges.

Carole Frève arrived from Montreal and was all smiles when she reached the studio located in the keeper's dwelling. She is our next artist-in-residence, and her style of art is unique in the sense that it uses printed circuit boards, lights combined with glasswork she blows.

Guide and hard-working volunteer, Donny Wabasse, provided Frève with an orientation to the island. Quickly acclimatizing the artist to the island helps provide more options for the creative process to flourish.

A project completed this week by the CLLS board of directors was to name the road from the boathouse to the main lighthouse compound. The road, built in 1960 of beach sand and gravel, stretches for 1.3 kilometres and bisects the Porphyry Island Provincial Park Nature Reserve. The purpose of the road was to allow the passage of supplies for the light station which had been off-loaded from the Canadian Coast Guard buoy tender, *Nokomis*, docked at the boatyard in the harbour. The *Nokomis* also brought a couple of cars (now rusted classics) by barge, which can still be seen at the top of the trail and which always warrant a second look from surprised visitors.

The sign for McKay Drive, named after Senator Bob McKay, an honorary member of CLLS, was installed this week to celebrate the McKay family as lightkeepers stretching back to 1922, with Edward and, later, in 1959, with Clifford. Bob McKay was on the crew that built the road, but he was also a keeper of several lights in the area, along with his wife Gloria.

Now a nature trail through the forest to the lighthouse, many visitors can be seen cycling on donated bicycles or walking along the road to the lighthouse.

Work is currently underway to again provide motorized transport. There are many memories of tractor rides in the past when the Graham family operated the lighthouse. Holding onto our history is important as we continue to preserve, protect and promote our nautical heritage.

Next week, assistant lightkeeper Iloe Ariss will be writing the "Lighthouse Dispatch" as part of her summer experience on the island.

Carole Frève, visiting artist-in-residence, displays components she will use in her artwork, while Iloe Ariss stands beside the McKay Drive sign recently installed on the road to the boathouse. [Photo: CLLS]

August 15, 2017

Lighthouse stands through stormy weather

by Iloe Ariss

The lighthouse stood strong through a fierce thunderstorm, just after the arrival of the new artist-in-residence, Chris Wilson.

The rain continued for the next few days, delaying the painting of the helicopter pad. The rain did not stop visitors from braving the mosquitoes and coming up the trail to explore the light station.

The view from the top of the tower on a stormy day is very impressive, as one is closer to the level of the clouds and can see the wispy lines of rain out on the lake while dark skies are overhead.

The storm brought large waves that crashed against the cliff along the southeast side of the island. New cautionary ropes and signs mark this side of the island; as the steep drop-off is dangerous.

A few feathery friends were seen flying in and out of the birches and tall pines on the island this week. These birds are yellow-breasted and have comical tufts of feathers on the back of their heads, and their tails are marked with a bright yellow line. They are commonly called cedar waxwings, and their playful fluttering further brightens the island landscape.

Though the rainy and grey weather lasted most of the week, it did not stop Chris from producing art. He began with a carefully detailed watercolour painting of the assistant keeper's abode, and continued to work on another while also finding time to explore the island's beaches and collect various colours of beach glass, which he plans to incorporate into his artwork.

The Gordon Graham Gallery not only has additional pieces from this summer's artists, but houses a newly-built display shelf which was installed for sculptures and other objects. There is a place on the island for every type of art medium.

The garden continues to flourish and some of the kale has been harvested, cooked and eaten. The rhubarb is not quite red enough yet to be picked, but there are hopes that it will soon be ready.

Many garter snakes have been spotted on the island in the past few weeks. These thin, sliding creatures are not dangerous for humans but may eat small rodents and insects. One snake was seen chomping into a large minnow, which it proceeded to swallow whole.

Luckily, Friday was a bright and sunny day, and the painting of the helicopter pad began.

The labours continued into Saturday and, after many hours of work, the bright red and white of the helicopter pad could be seen even more distinctly than before.

Managing director, Paul Morralee, returned to the island on Saturday. He brought out with him Matthew Sloan, a summer student working for Canadian Lighthouses of Lake Superior in Thunder Bay. Matthew enjoyed the tour of the island and happily watched the lighthouse flashing among the stars on Saturday night.

The island's residents, re-fueled and re-stocked over the weekend, are looking forward to the last few weeks of August.

Next week, we will hear about the addition of new floating docks to Porphyry Island and also, weather permitting, take a visit to Trowbridge Island and hear about some of the work taking place there.

Iloe Ariss was an assistant lightkeeper for the summer for Canadian Lighthouses of Lake Superior.

Waves roll in on the other side of the Sleeping Giant.   [Photo: Donny Wabasse]

LIGHTHOUSE DISPATCHES

August 22, 2017

No shortage of visitors at Porphyry Island

The sun's reflection on the paddle blade swinging over the water signalled from a distance that our adventurer was about to arrive. Dianne Whelan is on a 23,000 kilometre odyssey along The Great Trail (TransCanada Trail); hiking, biking, snowshoeing, skiing... and canoeing 7,000 kilometres of it by water.

This solo adventure started at the Atlantic Ocean and will finish at the Pacific, and the journey will be featured in her documentary "500 Days In the Wild".

During her visit, she touched on the stories of the land and people she had connected with along the way. She shared with us, at the dinner table, her unique view of the journey thus far.

Whelan, paddling her canoe, is tracing the route of the voyageurs using the preferred method of transportation at the time; but now the modern ways of travel are quicker. Whelan enjoys the slower pace, as it reflects a perspective that brings her closer to the land and its meaning.

It was a pleasure for the lighthouse staff to be educated and entertained by such a timely journey on the Great Trail and The Lake Superior Water Trail that will have an official opening across the country, and at Porphyry Island, on Saturday.

Not far behind were another 11 intrepid paddlers from the Voyageur Outward Bound School, who were on a kayak trip west from Rossport. When the weather closed in with torrential rain, the spirits of these young travellers were not dampened. As part of their routine, they give back to the lighthouse through volunteer work activities which, this time, included cleaning the boathouse grounds and replenishing the firewood for the next visitors.

Their reward came after many hours of work when the crew was invited to the guesthouse for banana bread and hot chocolate, with marshmallows to cap things off.

With their work completed, the Outward Bound crew departed across Black Bay for a final night on the shores of Lake Superior, from which they could watch the beam of light from the Point Porphyry Lighthouse from afar.

Next to arrive was an armada of vessels from the Silver Islet Yacht Club, which pitched and yawed before reaching the new docks at Porphyry Island. Every bit of dock space available was taken-up and, in total, eight boats were accommodated for the yacht club's Annual Rendezvous which, for the past few years, has been held elsewhere.

The Silver Islet Yacht Club, and the Friends of Porphyry had played a role in helping maintain the boatyard, docks and exteriors of the keeper's dwellings for several years. It's again through the efforts of many that the facilities are in operation today. Now, Canadian Lighthouses of Lake Superior's volunteers, staff and board manage the facilities for equal access, and continue to gather support from many other community members and allies.

The lighthouse crew also spent a day at the Trowbridge Island Lighthouse, situated at the feet of the Sleeping Giant. Trowbridge's accessibility is certainly challenging from a water perspective, and work is ongoing to provide a day-dock for visitors; but that will happen later in the season.

Finally, the lighthouse group and the Thunder Bay Yacht Club hosted an On-the-Water Rendezvous at Tee Harbour that combined a tour of the Trowbridge Island Lighthouse, access to Sleeping Giant Provincial Park and a delicious BBQ.

This weekend, we'll share with our volunteers, members, and board of directors a national celebration of the opening of The Great Trail here at Porphyry.

Dianne Whelan, "500 Days in the Wild" documentary filmmaker, crosses Black Bay, west towards the Sleeping Giant. [Photo: Donny Wabasse]

August 29, 2017

Books and art at Point Porphyry Lighthouse

The shuttle returned to Porphyry Island with another group of people ready to disembark to start a new adventure. One visitor, Jean E. Pendziwol, author of a top-ten bestseller, *The Lightkeeper's Daughters*, surprised the guests with her appearance as many were attending a book club gathering.

The banners were up and the BBQ set for the guests. This was a day of celebration for The Great Trail (TransCanada Trail). Porphyry Island is part of the Lake Superior Water Trail that starts in Thunder Bay's Lorne Allard Fisherman's Park and ends in Sault Ste. Marie, Ontario, 750 kilometres away. The national celebration at Porphyry was to identify one of the stops on the Great Trail that kayakers and canoeists can now visit.

Paddlers will be assisted by new signage that was produced to showcase the local and regional histories while also acclimatizing the public to the issues specific to water safety on Lake Superior.

Eight members of the Catherine Street Book Society were on board to learn more about the water trail, but were also excited to learn more about the history of the island. The tour of the island began with a brief outline of how our lighthouse group, Canadian Lighthouses of Lake Superior (CLLS), had acquired, and how today it manages the leased property. This was followed by an extensive tour of the main site, light tower, mini-museum and the Gordon Graham Gallery.

A short video was shown — CBC Television's series "Heartland", introduced by Sylvia Tyson — which focuses on the life of a lightkeeper in the early 1980s. After the film, Jean E. Pendziwol did a reading from her recently published book to a quiet and attentive crowd.

Hiking back down the trail, Paul Capon, Chair of CLLS, cooked hamburgers and hot dogs while others brought appetizers and desserts for everyone to share. When the conversation lulled for a moment, presentations were made, and a short speech was given about the significance of the Lake Superior Water Trail and how it works with the Lighthouse Trail across the north shore.

Michel Dumont, our artist-in-residence, also provided a sneak peak of his work — a hand-crafted ceramic tile mosaic map of Porphyry Island, decorated on an animal form. The tile pieces were organized in great detail to provide a guide map to many of the beautiful things to see on the island.

When the shuttle returned to pick-up the next load of guests, our visitors were reluctant to leave as everyone knew there was even more to be discovered than time would allow. Luckily for most, they have a copy of *The Lightkeeper's Daughters* to refresh their memory in the winter months.

Our weekend ended with heavy southeasterly winds, two-meter waves, and a few logs on the fire at the keeper's dwelling.

Next week, we will look at some of the visitors that came this past summer and share how the community continues to come together to support history, economy and goodwill on Lake Superior.

Michel Dumont's sculpture can be seen creatively perched on Point Porphyry rocks.

[Photo: Donny Wabasse]

LIGHTHOUSE DISPATCHES

September 8, 2017

Porphyry Island lightkeepers reflect on successful summer

More wind and waves have come to Porphyry Island as the change of season starts to take place. With a fire in the furnace of the lightkeepers' dwelling, hot tea just off the stove, and windows washed by driving rain, it's nice to be indoors. Time to pause and reflect on the lighthouse group's work this past season and to draw upon the sense of community we felt this summer on the island. It's a challenge to capture the energy and excitement, but it was through the commitment of many that this lighthouse island continues to grow and slowly evolve.

Our Great Trail (TransCanada Trail) event last weekend brought together many members, volunteers, board directors, and guests to witness our achievement in managing a lighthouse destination for all visitors.

This year, we saw an increase of 25 per cent more visitors to the island than last year. They came to experience the well-manicured nature trails, panoramic views of Lake Superior and learn more about our history.

Our assistant lightkeeper summer staff, Iloe Ariss and Mathew Sloan, provided guests with activities, events and opportunities to interpret further our connection to this great lake. Without the support of the Canada Summer Jobs program, we would have been challenged to provide this wonderful support for our many visitors.

The benefit that our artist-in-residence brought to us was a refreshed view of the lake and island. The many views witnessed through the artists' eyes brought us closer to an understanding of what people are attracted to and enjoy.

This year's dock work was helped substantially through the kind assistance of volunteers from the Thunder Bay Yacht Club. The new floating docks now allow bigger boats a place to tie up for the night before continuing their journey east or west, and occasionally south to the United States.

The Voyageur Outward Bound Group from Ely, Minnesota, made a great contribution to our operation this summer by clearing our main trail of blowdown, and securing a wood supply for next season. We also saw the Ministry of Natural Resources and Forestry Youth Rangers clear a new coastal nature trail so visitors can see the beauty of our lake from another angle.

Whether arriving by paddle, sail or power, the island always transforms from a destination to an exploration. Most of our visitors were immediately aligned to the natural beauty the island had to offer, but surprises occasionally appeared. For example, found this week in the black, rocky shoreline was a ribbon of white quartz, three-centimeters wide and 30-meters long before sinking and being lost below the waves; begging more questions than we have answers.

To everyone who visited this season: thanks for your input, your support and your assistance to continue to provide a destination for all visitors. The board of directors of Canadian Lighthouses of Lake Superior appreciates your feedback and comments at anytime.

As the season winds down, we will all assess our summer and prepare again to bring the best of Lake Superior to our members and friends.

2018

A Sense of Peace and Tranquility.

June 5, 2018

Shuttle service a welcome addition to lighthouse

Situated on the east side of Black Bay, Point Porphyry Lighthouse on Porphyry Island is again gearing up for the summer, thanks to many helping hands.

On the rugged north shore of Lake Superior, Canadian Lighthouses of Lake Superior (CLLS) is providing public access to three surplus lighthouses leased from the Department of Fisheries and Oceans Canada.

This past winter had been busy with three grant applications confirmed, leaving the group with several key assignments to be completed by end of the season.

Upon arrival at the island this past weekend, many volunteers spoke of the thrill of traveling on the new shuttle service that will be offered every Monday this summer. Volunteers are key to making this happen, along with many levels of government and small businesses.

This weekend, the new *Superior Rocket*, operated by Sail Superior Inc. helped out by providing transport to volunteers so that they could make the trip to Porphyry Island for the day. The *Superior Rocket*, captained by Greg Heroux, is a welcome addition to the lighthouse experience as it will fulfill the lighthouse mandate of providing public access to the site, especially to Porphyry Island, this summer.

For a company like Sail Superior, which has for years offered tourists and locals with vistas from the water, these island lighthouses are a great historic destination. For more than 140 years, lighthouses have guided commerce in our area, helping make Canada a more prosperous country.

With tourist destinations on Lake Superior in short supply, Porphyry this summer will provide visitors with more amenities than ever before. New docks were brought out by the tugboat, *Rugged*, offering another 72 feet for boaters to tie up to, and also a new 8-by-14-foot prefabricated sauna. The sauna is in response to a request made to the Paterson Foundation which has generously provided funds for this facility both for safety and convenience.

Thanks also to the Thunder Bay Yacht Club volunteers and to Joe Marcella for designing and building the sauna.

Destinations on Lake Superior are difficult to access due to a lack of infrastructure investment and maintenance. Through five years of work, the lighthouse group is continuing to ask provincial and federal levels of government to help provide access to these historic lighthouse sites.

This season, we are expecting over 800 visitors who can come and enjoy the interpretive programming that the lighthouse offers, along with long-standing programs such as the artist-in-residence, the Gordon Graham Gallery and the panoramic light tower tour.

It's hoped that, again this season, CLLS can share the facilities with other organizations such as the Save Ontario Shipwrecks, Thunder Bay and Silver Islet Yacht Clubs, and Outward Bound expedition groups.

Next week we will share progress of our gear-up for the season, and chat with some kayakers visiting from Naturally Superior Adventures, in Wawa, about their explorations into these waters.

The tugboat, *Rugged*, floats three docks and a prefabricated sauna out to Porphyry Island during a break in the weather.
[Photo: CLLS]

June 12, 2018

Adventurists arrive on island

Adventure on Lake Superior is always best when surrounded by friends and familiar faces.

The 35-foot freighter canoe rounded the corner after traveling for part of the day up the shore of the Black Bay Peninsula, passing Edward Island to finally reach Porphyry Island. David Wells from Naturally Superior Adventures of Wawa, Ontario, was heading up a group that has travelled annually together for the past four years on Lake Superior. The youngest in the group was 60 years of age, and they were all in great spirits upon landing after a rather calm crossing.

Quickly, and like a well-oiled machine, tents were set up, wash stations installed and duties assigned at Porphyry's harbour. First off was a tour of the ever-expanding amenities located at the Point Porphyry Lighthouse.

Witnessed upon arrival, a new 80-foot dock has just been installed as part of a Parks Canada Lake Superior National Marine Conservation Area (NMCA) destination development, under a contribution agreement.

With the sauna construction work well underway, these adventure enthusiasts were quick to understand the value of a sauna on an extended wilderness trip. Not only do saunas provide an opportunity to clean up, they also can be used as a refuge in an emergency to provide warmth and shelter. Other than the practical use of a sauna, the back-story tells us saunas like this that stretch along the north shore of Lake Superior are a feature that visitors are interested in knowing more about and, of course, using.

When Parks Canada recently explored the NMCA's visitor experience strategy, this question was asked: "What attractions might entice visitors to experience further this new area in development?" Island saunas were one of the recommendations made in the strategy.

In a few more weeks, the Porphyry sauna work should be completed thanks to some very hard-working volunteers!

Simon Cohen, from the state of Georgia, whose family's summer camp is at Silver Harbour, has spent the last week volunteering his time during his summer break. He's studying anthropology and biology at the University of Georgia and has adapted well to the cool temperatures of Superior. He will later be going to Israel on an archaeological dig, but will continue helping out here for another week; chopping wood, clearing trails, and helping with daily lighthouse chores.

Meanwhile, the 13 freighter canoeists have made it up to the top of the lighthouse tower on Point Porphyry and are amazed at the 360-degree view. Most are visiting from southern Ontario, and they all relished the serenity that is offered with calm winds and flat seas.

Bob Fisher from Toronto said, "I am amazed at the dedication demonstrated by the lighthouse group, and wonder why other levels of government are short-sighted to fully support these heritage sites?"

With weekly Monday shuttles transporting the public from Prince Arthur's Landing in the City of Thunder Bay, it's hoped that more people can come and enjoy the quarter-million dollar investment made over the past five years for this and other Lake Superior destinations.

Next week, we will share more on the work that is taking place on Porphyry Island and tell you about the start of a cleanup and painting party on Trowbridge Island.

A freighter canoe arrives at Porphyry Island for an overnight stopover. [Photo: Donny Wabasse]

June 19, 2018

More exciting activity on Porphyry Island

Fog, rain, sun, waves and wind are all the order of the day while living out on the lake for the season. Each day, we can expect to get a taste of everything at Porphyry Island. With this type of weather, you must carry a hat/glasses for the sun, windbreaker for the wind and rain, and extra layers you peel off all day, only to be layered back on at day's end. If you are lucky, in the morning your boots are dry, and your work clothes that were hung by the fire the night before, are comfortable to wear. Nothing uncomfortable deteriorates your work mood faster than having wet feet.

This week's adventures included a paint party at Trowbridge Island, a grandfather and grandson building team, and our first book-tour of the season.

This past Saturday morning, 16 volunteers started to work on painting the Trowbridge Island Lighthouse. It is situated near the feet of the Sleeping Giant and was built in 1924. This important aid to navigation guides marine traffic along the shipping corridor past Isle Royale to the Port of Thunder Bay. It's been a few years since the place saw some paint and, to manage our lease with the Department of Fisheries and Oceans Canada, it's our goal as an organization to be good tenants and keep the place in order. Painting is a good motivator for our volunteers because right in front of their eyes they can see change happening and that their efforts are making a difference. It's with thanks to sponsorship by Dulux Paint, a Colourful Communities project, that our two family painting teams and members of our board of directors could get the work started.

Later, we were all chased away due to some impending storm cells from the south, but we managed, working together as a group of volunteers, to get the work underway.

Upon completion of this stage of the day, *Nina*, built in 1955 as a wooden cruiser, returned from Trowbridge Island to Porphyry Harbour; a two-hour cruise to the east across Black Bay. Following the compass as thick fog enveloped the vessel, we gingerly made our way in. Waiting on the dock to greet us was Joe Marcella and his grandson, Dustin, who had been very busy closing in the sauna from the elements of Lake Superior. Seeing the dedication of volunteers makes everyone feel good.

One other project waiting to be installed is a new dock extension on the original concrete footing near Point Porphyry. This effort is sponsored by the Thunder Bay Yacht Club and it will allow visitors to tie up during the day near the historic lighthouse. Through simple adaptations, we can work to make the lighthouse safer to access during calm weather and create a unique interpretive opportunity for visitors.

We live our lives to make a difference in our society, and before our eyes the sauna is being erected to showcase, in some respects, the lives of Northerners on Lake Superior. Yes, we have it tough sometimes, but soon we will have the comforts of a new sauna to share with hundreds of visitors.

Jean E. Pendziwol, author of a best seller, *The Lightkeeper's Daughters*, took a group of hungry adventurers around Porphyry Island to hand-feed them some of her inspiration and nuggets of distilled information to satisfy their desire for the book's background — another example of continuing to share the stories of lightkeepers and their families who toiled on this rugged and changing coastline.

Next week, we will share with you the story of how the work that's taking place on these remote islands on Superior is making an impact in Toronto.

Volunteers clean up the façade of the Trowbridge lightkeeper's dwelling prior to adding a coat of paint.
[Photo: Donny Wabasse]

June 26, 2018

Historical society recognizes Lake Superior lighthouses

Preparing for the summer continues at Porphyry Island with many hands lightening the load. Our volunteers have been working extra time to facilitate the visiting public on the island this summer.

It's the little deeds that don't go unnoticed. For example, the Saunders family arrived last week with a new artifact for the lighthouse museum: a child's leather shoe. Washed up in a storm years ago, each little artifact like this helps to share a story of the island's lighthouse history.

The Ontario Historical Society recognized Canadian Lighthouses of Lake Superior (CLLS) in Toronto on Saturday, and I had the opportunity, on behalf of the group, to receive the award. "The OHS is pleased to present the 2017 Scadding Award of Excellence to the Canadian Lighthouses of Lake Superior," said Kristin Ives, a director of the Ontario Historical Society. The Scadding Award is presented to a historical society or heritage group that has made an outstanding contribution to the field of history. The CLLS was formed in 2012 by volunteers with a mandate to preserve, protect and promote public access to the lighthouses on the north shore of Lake Superior.

"The CLLS organization recognizes, as unique heritage resources, these historic maritime structures which stretch over an 800-kilometre shoreline from Thunder Bay to Sault Ste. Marie," said Ives. "Impressively, CLLS has gained leases from the federal Department of Fisheries and Oceans Canada to access and maintain three lighthouses in the region: Porphyry, No.10 (Shaganash) and Trowbridge. Along with access to and maintenance of these physical structures, this group is dedicated to restoring the navigational history and sharing these rich stories of the area's history with locals and visitors alike."

Ives noted that CLLS has welcomed tourists, artists, painters, outdoor enthusiasts, birders, kayakers, sailors and powerboaters to enjoy the lighthouses and the region. Among other things, the group has developed an annual lighthouse symposium, spearheaded the heritage designation of the Lamb Island Lighthouse, developed and hosted the Porphyry Island Superior Rendezvous event, engaged volunteers, created summer jobs for students, developed an artist-in-residence program and engaged citizen scientists to catalogue native plants.

"Through their significant efforts to preserve and promote their region's lighthouses, CLLS has forged strong ties and encouraged partnerships between communities, heritage organizations and other agencies," said Ives. "The Honours and Awards Committee of the Ontario Historical Society is pleased to recognize these contributions with the Scadding Award of Excellence."

On behalf of the board of directors and the volunteers, I accepted the award. We were in good company with CBC's Carol Off and "Murdoch Mysteries" (Shaftesbury Films) also being recognized, among many others.

This coming week, we are back at the island getting ready for our first *Superior Rocket* shuttle on Monday. We are hoping, as an organization, to make the island more accessible to the general public with extra seats available on our Monday charter service.

Soon, we shall share with you our Canada Day celebrations and update you on our sauna project.

Ontario Historical Society honours & awards committee chairman Ian Radforth, left, and director Kristin Ives, right, present the Scadding Award for Excellence to Paul Morralee of Canadian Lighthouses of Lake Superior.
[Photo: Daniel Dishaw]

CLLS and the Ontario Historical Society

Building of a non-profit organization requires a good foundation to begin the process of attracting the right people and affiliations that help to build capacity and sustainability. The enthusiasm at the launch of Canadian Lighthouses of Lake Superior (CLLS) in October, 2012, was infectious, but also came with the tall order of incorporating the organization and gaining charitable status. For this, CLLS was advised to approach the Ontario Historical Society (OHS).

Upon meeting the OHS executive director, Robert Leverty, the board of directors quickly recognized that they were in capable hands. Rob expertly guided CLLS through the process of creating the articles of incorporation and bylaws. This was also accompanied by an application to the government for charitable status.

The OHS helps groups network by connecting them through a forum for individuals, organizations and institutions to exchange ideas, research and experiences related to the rich history of the province. The society provides educational materials, resources, and professional development opportunities to encourage the sharing and celebration of Ontario's history in classrooms and museums. It was founded as a non-profit organization in 1888, working to bring people together — all ages, walks of life and cultural backgrounds — with the goal of preserving Ontario's history. Now, the society has over 350 member groups, all of which connect people to the history of the province.

The assistance provided to the CLLS has been immeasurable as each barrier or issue was resolved. In 2018, Canadian Lighthouses of Lake Superior won the OHS Scadding Award of Excellence. This is presented to a historical society or heritage group that has made an outstanding contribution to the field of history.

The award read as follows:"Through their significant efforts to preserve and promote their region's lighthouses, Canadian Lighthouses of Lake Superior has forged strong ties and encouraged partnerships between communities, heritage organizations, and other agencies. The Honours and Awards Committee of the Ontario Historical Society is pleased to recognize these contributions with the Scadding Award of Excellence."

July 3, 2018

Summer crew starts – guests arrive

Life at the lighthouse is starting to take shape with the arrival of this year's crew ready to make the light station home for their tenure.

Through the dense fog, Captain Gregory Heroux of the *Superior Rocket* makes the dock after a 1-hour and 20-minute run from Thunder Bay.

The *Superior Rocket* is a military-grade Zodiac vessel capable of transporting 12 guests every Monday. Supplies piled high and guests jacketed up in bright orange waterproof survival suits with gloves and matching goggles, all arrived safely and everyone is excited about the pending tour.

Since our summer crew started today, introductions were made to our guests, which includes our artist-in-residence, host-keeper family, and summer students.

This was an ideal opportunity for us to share with our visitors the many programs and to explore the site, which includes a 15-minute walk up the old lighthouse road.

Splitting the group into two, the lighthouse tour began with an orientation of the site, the many players, and the role of the organization. Our boathouse has become a reception area for our guests, with a little gift shop filled with postcards, fridge magnets, T-shirts and mugs.

Periodically, hammering and sawing could be heard in the background as volunteers continue working on finishing up the sauna to have it ready for the season.

Walking through the forest was a treat as a spot of sunshine flickered through the trees to the carpet of moss below. "Old Man's Beard" (*Usnea florida* lichen) is dripping water droplets collected from the rolling fog that keeps coming and going. The weather has been very unsettled for several days on the lake with the last 48 hours accompanied by wind, rain, fog and amazing thunder and lightning shows.

Arriving at the main lighthouse site, our new Parks Canada interpretive signs are a hit with visitors, as they clearly explain the role of the lightkeeper and include some shipwreck stories on this part of the Lake Superior coast.

The light today is magic, with deep blues in the water, bright whitecaps, and green forests with the leaves only just recently making an appearance.

LIGHTHOUSE DISPATCHES

It's nice to look out the window to see the site full of activity again. Now, the whistle of the kettle signals teatime. Time to go!

Next week, we will learn more about our summer students and what projects are being undertaken, and hear about the happenings on the island.

The *Superior Rocket* arrives at Porphyry Island Harbour with lighthouse tour guests, summer students, host-keepers and the artist-in-residence.
[Photo: Donny Wabasse]

July 10, 2018

Island life at Porphyry

Through the eyes of others we can experience island life once again afresh and anew.

Our summer students, Ben and Emily, have settled into a routine, and so have Marsha and Jess our visiting host-keepers. Betty, our artist-in-residence, is also becoming comfortable in her new surroundings.

As a matter of course, there is always that significant moment where the shift from the electricity grid to living off-grid can create some experiences that leave a mark. The inter-relationship between living on the island or off is that you still need to eat, have a shelter over your head and be surrounded by some comforts of home.

Moving resources from the mainland to the island is reminiscent of the lightkeeper's life, and is often mentioned in lightkeepers' diaries. With Monday's *Superior Rocket* shuttle running from the Marina, we can now better accommodate our needs.

Marsha Reinikka and her daughter Jess have done a wonderful job of keeping the home fires burning bright. Marsha's family once occupied the Lamb Island Lighthouse, so this territory is far from new, and what better way to share family history with her daughter.

Ben Heywood-MacLeod and Emily Hunt, assistant lightkeepers for the summer, are amazed at the wide variety of things to do and see on-site. Ben arrived from Montreal and immediately enjoyed the island setting where, on his time off, he gravitates to playing ballads of Lake Superior on his guitar. Emily's view is similar as she experiences new things and is anticipating more visitors to the island. She's also attempting a world record on the slack line, which is a long strap supported near the ground by two trees, and is similar to a high wire act — good cross-training for the upcoming ski season I suppose.

This week has been mainly about orientating the staff as to what to expect in the coming summer months. The sauna is near completion and the docks and the boathouse visitor reception centre are ready for vessels to arrive.

Each of our crew at the lighthouse has tasks to complete during their stays. Jess has been reviewing Porphyry lightkeeper Andrew Dick's diaries. Written at the end of the 1800s, it's an interesting read as to the similarities and differences we now experience here on the island. Betty Carpick, our resident artist is stitching up a storm on fabric. Visitors are asked to grab a needle and thread and cast a line of stitches onto the emerging map of Porphyry. It might not be the stitching that's ultimately important, but the exchange of ideas and thoughts as people work together — the moment to put your mind to a task, and in that moment find a new avenue to explore. Betty's art is allowing people space to explore, and it creates new frontiers and builds upon previous experiences.

One of our loyal volunteers asked his friends and family to donate money in lieu of birthday gifts and he raised a significant contribution to the lighthouse. Thank you so much William Vanderwees, and Happy Birthday from your lighthouse friends.

Next week, we will share a finished picture of the completed sauna and share with you an update on our visitor stories.

Emily Hunt (right) and Ben Heywood-MacLeod load the hand cart with wood for the sauna.

[Photo: CLLS]

July 17, 2018

Excitement builds for opening of island sauna

Black Bay this weekend came alive as the Thunder Bay Salmon Association held their annual fishing derby. From the point at Porphyry Island, boats could be seen bobbing about, trolling for the winning catch. As it was a weekend event, some fishermen stayed overnight at the dock, and all for free.

Later, we were able to meet up with three young Northern Michigan University students from Marquette who are circumnavigating Lake Superior by kayak. Three pairs of eyes were watching expectantly their catch-of-the-day wrapped in tinfoil being cooked over the fire. The crew was excited to be on the island to share their adventure and to stretch their legs.

The excitement on the island continues to build for the opening of the sauna, which is still in the fine-detail stage with doors being hung, windows being shimmed, and paint applied. Every visitor is impressed with the quality of the work so far, including members of the Paterson Foundation which granted funds to build this amenity. The attraction will provide comfort for travelers, a place to warm up or, interestingly, a story of how a sauna impacts life on the North Shore.

With work well underway at Porphyry, our team of volunteers is also working hard painting and cleaning up the Trowbridge Island Lighthouse, located near the feet of the Sleeping Giant. For anyone who has been to Silver Islet, the light can be seen across the water every five seconds. Built in 1924, the lighthouse is important to shipping as it provides direction for big vessels to find their way into Thunder Bay.

Across the feet of the Sleeping Giant a small red helicopter could be seen approaching Trowbridge. After circling the island, Liam Dowds, owner and pilot of Northwest Heli-Tours and Adventures, set down on the landing pad. He brought with him three gentlemen — the Singh brothers. Dowds said, "Visiting the lighthouses of Lake Superior offers a fantastic experience. Getting there by helicopter in 15 minutes with views of Thunder Bay, the Sleeping Giant and the lighthouses from above is incredible!" All were amazed at the beauty that the lake offers and were very happily snapping pictures for Facebook and to share with friends.

As our week begins, we thank artist-in-residence Betty Carpick as she leaves the island, and welcome our new resident artist, Cynthia Nault.

We also have a new host-keeper, eager to get started on helping the marketing of our story online. This week's shuttle also brought us two tourists from Scotland who were so full of superlatives about their visit that we've run out of space to share all their words.

Excitement is building as Canadian Lighthouses of Lake Superior's exhibit aboard the *Alexander Henry* Museum Ship will be opening to the public on July 18. The exhibit is housed in one of the seaman's cabins and features the ship's role as a lighthouse supply ship many years ago. Also showcased are two new replicas of the Shaganash Lighthouse on Number 10 Island. These model lighthouses were built by the woodworking shop at Hammarskjold High School and capped off by some steel works from the welding class at Superior Collegiate and Vocational Institute. The ship will also feature some brand new gift items made especially for visitors.

Next week, we will further explore Cynthia Nault's art experience and hear how our host-keeper is getting along with her lighthouse keeping chores.

Canadian Lighthouses of Lake Superior Chair, Paul Capon, poses along with Xammy Singh, Sartaj Singh, Amrik Singh and Paul Morralee on the helipad with the Trowbridge Island Lighthouse in the background.

[Photo: Ben Heywood-MacLeod]

July 24, 2018

Island offers "breathtaking panoramic views"

Now that the swirling fog of Superior is behind us, the summer sunshine is finally drying us out.

Long walks along the black sand beach and hiking through the moss-covered forest floor leave visitors with a sense of belonging. This is their island; this is their place to explore, and more people continue to do just that.

With the Superior shuttle in full operation, the vessel brings another wave of visitors who are surprised by the experience. As the clock ticks down the summer days, visitors are happy to let time pass them by, and take it all in. Kayakers are coming to visit now that the waters are calmer and the breeze is not so fresh as to leave you shivering. Setting up camp with fresh-cut firewood, with room to roam free and stunning sunsets, what could be better? Boaters continue to take advantage of the new docking facilities and the visitors' experience centre which entices them to stay longer and spend another night.

Our host-keeper, Cyndi Fecteau, enjoyed her experience working on refreshing the lighthouse media pages with a visitor's insight. She writes, "Porphyry Island offers breathtaking panoramic views that will have you thirsty for more. The Sleeping Giant lies at the foot of the Porphyry Point and is a sight you will enjoy any time of the day or night."

For Cynthia Nault, our local resident artist, she said, "The opportunity to stay on this island and learn about the life of a lightkeeper has been such a gift. It's hard to capture the magic and mystery of Porphyry without spending time immersed in its majestic scenery, surrounded by Lake Superior."

During her first week as artist-in-residence, she's learned how to identify cedar waxwings by their calls. The haunting beauty of their soft whistles feels very much on-point with the loneliness and isolation an early light keeper must have felt. However, their sense of community, as can be seen in the way they travel in flocks, reminds her of the family atmosphere here on the island. These beautiful birds have made their way into her painting, which will be auctioned off at next year's fundraising dinner.

This past weekend at the Trowbridge Island Lighthouse, visitors from the Thunder Bay Yacht club received a personalized tour of the site, while a crew of volunteers worked hard to continue to conserve the lighthouse and area. Their conservation work included moving the outhouse, installing a new compost toilet and repainting the exterior of the buildings.

Next week, we will share with you the adventures of the Save Ontario Shipwrecks crew that is coming to explore the wrecks just offshore from the island.

Cynthia Nault, artist-in-residence at Porphyry Island, creates layers on her canvas to capture the surrounding experiences she has witnessed in the last week of exploration. [Photo: CLLS]

July 31, 2018

Stories from the past at Porphyry

The sparkling waters off the point ebbed and flowed as the gentle breeze of summer moves us along through another beautiful day. The voices of people can be heard in the forest as laughter permeates the constant rhythm of water washing upon the rocks; echoing times from the past.

Eve Graham, former lightkeeper on Porphyry Island, tells us the stories of lighthouse duties as many gather around to listen during one of our afternoon tours. She shares with us her feelings about returning to the lighthouse after many years of being away. "I'm happy to see all the work that's gone into keeping this place maintained, which helps visitors to remember the families that once served here," she says.

Later, for the very first time, Eve tours the Gordon Graham Gallery — named in memory of her husband — and also views, in the museum, some of the artifacts of a bygone era. For her, this was part of her past life. Raising two young boys on Porphyry Island was not easy, and she also home-schooled them. Some of their toys are still in the basement of the old house, waiting to be animated again by a youthful hand.

Gordon Graham's photographic images stand as a testament to the final chapter of lightkeepers manning the light station, and provide people with a glimpse back to another time.

Venturing along the North Shore towards Rossport is Zack Kruzins, whose company, Such A Nice Day Adventures, stops at Porphyry Harbour. He and his crew of seven kayakers are excited to be on the water and to experience the first major attraction on their eight-day trip. After a delicious meal cooked over a wood fire, the group of kayakers head up to see the big, panoramic view of the lake from the light tower. In every direction you can see for many miles, helping them to chart their course towards the east.

In the distance, a swirl of smoke can be seen as the sauna is in its final testing phases. Thanks to brothers Mark and Steve Daley for installing the smokestack, and to brothers Richard and Joe Marcella for assembling the benches and doors, among other unnamed tasks.

With tours now happening daily, the assistant lightkeepers are happy to continue to build upon their narratives. Each tour allows the summer students to test their method of delivery and to glean new facts from visitors or to respond to interesting questions about the lighthouse.

The volunteer host-keeper family has moved in, and our newest artist-in-residence has arrived. We are ready to educate and entertain once again.

Next week, we will be hosting an informal awards night at Porphyry for the SUNORA regatta made up of ten boats and twenty-five participants.

Seen in the front of the boathouse after a day paddling Lake Superior are Cesar J. Heriandez, Zack Kruzins, Barb Adderley, Wendy Heron, Anna Lagre, Jen Coyne and Melissa Allin. [Photo: CLLS]

August 7, 2018

Lineups forming for new sauna on island

Rumors have been circulating along the North Shore about the impending opening of the sauna on Porphyry Island, and today we can announce that it's open. After three months of prepping, pre-fabricating, building and installing, the response has been very positive. Considering our weather here has been cool this summer, the addition of a hot, functioning sauna has meant that, for the past four nights, lineups have been forming. Comments from visitors have been coming in and it's two thumbs-up from everyone. One family stayed two extra days just to get in more sauna time.

Fifteen visiting engineers from England spent the afternoon on guided tours, and finished up their visit with a dunking in Lake Superior after a sauna. Wide-eyed and with frantic strokes, they managed to recover to the safety of the docks. Through these visitors' eyes, we know how lucky we are to live here; on this island; in this adventure playground.

The annual SUNORA sailboat regatta that was traveling back to Thunder Bay after a week on the water took advantage of the Porphyry Harbour grounds for a final night before heading home. Each year, the regatta attracts new and old boaters and shares in a North Shore experience of camaraderie around the fire. It's great to see everyone together swapping stories and having a laugh.

Our artist-in-residence and his spouse hail from Oxford, England. Adrian and Jane Brooks have been shocked and awed by the beauty of the area. Adrian said his first impressions were, "...the sheer scale of the lake, the grandeur of the Sleeping Giant and the awesome Milky Way; truly magnificent." Coming from the landlocked County of Oxfordshire, he says, "There is not a lighthouse in sight, and so to hear the tales of lighthouse families from past years at the kitchen table over lunch is haunting." Adrian will be designing a wall-mounted painted theatre that will illustrate his experience on Porphyry.

Our summer continues to forge a path towards connecting people to our history, to sharing our culture and celebrating the rituals of summer.

It's wonderful to not only witness boaters, sailors and kayakers enjoying the experience but, now, the general public arriving aboard the *Superior Rocket*. Many of the visitors are floored to find cars at the top of the Porphyry Island road, and giant "Devil's Club" plants infringing upon their path, or to spot the rabbit that lives by the swamp.

Like the layers of an onion, the experience is always fortified with more levels to explore, to inspire people to continue the journey to celebrate our history.

Artist-in-residence, Adrian Brooks, shares with U.K. visitors his approach to capturing the lighthouses in watercolour. [Photo: CLLS]

August 14, 2018

Allure of Porphyry – Hundreds of people visiting

In the dusk, as one of our team members was returning to their overnight accommodation on Porphyry Island, he came upon a bull moose on the trail. The moose was startled dining out on swamp cuisine. After a moment of consideration, it departed down the trail quickly, leaving sliding hoof marks.

Over breakfast, everyone on the lighthouse team was talking about the moose sighting the night before and wondering where he might appear next. It was not long before the moose was spotted again, this time swimming in the water. The inbound Superior shuttle guests were very happy to have seen this rare occurrence. Spilling their words of glee, they shared the experience of seeing the huge beast powering its way through the water, reporting its final destination to be Hardscrabble Island. Meanwhile, island life continues to percolate, along with a variety of events that have left some visitors wondering: what's happening here?

Take Friday for example... The Air Ambulance visited our helipad on a touch-and-go exercise. The lighthouse group had asked for a site survey to be conducted to be prepared in case of an accident. The RCMP in their RIB vessel followed the helicopter, checking in to see how our summer was transpiring and to check for foreign vessels. This was then followed by a float plane circling the island before landing in the cove. The visitors had come to see the island from top to bottom and side to side. Finally, with all the commotion around the island, we had the neighbours boating over to see what was going on! We nonchalantly answered that everything was fine.

Our second expedition from the Voyageur Outward Bound School came through and they were very willing to help cut and pile firewood. Helping hands lighten the load.

The Mallon, Sargent, and Leduc families enjoyed the camping area during the week, and were happy to test out the brand new sauna.

Our artist-in-residence program says goodbye today to Adrian Brooks, and is now welcoming Kaija Savinainen-Mountain as she begins her two-week stint. Our host-keeper family of Heather McLeod and sons Sam and Ben enjoyed endless days of summer in their week on the island; finding adventure at the beach and contributing to the operation of the lighthouse. Thanks to the previous families who had left sand pails and spades for the children to play with, and to the Silver Islet families who donated the picnic tables years ago for people to relax upon. Every little bit helps create a welcoming atmosphere. We continue to see increased traffic to the island from all walks of life. Our guests are helpful in giving us direction to make this a fun place to visit.

This week, Canadian Lighthouses of Lake Superior will be attending a meeting in Nipigon to discuss access to the National Marine Conservation Area through marinas and docks. So far this summer the lighthouse group has counted 480 visitors to Porphyry Island. They came by sail, power-boat, floatplane, voyageur canoe and kayak. These reported numbers will help us continue to garner support for this as a visitor destination. The lighthouse group is excited about these consultations as the future is upon us, and people are looking for things to do.

Next week, we will share with you reactions from our new artist-in-residence and host-keeper family.

The Voyageur Outward Bound School prepares for their final leg back to the mainland as four families in the background enjoy their summer visit at Porphyry Harbour. [Photo: Donny Wabasse]

August 21, 2018

Good times all 'round

The glow of the campfire could be seen from a distance as music gently flowed into the clear night sky. Silver Islet Yacht Club (SIYC) members and friends had come together for their Annual Rendezvous, which meant good times all 'round. Sitting around the fire listening to stories from the past or watching revelers dance by the firelight made the evening memorable. It was a sight to see and to acknowledge that, through their own efforts, they'd made this opportunity possible.

Years ago, SIYC members recognized the island as a destination to share in family traditions, and catch the odd fish too. Upon departure, someone's fishing rod would not let go of the dock, and was whipped out of the boat to sink to a watery grave. It's difficult to leave.

As the programs at Porphyry Island continue to operate tours and entertain tourist, there's ample room to explore.

Elaine Lynch and Jim Dacey enjoyed immensely their adventures as host-keepers for the past week. Lynch said, "We have so much respect for this site and admiration for the care, tending and heritage restorations by Canadian Lighthouses of Lake Superior, in sharing their efforts with people from all over the world." It's through the efforts of these volunteers that CLLS, as an organization, can continue to operate and provide a small level of service. Meals are prepared and grounds maintained to give visiting tourists the opportunity to understand what was required to tend to the light and survive on these treacherous shores.

Kaija Savinainen-Mountain, our visiting artist-in-residence, is everywhere. She sees the big lake and rugged nature through enthusiastic eyes. Savinainen-Mountain said, "I jump into drawing and painting, attempting to catch the essence of what lies before me. The island is magical with her almost impenetrable forests and the black sand beach interspersed always with the sound of waves — an artists paradise."

When we witness artists taking the time to explore, to discover the inner mysteries of the Lake Superior wilderness, it's satisfying to know their art will reflect these themes.

Our visitors keep coming, but there's still lots of room for more. Besides the Porphyry Harbour, many boaters moor off of Edward Island or stay near Walkers Channel. It is always a balancing act among power-boaters, sailors and kayakers. Dropping barriers and pretense happens all the time in the challenges of being in the wilds. It's refreshing to see everyone getting along together and enjoying the moment.

As the summer starts to wane, our garden continues to flourish, although well behind in the season. We may never see tomatoes ripen as they are just flowering now, but our zucchinis are doing well. Porphyry zucchini anyone?

The lighthouse team has been engaged in berry-picking too, which has meant many pies being cooked. The past two weeks, we've had gooseberry and raspberry pie mixed in with apples from the mainland. Now all we need is to get some ice-cream!

Next week, we will share with you some of the CLLS accomplishments as the summer starts to draw to a close.

Jim and George strum away the evening playing many favourite campfire hits. [Photo: CLLS]

August 28, 2018

Retracing route from the past – Resurrecting history at Porphyry Island

Summer fun continues with warm weather, great sunsets and a parade of new guests out to explore.

This week, the Thunder Bay Yacht Club with their annual On-the-Water Rendezvous made it to the island to retreat from the city and enjoy some nature. As the campfire roared on, people were taking turns using the sauna and exploring the lighthouse site. Thanks to all the yacht club members who helped build docks and maintain the site. Returning visitors are often impressed at the changes that have taken place from one year to the next.

This year, for example, we have been celebrating the seven Parks Canada interpretive signs that helped keep the lighthouse story alive. The lighthouse group is happy for the support from the Paterson Foundation for the sauna that is getting lots of good use. And finally, we are excited for the future of the hostkeeper program after its first run this year. This gave visiting families the opportunity to live and work at the lighthouse for a one-week term.

Our tourist numbers are up in comparison to last year, and our power-boater, kayak and sailor numbers have also increased slightly over the previous year.

We say goodbye and thank you to our summer staff, Ben, Emily and Tazi, for their hard work and dedication to the cause. It's wonderful to work with youth today who help us stay current and engaged in telling our story. Soon, we will be releasing a short film on the summer staff experience dedicated to the Canada Summer Jobs program of the federal government .

Also, thanks to our dedicated volunteers who are still hard at work on a Great Lakes Guardian Community Fund project to restore the Trowbridge Island habitat and grounds for future visitors. Concrete pathways, painting and septic upgrades have already been done on-site.

This week at Porphyry, we had a visitor, Frances Anne Hopkins, a.k.a. Naomi Harris, a well-known photographer retracing the 19th Century travels of painter Hopkins from the fur-trading era. Hopkins, in her day, had painted her way from Montreal to Fort William, following the route of the voyageurs. Her paintings showed the last days of voyageur life prior to the age of steam locomotion.

LIGHTHOUSE DISPATCHES

Traveling by canoe with one guide, Naomi Harris, modeling herself after Hopkins, followed the same route the 19th Century artist took over 150 years ago. Watching Harris recreate the path of Hopkins is parallel to the work undertaken by Canadian Lighthouses of Lake Superior, in that we are also resurrecting history and animating it for visitors today.

As we work hard to make history come alive, we are reminded of all the help we have received from the lightkeeper families that are still in the area. Everyday, we share with visitors some piece of history that we've learned, and most are interested to learn that some things remain the same and never change; like the breathtaking view, the cool clean air and the panoramic vistas.

Next week, we will share with you some of the observations that visitors have shared with lighthouse staff and members.

Naomi Harris stands in front of Porphyry Island Light tower in 1800's-era dress, while on her journey to Fort William.   [Photo: CLLS]

Porphyry Island's New Light Tower

At the heart of the current Porphyry light station stands the island's operational navigational structure: the light tower. For both visitors and tourists, this tower symbolizes the essence of the lighthouse's story. Over time, technological advancements have led to significant downsizing, requiring less manpower. For instance, the original light used lamps fuelled by kerosene which were labouriously maintained and manually lighted on a daily basis. Today, the electric light in the tower is powered by a solar panel and battery, activating automatically at night.

The light tower's story began with the remodelling of the light station in 1960, which included the addition of new living quarters for the keepers along with other auxiliary buildings. The original 1873 lighthouse, built in 1873 was demolished. The new tower was constructed on a high point of land and rises 80 feet into the air. Using a 500-watt Crouse-Hinds electric light originally powered by a diesel generator, the lighthouse now provides illumination that reaches 15 miles into the navigation channel.

The construction was carried out by a crew from the Canadian Coast Guard Ship *Alexander Henry*, which had just been commissioned into service. With large steel trusses suspended high above the ground, skilled workers bolted the structure together and covered it with sheets of tin to enclose the climbing ladder within. At the top, an aluminum, prefabricated, eight-sided cupola with large glass panels, was installed. A vent in the roof was included to release any fumes if gas-powered lamps had to be used.

The tower serves as a navigation aid both at night and during day as it includes a white wooden signboard as a day-mark fixed to the south-facing side of the tower allowing vessels navigating the channel to spot the structure during the day.

Today, the automated tower also serves as a fantastic observation platform, granting visitors stunning views of the clear waters and panoramic vistas, as well as the volcanic basalt that composes the island.

Light tower construction, 1960. The original 1873 lighthouse can be seen in the background.
[Photo: McKay Family Collection]

LIGHTHOUSE DISPATCHES

September 4, 2018

Summer's end: An opportunity for lighthouse reflections

You may be asking the same question our volunteers, board members and visitors are asking: "Where did the summer go?"

Sitting in the lightkeeper's dwelling with the sound of waves coming across the window sashes and spilling into my writing space reminds me of the perpetual motion of time. The weather, the waves, the sounds of the seagulls; all keep bringing me back to the sense of peace and tranquility that this space generates.

Away from the buzz of the internet or fake news from the south, many have sought sanctuary by visiting Lake Superior; especially the three islands that Canadian Lighthouses of Lake Superior manages.

Turning the pages of the Porphyry Island guest book reminds us of the passage of time and how people have responded to their experiences.

Let's start with the Glennie twins, originally from Scotland, who wrote, "Walking along the Marina Park in Thunder Bay, and there was this sign 'Superior Tours'. Called, and we got on the Zodiac tour to Porphyry Island. The most amazing trip on Lake Superior and the lighthouse. Well worth the journey!"

Michael Luhrsen from Duluth, Minnesota writes, "Spent a great night here returning from a fishing trip. Had a very informative tour. I've been wanting to check this place out and am very impressed. I'll be back."

Elissa Field said, " Had a great time exploring my roots. I love reminiscing in a place I saw as a child."

Or how about the "Four the Water Crew" of kayakers who arrived with only three members. I'm not sure what the back story was, but they said, " Paddled in last night during our circumnavigation of Mother Superior and was welcomed and given an excellent tour. Very cool spot here and look forward to being back one day. Jared, Ryan and Karol."

John Stevenson and Mary Wood of Thunder Bay, aboard a sailboat said, "From Loon Harbour – beautiful day sailing – 12 knot winds – sunny – light chop. Great to be at the (Porphyry) dock! Looks fantastic. Can't wait for a sauna."

And who could forget Dave Bradley's maiden voyage to Porphyry Island by Sea-Doo: "Great work everyone! Can't wait to be back soon."

Finally, Max Bailey writes, "Love coming back here, and always seem to learn something new each time. We slept in tents last night and were treated to the most intense thunderstorm I've seen in years. We somehow managed to keep dry. Island is in better shape than I have ever seen. Thank you to the team. Until next time!"

And now for my personal words of thanks to all who made this summer happen. It takes many in a community to come together to realize a goal, and to keep moving the goal posts forward. To our supporters, volunteers, host-keepers, artist-in-residence, Canada Summer Students. our guests and visitors; thank you for your support and encouragement to maintain this historical asset.

As this is the final Lighthouse Dispatch in this series, I'd like to thank you, the reader who have often quietly pulled me aside to share with me your thoughts. It's great to know that you came along for the journey, to embrace our history, to engage with our nature, and to celebrate our magnificent Lake Superior lighthouses.

Sunrise over the black sand beaches of Porphyry Island. [Photo: Donny Wabasse]

2019

Monarch Butterflies and Crashing Waves

July 9, 2019

Porphyry site receives more visitors so far

While seated at the lightkeeper's dinner table, the cool winds lift up off of Lake Superior and through a small crack in the window frame, reminding us of how refreshing it is to be back for another summer. New and old faces appear, but some are more than familiar with the hardships of living on a Lake Superior island than most would first guess. In a family-style setting, host-keepers, previous assistant keepers, lighthouse navigators (our new designation for our summer students) and an artist-in-residence come together to share the moments of the day.

Perspectives are shared, and Judith Appleton from Israel speaks about the arid conditions she's used to and now she is bathed and ensnarled by Lake Superior's cool tentacles. Others come from the west side of the continent where the waters are salty and whales can be seen, and living on an island is no big deal. For the few seated at the table who come from the city of Thunder Bay, listening to the views of others and hearing about people's lives makes for interesting conversation and reflection.

It is through these exchanges that, as a group, we start to staff this light station and begin to understand that we must work together to provide visitors with a memorable experience to keep things running; sometimes again the odds.

For three days, our lighthouse navigators were grilled on the daily chores of station life, and taught about narratives that will interest the pending run of tourist and locals this season.

The island's visitor numbers are already 30 percent higher than last year at this time, due in part to some large eco-groups accessing the site. Host-keeper Betty Carpick returns after being an artist-in-residence last season, and she is enjoying the fresh-air and open expanses that Superior brings. Being a host-keeper offers another perspective of several roles necessary to play to keep the operation going.

Eve Graham and her recently dearly departed husband, Gordon Graham, both operated the light station with their family in tow. In the late 1980s, prior to the light becoming automated, times were different. Eve's perspective and story-telling made a big impact on the summer staff.

As the students prepared their narratives for the coming visitors, they were able to not only hear the stories but also taste the same bread recipe Eve used years before.

These connections form a powerful motivation to help share the life of a family on an isolated Lake Superior Island... along with many laughs.

Sandor Turcsanyi and Katelyn Jefford, both lighthouse navigators, are enjoying some amenities, including the new sauna to which they will be introducing visitors this season. A hundred volunteer hours have already been expended to get the site up and running this year.

As a non-profit, charity-based operation, Canadian Lighthouses of Lake Superior is dedicated to preserving, promoting and protecting these assets for years to come. Volunteers help move us there.

The *Superior Rocket*, operated by Sail Superior, will help others who are interested in seeing the preservation work and provide them with an opportunity to take an intimate step back in time to the story of lightkeepers from long ago. There are some wonderful stories to share including the time the *Thordoc* arrived unexpectedly on one of Porphyry Island's many reefs in 1929; leaving everyone in the local vicinity with bags and bags of flour, as lightening the ship's load was the only way to float the vessel off the reef.

Chat around the dinner table this summer will be filled with adventures and points of interest to share.

Providing a destination on Lake Superior is a challenge for many reasons, but for those that make it here, they understand the value of conviction to help people understand our storied past.

People sitting around the light keeper's dinner table on Porphyry Island are, from left, Donny Wabasse, Sandor Turcsanyi, Eve Graham, Katelyn Jefford, Maya Vanderheide, Judith Appleton and Betty Carpick.
[Photo: CLLS]

LIGHTHOUSE DISPATCHES

July 16, 2019

Capturing the imagination of people each year

"Porphyry, Poor Porphyry" are the opening lines from Doug Gould's poem about the state of Porphyry Island in 2010. Now, nine years later, Gould, a retired teacher, writes a new poem titled "Porphyry – A Crowning":

> Porphyry, oh Porphyry, look at you now!
> Transformed by good people
> And lots of hard work.
> By CLLS staffers, Silver Islet crew,
> Plus many a boater, there was much to do.

His words reflect today the transformation of this property that is leased from the Department of Fisheries and Oceans Canada. The lighthouse group was formed in 2012 with a mandate to preserve, protect and promote, with much effort and dedication, the Canadian Lighthouses of Lake Superior (CLLS).

The group maintains lighthouses from Thunder Bay to the east, including the Trowbridge Island light located at the feet of the Sleeping Giant, the Point Porphyry light on Black Bay and the Shaganash light on Number 10 Island on the inside North Channel.

Through fundraisers, donations and membership, CLLS operates with an $80,000 annual budget that is used to educate, entertain, and capture the imaginations of 1,000 visitors annually, and also includes many Thunder Bay community events during the winter months.

In Gould's opening lines, he captures the essence of destruction at Porphyry, "Mindless hoodlums and senseless acts," and it is because of the past vandalism that he now sees the change, and a promising future.

Arriving from Black Bay's Sibley Peninsula, eight numb kayakers from Naturally Superior Adventures arrive at Porphyry's Paterson Sauna to warm up after chilling splashes during their transit. With smiles and warm hands, they are welcomed to the lightkeeper's dwelling where the stove heats a delicious meal that wafts throughout the homestead.

The weekend had been busy with many sailors from the Thunder Bay and Silver Islet yacht clubs to start the wind-up into a summer rhythm. Our weekly charter is operating again and picking up and delivering tourists, volunteers, artists and host-keepers.

Judith Appleton, our visiting artist from Israel, was busy packing up and lamenting about leaving, as our new artist-in-residence arrived. Margaret Mol, from the nearby Slate River Valley, is very enthusiastic about the opportunities already presented to her blank canvas. With paint and easel in tow, her eyes settle upon the Sleeping Giant at sunset across Black Bay.

Our two host-keepers, from Terrace Bay and Nicol Island, are enthusiastically lining up their work duties for the week. Gerri Turner and Claire Belliveau are excited to dedicate some time to learning more about the lighthouse experience and enjoying the panoramic scenery.

Our previous host-keeper, Betty Carpick, provided an abundance of support and also cooked some amazing meals during her stay. She was part of the artist program last year and has made a significant contribution in time and expertise to the organization. Her efforts did not go unnoticed and were appreciated by the lighthouse team.

One little bit of news... We did get a call last week to say that our dock from Trowbridge Island had been found. This was exciting news. The culprit had been the winter ice, which had drawn the dock down into 40 feet of water in front of the light.

We'd like to thank everyone who searched for the dock and, until further notice, the dock at Trowbridge is under repair and closed for safety reasons.

Kayakers are ready to depart for the No.10 Lighthouse after staying in the lightkeeper's dwelling on Porphyry Island. At rear, from left, Otto Bedard, Jim Schritmeyer, Randy Barnhatt and Wolf Meingast. In front, from left, Ann Bellman, Carolyn Meingast, Harold Simon and Kim Kilpatrick. [Photo: CLLS]

July 23, 2019

Memorable stories shared over lighthouse meals

Lighthouse living continues with the comings and goings of people in all modes of transport from early in the morning to, sometimes, late at night. Take for instance the young couple last night who flew in by NorthWest Heli-Tour and Adventures to delve into our marine history and natural landscapes, or many who have come to witness Jean E. Pendziwol address a group of budding writers in a weekend retreat, and hang upon her every word.

What joy when art and history and nature come together in literacy right here on the island after being fallow for so many years.

People continue arriving by sailing craft, fishing boats, motor cruisers and kayaks to explore this Lake Superior destination and to hear the stories of days gone by. Our on-site crew of lighthouse enthusiasts that manage the light station as lighthouse navigators, host-keepers and artists-in-residence learn new and dynamic narratives to keep visitors engaged. Everyone plays a role to keep visitors orientated, questioning and connected to our legacy and pristine wilderness.

Artist-in-residence, Margaret Mol, has played many roles, including conducting a baking lesson on baguette making, which I'm anxious to test out later. It's always a pleasant surprise when our staff try out a new recipe or experiment under the watchful eyes of an experienced cook; it gives us variety.

Our mealtimes are a feast for the eyes and the mind as we receive a diverse group of visitors on our commercial tour days. Dining at the lighthouse table allows the door to the past to creak open and provide an insight into life on the island. Each dinner consists of searching out ingredients in the pantry and looking to build the best meal possible with whatever is on hand. Thanks to some sailors for us to have extra treats — cheese or goodies they don't need on their return journey home. It feels very much like a community out here where everyone is surviving the elements of a sometimes-tempestuous Lake Superior.

Satisfaction comes after the meal when the conversation floats around the day's activities and we share meaningful moments that we've encountered. There's also levity in the moments on the island as we all work hard to make the site attractive and inviting to our visitors. We know the importance of providing a destination, as some boaters come to us for a safe harbour overnight; especially considering some of the weather conditions we experience here.

The other night, Porphyry Island was engulfed by a huge thunderstorm that had escaped from Thunder Bay. It rattled the windows, giving visitors something to talk about in the morning. Bright flashes over leaden waters followed immediately by a thunderous clap. Safe in the keeper's dwelling, warm from the elements — now this is life! Lighthouse living is filling up the senses and overloading us with a lifetime of memories that we share with others.

Under the watchful eye of their father Peter, three-year-old Emil and his seven-year-old sister, Audrey, explore the island. This tells us all one thing: life goes on.

The whistle of the kettle cuts me off now; it's tea time. Time to go.

From left, Maya Vanderheide, Katelyn Jefford and Margaret Mol prepare the boat house gift shop for visitors to Porphyry Island.
[Photo: Donny Wabasse]

LIGHTHOUSE DISPATCHES

July 30, 2019

Light still plays big role guiding mariners

Being chased by an oncoming storm, *Nina*, my wooden boat, along with a guest, ventured trustingly across Black Bay. Today's destination is Porphyry Island, 15 kilometres east of Silver Islet, which means crossing some open water and passing a half-dozen islands.

I'd been tracking this storm cell for sometime and thought that it would pass either to the north or south of us as it tracked northeast, but things quickly changed. There was lightning coming down at the feet of the Sleeping Giant some 15 kilometres to the west, and as we moved along, the clouds and the fog started to meet up in the middle, offering little – then no – visual guidance.

With a GPS plotter and compass, *Nina* took some wind from the northeast and a tiny chop, to then finally be engulfed in the storm with half-an-hour still before reaching land. With the storm catching up, it ended up tracking south and dissipating over the water, but that didn't change the fact that we couldn't see because of heavy rain, thick cloud cover and fog.

Watching the clock and figuring out our destination time we knew we were getting close. The compass bearing was held steady but we felt a little disoriented, as there were no visual cues, no familiar landmarks. Nothing!

Aboard was my best friend, Rob Logan, from Vancouver, who had wanted to visit the island for some time and was coming to look at our business model while being a tourist. To him, this was an adventure of a magnitude equal to that of the West Coast Trail or one of the many southern Caribbean Islands he'd visited.

Pent up in the fog, looking for guidance, we then saw the calming flash of Porphyry light to the south. This reminded my guest and me that the light still plays a significant role in providing help for mariners on this big lake. Guided by the flash every 11 seconds, we found our way into Porphyry Harbour as the daylight was completely fading. The lighthouse navigator team was there to greet us and off-loaded our supplies and helped us up to the lightkeepers' dwellings.

As Sunday rolled around — our busiest day — we greeted more tourists, sailors, and our new artist-in-residence and hostkeepers.

Helen Solmes is looking forward to, "Porphyry Island's remoteness and lack of urban light pollution," as she is our resident artist who is delving into night photography. Solmes is thrilled by "...the prospect of being in place to capture Lake Superior summer storms." The objective of her stay is to produce a coffee table book of images from her Porphyry visit.

Bruce and Sandy Hansen are equally excited to explore lighthouse living as host-keepers. As they steady their footing, being avid sailors, Bruce is looking to develop some musical renditions from his island life experience during the week. The goal is to develop an encore to 2018's music festival held at the Urban Abbey.

For the first time, we hosted a small group of yogis who came to commune with nature. What a spectacular day to see turquoise waters, feel the cool winds and remind us of being part of nature; not just an observer. They had come for the lighthouse experience and to explore other opportunities.

It's through these small community steps, and through outside business interest that the island destination keeps receiving added traction. As for my friend who was visiting, he now understood the relevance of a light in a storm, and for me it was a reminder that changing perspectives is invigorating.

A moose walks along the beach as a merganser travels the other direction one morning at Porphyry Harbour.
[Photo: Donny Wabasse]

August 6, 2019

Travellers coming from all over

Our artist-in-residence, Helen Solmes, met long-time lighthouse volunteer, William Vanderwees and his wife Betty on the front steps of the keeper's dwelling at the Point Porphyry light station. Vanderwees has been an active volunteer with the lighthouse group for five years and had decided to take a tourist trip to Porphyry Island to catch up on all the new developments.

The first thing to catch his eye was the budding garden, with peas, beans, rhubarb and radishes all well under way. He remarked that he had tilled the soil and helped construct the fence that now holds back the garden from the rabbits. Solmes, a photographer, invited the Vanderwees' into the homestead for a chat about her work and to reflect on her two-week term. Upon entering the dwelling, Donny Wabasse was busy preparing lunch for a work gang building a shed outside. Recollecting his thoughts, Vanderwees remarked that he remembers 41 panes of glass having to be replaced in the house, and today he was happy to see how the home was very much in use.

Visitors this week range from Costa Rica to Texas, and from San Francisco to Minneapolis. They bring with them a wealth of questions about the island and how it came to be this way. Each part of the visitor's journey is tailored to ensure that people understand the significance of the work that's been undertaken to restore this historic site. Imagine the hardships to survive on this unforgiving lake? Rebekka Redd an outdoors enthusiast, visited the island and said that the experience was, "...a cross between the Galapagos Islands and the east coast of Canada."

CLLS board members, Vic Miller and Joe Marcella, also brought out family members to help with the ongoing work to ensure that the site stays open to the public. The place is abuzz with travelers from all over, doing many things from sitting by the fire, walking through the forest, taking in a sauna or listening to an acoustic music set by Larry Carpenter on his way to the Red Rock Music Festival.

The Thunder Bay Yacht Club's annual SUNORA regatta final barbecue and awards night took place at the harbour. This year, nine boats participated and were able to cross the archipelago of islands to explore many destinations; some old and some new.

It's the family atmosphere of people sharing time while acknowledging the beautiful surroundings that makes it a destination to remember.

A fisherman offers up a couple of salmon for the lighthouse dinner for the volunteers and staff. First, it's the buzz of getting some fresh fish that hits the antennae of the staff. Then, like Pavlov's experiments, everyone is savoring the thought of fresh salmon. Questions are raised as how to best cook the four large fillets. Should it be roasted, fried or baked on a cedar plank? The aroma hits the ceiling and wafts through the room. Now, I can imagine Vanderwees saying, "I could never fathom having such a fine meal in a house that five-years ago was vandalized, neglected and abandoned."

Today, both inside and out, a joy persists that we are fortunate to share in these experiences that our surroundings have provided us.

From left, Maya Vanderheide, Sandor Turcsanyi and Paul Morralee film a sequence on Porphyry Harbour for Bruce Hansen's music video.
[Photo: Donny Wabasse]

August 13, 2019

Island experience "a perfect getaway"

Turquoise waters surround Porphyry Island as summer continues to gently move along. Many guests continue to venture to this island paradise to experience new perspectives, including some of my relatives from Great Britain. It is through their eyes that we can refresh our view and see things that are right in front of our nose.

Bea Pratt said, "The island is very calming and the community spirit is strong. It's an unforgettable experience that will live a long time in our memories." Her husband Jerald says, "The alternate lifestyle is a perfect getaway from a busy life, where we can relax, read a book and be in contact with nature."

Transient boaters continue to arrive, and the boats seem to be getting larger and larger. Many tours of the island are being offered and the donated bikes have been handy for people to commute from the harbour to the lighthouse point.

Summer staff, our lighthouse navigators, are also keeping busy finishing projects started earlier in the summer. A catch phrase used by former lightkeepers was: "If it moves, oil it; if not, paint it!" Our shed is also completed after three days of hard work and will be getting some paint on it soon. We've had a few kayakers throughout this summer, but it's been slower than normal, possibly due to cooler weather on the lake this season. When kayakers arrive, their boats that carry their tents, food and sleeping bags, seem to explode upon landing. This is to dry things out while also organizing the load for the next leg of the journey.

Fortunately, the stocked wood is ready and the sauna will soon be hot to sooth their aching muscles after a 13-kilometre crossing. The group is from Duluth, Minnesota, and New York City.

Our second session of yoga took place thanks to transportation by the *Superior Rocket*. Walking in silence through the forest to the heliport platform, thoughts were gathered for the practice of many moves. The calm waters help to draw their focus in to concentrate on their poses. Like poetry in motion, the camera captures a moment in time to be shared later.

As always, the team lunch at the lightkeeper's table was a lively affair. Helen Solmes, our artist-in-residence, departed on Sunday and gave us a preview of the photos she had taken of the night sky. In the next few months, she will create a coffee table book of her time on the island, and it will be auctioned off at the next fundraiser.

Sean Kim sailed in with his family to take the next artist-in-residence post. Over the next two weeks, he will be composing some Superior magic from the soundscapes he captures from the waves.

It's great to see Kim's children enjoying the fishing, splashing about in the water, and chasing minnows, for, in these moments, family memories are made that can be relived for years to come.

Porphyry Island continues to evolve in the cool lapping waters and is becoming a select destination by a stronger and stronger community of mariners.

Yoga Session On Helipad. Curnis McGoldrick demonstrates some yoga moves on the helipad at the Point Porphyry Lighthouse.
[Photo: CLLS]

LIGHTHOUSE DISPATCHES

August 20, 2019

Waves continue to crash upon the shore

The light tower rattles in the wind as the waves crash on the shore. Water is everywhere; infused in the air as 40-kilometre per hour winds and two-meter waves eject cool water skyward after deflecting off the rocks.

Lighthouse life continues on this isolated island 43 kilometres (as the crow flies) east of the city of Thunder Bay.

Eve Graham, former assistant lightkeeper and member of our board of directors, returns for a visit to see how things are operating on the island. Canadian Lighthouses of Lake Superior is fortunate to have someone who understands the lighthouse history. She has lived it.

Since her last visit, there have been many improvements to the light station, including a tool shed, pump-house, sauna and some more interpretive displays. Graham has met the new host-keeper family and reminisced about when she home-schooled her children on this very island in the 1980s.

Visitors this week had two surprises to contend with: first, a past lightkeeper was on-site to share stories, and secondly, a film done by the CBC Television 37 years ago documenting the Graham family's life on the island. The film depicts a time when the lighthouses were being shut down due to automation and better navigation tools were available to mariners. It was a time when the systems were being put in place and the buildings on-site were to be terminated, closed or destroyed. It was a time of uncertainty for the Graham family too, with losing a career and a lifestyle.

It was 20 years ago this month that I had first set foot on this isolated island to see the destruction caused by vandals. As I walked the site, I did see the beauty in the landscape and the panoramic views, and I imagined that, once, people used to laugh and live here.

My trusted wooden boat, *Nina*, has since that time ventured to Montreal and back; traveled the North Shore up from Sault Ste. Marie to Thunder Bay, voyaging some 20,000 kilometres.

As a destination, Porphyry's perspective — seeing the Sleeping Giant from the east side — was first witnessed by the First Nations peoples, and it is impressive. Discoveries still happen today as young visitors ask questions about the reasons for having a lighthouse on a point, or what does a fog alarm do?

Connecting youth to the lighthouse journey opens them up to many other avenues that include the wildlife, natural history and, of course, the story of our founding peoples who lived on Black Bay. These stories allow for a rich learning experience that makes it more than a destination, but a place where memories are made; memories that will remain with our lighthouse navigators who have worked hard to provide visitors with both entertainment and facts about the regional lighthouses and the role they played and still play today.

This week, we said good by to Maya Vanderheide as she goes back to school on the West Coast after spending her summer with us. Not a dry eye was to be seen as we said our goodbyes. Now, we continue our story with young visitors and invite them to join us in future years to become lighthouse navigators and custodians of these once-vital monuments to commerce.

The waves continue to crash upon the shore. The tower still rattles, and again, my tea kettle whistles. It's time to take a break and take in the view.

August 27, 2019

Uncovering relics from the past

The storms clouds are gathering and so are some boaters and kayakers in the harbour below. Heavy winds are forecasted and everyone is busy battening down the hatches for the impending storm. Darrell Makin, a previous board member of the lighthouse group, is here with two kayakers on a journey across the Lake Superior archipelago to Rossport. One visitor is from Southern Ontario, and the other from a lot further south — Florida

Imagine the days of yore when people traveled in small wooden boats to and fro for supplies. They also watched the weather closely; hardy individuals who knew the waters well and how to navigate, bringing supplies to the lighthouse, as did the coast guard vessel, *Nokomis*.

Today of course, it's different with all of the technology, but some things on the island remain the same; like ordering in food. Each week. we send our food order to Renco's on Court Street in Thunder Bay, not unlike the Graham family who used to order from the Walberg's store on Brock Street. Forty years later, Eve Graham, past assistant lightkeeper, is meeting Barb, the daughter of store founders Lloyd and Lena Walberg, for the very first time. It's in these special moments that we realize that history continues to live on.

Libby Dahl has also signed on to be a host-keeper this week at the lighthouse situated some 43 kilometres east of Thunder Bay. Duties for the duo are to paint, paint and paint, but in red and white only. These are still duties of the lightkeepers as they help to keep up the appearance of the light station.

In the old days, the foreman at the Thunder Bay Coast Guard Base would only send out a couple of brushes to each lighthouse, so the keepers were forced to clean and reuse the brushes, much like we do today.

We received an interesting email from Beth-Anna Van Dellen from out West, who is a descendent of the Merritt family. Charles Merritt was a keeper of the lighthouse in the 1940s up to 1959. After receiving some direction from Beth-Anna, we were able to locate a concrete block that was once used as a base for a radio antenna. We were looking for an impression of a baby's footprint that belonged to her mother — and there it was, with the inscription "Charleen Merritt, Sept. 10, 1950" etched in the concrete.

Uncovering items from the past is exciting and keeps us motivated to find more.

Also, Van Dellen spoke about Rum Bottle Bay, located near the point and

Canadian Coast Guard Supply Ships

Over the years, numerous ships have provided essential support and supplies to all of the light stations along Lake Superior's north shore. In the early days of lightkeeping in the region, the tugboat, *James Whalen*, was instrumental in breaking ice in the Port Arthur harbour (now Thunder Bay) each spring and then transporting the keepers, their families, and belongings to the lighthouses. This ship operated in the area starting in 1905. Each year, families would gather at the city dock to bid farewell to their loved ones as they headed to the lighthouse for the season. Mr. James Whalen was an industrialist who owned 21 vessels. He played a significant role in the development of the Port Arthur harbour.

Transportation was not always guaranteed in the early days. Initially, keepers were often left to their own devices after being dropped off, needing to make their way back to the mainland before the freeze-up. This was a risky undertaking and could end in tragedy in the icy waters of Lake Superior.

The Canadian Coast Guard vessel *C.P. Edwards* served as a buoy tender and supply ship from 1946 until its sale in 1972. Built in the Collingwood shipyard, it often provided support to the Point Porphyry Lighthouse during a major facility update when a new light tower was constructed and the old lighthouse demolished

In 1959, the Coast Guard commissioned the *Alexander Henry*, constructed at the Port Arthur Shipyards, and named after a notable Canadian explorer. This unique ship featured a heliport on its aft deck, allowing a small helicopter to transport keepers and their supplies, effectively avoiding the perilous ice. It functioned as an icebreaker, aid to navigation, and occasionally as a search and rescue vessel.

In 1960, the Coast Guard tender *Nokomis* played a crucial role in delivering two 1950s cars and construction equipment on a barge to Porphyry Island. Today, many curious visitors wonder about the presence of these old abandoned cars on the island.

CCGS *Nokomis* at Silver Islet, c.1958.
[Photo: McKay Family Collection]

The 1.2-kilometre trail from the harbour to the point was widened into a usable road, thanks to assistant light keeper Robert (Bob) McKay, a founding member of Canadian Lighthouses of Lake Superior, who was compensated $300 to clear a path through the dense boreal forest.

which occasionally spits out remnants of broken glass that can be traced back to bootlegger days during the era of U.S. prohibition.

This week, we said goodbye to our most helpful and pleasant lighthouse navigators, Katelyn Jefford, Sandor Turcsanyi and Maya Vanderheide. We also were thankful for the Kim family's visit to the island as host-keepers. We are hoping to use some images of their stay here to encourage other families to come and visit.

It's going to be a delicious dinner tonight as Libby and Barb are working now on collecting gooseberries in the yard and mixing them with fresh peaches to make pie.

The storm continues to brew with winds blowing in the trees, and I am starting to imagine the aroma of baked pie.

Working on the Island. Maya Vanderheide, Katelyn Jefford and Sandor Turcsanyi, lighthouse navigators with Canadian Lighthouses of Lake Superior, spend a day at Trowbridge Island painting the exterior of the keeper's dwelling as a laker passes by in the distance. [Photo: CLLS]

September 3, 2019

Island helpers thanked

After a fifth day of constant bad weather this week, it was nice when the water calmed down and Labour Day boaters and travellers arrived at Porphyry Island for the weekend.

When the lake kicks up and waves crash constantly on the shores, the volume level is always high. Day upon day, the waves pounded the shore, leaving some travellers stranded while our host-keepers, with list and paintbrush in hand, kept busy. Libby Dahl and Barb Walberg worked hard to update high-traffic areas with fresh coats of paint and spruce up the two keepers' dwellings. From the floor of the tower to touch-ups around the site, the place now looks fantastic. It's wonderful to see these little tasks done in preparation for next season.

Other citizens and organizations also can take credit for making this black volcanic sand island come to life. Take for example a couch that was donated and delivered four years ago. Finally, it was mated up again with its matching recliner. Doug and Ruth Pantry from Black Bay reunited the couch and recliner to give comfort to our many volunteers and artists-in-residence.

Or consider the Superior Shores Gaming Association BINGOs that lighthouse volunteers attend. Funds from this source have afforded Canadian Lighthouses of Lake Superior new visitor information brochures and orientation signage. Now, people know how to get around the site safely and are informed of the variety of opportunities to explore.

And what about Chuck and Christine Sandford of Exquisite Gold & Gems Inc., who had, earlier in the season, identified the need to replace an old rusty barbecue with a new gleaming stainless steel one. Every little bit helps out to make the site inviting to the public who arrive to experience a lighthouse island on Lake Superior; a destination that evolves to open up doors and minds to new experiences.

"Four buds, two boats and one lake," is what a group of adventurers call themselves after two years of planning while attending Northland College in Ashland, Wisconsin. Upon graduation from an outdoor recreation program, and wanting an epic adventure, they set sail to circumnavigate Lake Superior in 30 days. Clair Emmons, Sarah Szymaniak, Brontë Gross, and Alec Malenfant are next headed to Loon Harbour and points east. Hearing their stories and living vicariously through their journey, it made me smile and remember that life is all about experiences.

These adventurers had set out onto a big lake to seek an experience, so when they arrived at the lighthouse on Porphyry, located 43 kilometres east of Thunder Bay, we were ready for them. First, we took an upside down cake that was prepared a day earlier with gooseberries and peach, added some hot tea, and they were immediately our friends for life as they dined at the lighthouse table. Later, this was followed up when Donny Wabasse, who has been the master of the household during the summer months, prepared a packaged bacon, lettuce and tomato sandwich for the crew. They were ecstatic.

Memories are made from moments like this; the smiles and goodwill fills the atmosphere and everyone leaves feeling part of something bigger than themselves.

As the summer winds down and people start to take into consideration their fall programs, schools and jobs, it's great to know that there are still weeks' worth of memories waiting to be created. For the next couple of weeks, we will remain dedicated to standing watch at the lighthouse to help people experience what Northwestern Ontario and Canada are famous for — water, rocks and trees... and some weather, too.

Seeing adventure on Lake Superior, Sarah Szymaniak, Brontë Gross, Clair Emmons and Alec Malenfant from Ashland, Wisconsin, are circumnavigating the lake on a 30-day trip. [Photo: CLLS]

September 10, 2019

Butterflies... something to behold on island

It was something you needed to see to believe — monarch butterflies smothering the trees as they rested for the night; bright orange-and-black wings accentuated by the bathing light of the setting sun against a forest of green.

Over the past five years, being on-site and restoring the human habitat — the keeper's dwelling for example — our staff and volunteers have always been conscious of wildlife habitat too. Each year, we chase the odd butterfly trying to get it to comply with having its picture taken; but slim chance of that happening as their goal is to find food.

As the day wore on and we completed our tasks, more and more butterflies arrived, making it, at times, difficult to concentrate on the work at hand.

Riding the lighthouse bicycle from the harbour below and rounding the corner to the light station, I had to stop. Above me were hundreds of butterflies beginning to roost for the evening. Fortunately for us at the lighthouse, Gloria and Bob McKay (previous lightkeepers) had donated part of their National Geographic magazine collection and, lo and behold, there was an article from August 1976 featuring monarch butterflies. The article, titled "Found at Last: the Monarch's Winter Home," by Fred A Urquhart, solved the mystery 46 years ago as to where the butterflies wintered each season: Mexico!

Now, we are preparing for winter by completing many jobs around the site. This weekend saw the refitting of docks to accommodate more boats, and with a new anchoring system attached.

Justin Ranta volunteered his time to install a propane fridge that was donated mid-summer, and it now provides another much-needed amenity to the guesthouse.

Our site has been getting added attention because of some interpretive artifacts including a fish netminder from the fishing tug *Grebe*. The netminder helped to bring in the nets over the bow after trawling for the day's catch. The vessel was scuttled in the harbour in 1965, with its burnt hull now submerged in the bay and its wood-fired boiler still poking its head out of the water.

Jim Dyson, who fished these waters for thirty-odd years, brought his family over to visit the lighthouse from Silver Islet and they were all smiles as the adventure opened up before their eyes.

There was also the Country Neighbour's Book Club, which charters Archie's tour boat to come and discover the location upon which the *Lightkeeper's Daughters* book was loosely based. Jean E. Pendziwol, the author, would be proud to know that yet another book group has been inspired by the book to visit Porphyry Island.

Every little bit helps to build our understanding of where we live, our history and the natural beauty that surrounds us. Time and time again I hear from people about their take on visiting the island, and time again I hear the same thing . . . "this is an amazing place."

Not many people venture onto Lake Superior and see, for example, the Sleeping Giant from the eastern side or witness the turquoise waters. Together, we can make connections to where we live by making a first step outside of our comfort zone towards the unknown.

I guess that's what the monarch butterflies do everyday? It's nature.

Archie Hoogsteen (left) from Archie's Charters is joined by the Country Neighbours Book Club, who are visiting Porphyry Island for a book tour. Pictured in the front row, Heather Conrad, Gertrud Belanger-Boeckermann, Tracy Gardner, Wanda Edwards, Barbara Krasemann, Diana Bockus, Sandy Graham, and lighthouse volunteer Justin Ranta. In the back row are Lisa Primavesi, Shelly Istiefson, Cindy Poulin and Rosalyn Dowhos.

[Photo: CLLS]

September 17, 2019

Visitors make memories at island lighthouse

The cistern below the house drains of water as the summer lighthouse season draws to a close. The daily log and guestbook are put back on the bookshelf, the homesteads are tidied up, the grounds are cleared and the lightkeeper's dinner bell has now fallen silent.

What will people say about this season? What memories were the best and what will remain in their mind's-eye for years to come? A guess might be the turquoise waters of Lake Superior, or the haunting call of the loon, or the furious storm-surges and pounding waves. From my standpoint, it might be watching visitors make memories as they meet new people, take in the incredible views, or enjoy a night singing by the campfire. Personally, the monarch butterflies would have to be my highlight.

At Porphyry Island, we received the same number of visitors as we'd seen last season — with a change to the mix. Kayakers were fewer but charter visitors were more, displacing any loss. Power boaters amounted to 60 per cent of the visitors, while sailing craft were about 26 per cent, growing slightly over last year. Half of all our visitors were from Thunder Bay, and half of those were from the Yacht Club. Silver Islet visitors to the lighthouse make up ten percent, with the remainder from further away. Four artists-in-residence, 13 host-keepers and three Canada Summer Jobs students attended to bring the total number to 660. Over 1,150 hours of on-site volunteer time was employed to build docks, do yard maintenance, build a shed and prepare meals.

Thanks to photographer, Donny Wabasse, who spent his whole summer here and never left the island once. This year, we saw some substantial gifts, including a new propane fridge, a golf-cart to move supplies and elderly visitors, and one donation of $1,000 cash made after a short visit. Oh, and a new percolator coffee maker. For a non-profit organization, these offers of support are important as we continue to provide for the general public to visit for free.

Lighthouse history, lightkeepers' histories and the surrounding lore of Black Bay, Silver Islet and Walkers Channel; all are animated through the collective work that Canadian Lighthouses of Lake Superior provides. Work continues to build interest in the lighthouse group's activities, and during the coming winter months there will be many opportunities to share in the experience.

Our speaker series again will be available to the public, and it will feature stories from this summer's host-keepers and artists-in-residence. A lighthouse music and film event are also planned in the new year and everyone is welcome to attend. To stay in touch, to donate or to help support this important and relevant cause in maintaining our nautical history and sense of place, please visit us at clls.ca

It's been a privilege to write to you every week this summer. Thank You.

The cistern has just finished draining now and I have a boat to catch back to the mainland, I will miss this place.

Beautiful monarch butterflies stop for the night to rest in the trees near the Point Porphyry Lighthouse.
[Photo: Donny Wabasse]

LIGHTHOUSE DISPATCHES

2020

Self-Isolating... Since 1873

June 10, 2020

Opportunities await at island

Leaving the city of Thunder Bay behind as *Nina* pushes towards Porphyry Island, nature returns.

It's been September of last year since I've seen the light station, situated on the east side of Black Bay. The water is clean and clear, the air cool to breath and some fog is seen in the transit across the bay. What memories will be created from this summer season? Will people venture far from homes to explore the wilds of Northwestern Ontario? Time will tell, and new opportunities await.

Arriving at the dock after a four-hour journey, no damage by ice can be seen, making our landing safe. Traversing the trail from the harbour to the lighthouse, we encountered many trees downed by the winter winds. Chainsaw in hand and a crew behind, we managed to clear a path to be rewarded with a view of the majestic Sleeping Giant. In the trees above the point, you could hear an earful of cedar waxwings as many monarch butterflies gained sustenance from spring dandelions.

Leaves are just starting to come out. A couple of loons could be seen feeding in the water, as an eagle left the rocks at the point, temporarily trading places with humans. The temperatures are below seasonal and the weather is inclement with strong winds from the east, all impacted by Superior's cool demeanor.

In the keeper's dwelling, a fire is started as many other chores come into play. Water is pumped into the cistern, while the house water-pump is primed and readied. Propane cylinders are hauled up and connected to start the cooking stove, and the fridge is messed about with for a couple of days to get the temperature setting right.

Down at the harbour, Jim Massey arrives from the Thunder Bay Yacht Club to lend a hand setting up the docks and mooring ball for the season. Phyllis, his wife, provides hot tea and coffee to keep spirits up and numb hands warm.

The beach sands have been lifted high into the grass from last season's high water levels, and since then the water has dropped more than a foot. As dusk approaches, two families of Canada geese make their approach to the quiet Porphyry Harbour as a beaver navigates on its nightly rounds, slightly confused, I'm sure, by a floating white ball in the middle of his bay! The sauna is stoked up and hot water is made for cleaning up and getting ready for another workday to get the site ready.

With uncertain times ahead (due to the COVID-19 pandemic), the facilities are now open for vessels in the area wanting to land for some respite from the storm. For passing boaters, kayakers and paddlers, the sauna and camping area are available and Canadian Lighthouses of Lake Superior (CLLS) will continue to keep the grounds open for visitors.

To assist in CLLS's endeavours, donations can be made online or at our donation box on the island to help keep the facility operational. The walking trails though Porphyry Island Provincial Park Nature Reserve are open, along with many interpretive displays by the Parks Canada National Marine Conservation Area.

Regarding our weekly charters and host-keeper program, we will see limited programming this season, and our artist-in-residence program returning, hopefully, next season. For lightkeepers here at Porphyry, they've experienced isolation since 1873, and times don't change.

We're looking forward during the summer to keeping you connected with activities at our lights, light stations and lighthouse on the breakwater in Thunder Bay. Stay safe everyone.

Return to the island: Arriving at the Porphyry Island docks, *Nina*, my 26-foot vessel, keeps the occupants warm with a wood fire. [Photo: CLLS]

The Wooden Boat *Nina*

Wooden boats have largely become a relic of the past as modern construction materials have emerged for boat building. In 1955, the wooden vessel, *Nina*, was built on the banks of the Kaministiquia River at Great Lakes Forest Products by lead hand Jon Olson. Her hull was crafted from yellow cedar, secured with steel screws to her framework, and showcasing a prominent bow reminiscent of east coast vessels. *Nina* was equipped with a four-cylinder, flat-top gasoline-powered Gray Marine engine, and she had a steel rail skeg to safeguard her against the rocks and shoals of Lake Superior.

Throughout her history, *Nina* has had four owners, including Paul Morralee, who purchased her in 1999 from a former member of the Thunder Bay Yacht Club. The vessel was equipped with all the essentials for extended journeys on Lake Superior, — a wood-stove, cooking stove, galley, and berth. At 26 feet long, she faired well in the waters of Superior, when conditions permitted, but she did run aground once during a fierce 90 kph windstorm in 2003, when the cleats tore off the dock at Marathon, Ontario, leaving her beached nearby. *Nina* later ventured to Montreal and up the Ottawa River to Lake Timiskaming, ultimately returning to Thunder Bay in 2009. Over the course of twenty years Paul Morralee has covered a total of 20,000 kilometres in his trusted wooden boat.

In 2012, Morralee was invited to join the board of directors for Canadian Lighthouses of Lake Superior, which allowed him to visit various lighthouses and develop a network of contacts. The following year, *Nina* journeyed along the North Shore to help produce a documentary film, titled "The Lighthouse Trail", which explored the history of the region's lighthouses.

As the years went by, visiting artists-in-residence and host-keepers on Porphyry Island experienced the true essence of Superior by traveling aboard *Nina*. She moves at a leisurely pace of five knots, taking an hour and fifteen minutes to travel from Silver Islet to Porphyry Island. Each summer, as activities on the island increased and people stayed in the keeper's dwelling, *Nina* became Morralee's primary accommodation, providing a welcome separation between lighthouse duties and a space to unwind, Currently, Nina is 'on the hard' (out of the water), awaiting restoration of her bottom and superstructure. She will once again sail the waves of Superior, serving as a nostalgic reminder of days gone and of families who once used her to explore this beautiful coastline.

Nina appeared in Thunder Bay's Annual Tulip Festival Boaters Parade dressed up like a Mayan Pyramid with accompanying women dressed in traditional Mexican clothing. [Photo: Paul Morralee]

June 16, 2020

Island starts to come alive

After contending with weather from post-tropical storm Cristobal, work continues at the lighthouse. Situated some 43 kilometres east of Thunder Bay, Porphyry Island is starting to come alive with leaves unfurling ready for the summer season, and our Canadian flag flying happily over the point.

For four days last week, we were thrashed with strong easterly winds, and then for another three days from the northwest, forcing us indoors for some time. Thankfully our wood stove kept everything warm and some of our visitors even took advantage of the sauna, as they were the only ones here. We had a visit by two conservation officers with the MNR, who were out on patrol looking for fishermen and checking their catch.

Archie Hoogsteen of Archie's Fishing Charters fame dropped in for a visit and brought with him a large salmon he hooked just for our dinner. In exchange, Donny Wabasse cooked up a tasty rhubarb crumble pie! This reminds me of past keepers' stories of survival on Superior. In years gone by the Dick, McKay, Merritt and Graham families would all share with fishermen and visitors to the island, and so the tradition continues.

The Grahams told us recently during some research, that local boaters used to visit them and, in the fall, the family would organize a corn roast. I can taste the corn with butter and salt now as I write this!

When you think of the isolation these keepers must have felt at times; to have people come and visit them would be something to look forward to.

In our realm of self-isolation and safe distancing, you cannot help but to be reminded of the nature that we live in — we are part of it. As a result of the pandemic, the summer season is going to be different this year, but we have some glimmers of hope on the horizon. The Silver Islet Harbour Association is in its finishing steps of formalizing and providing a service to visitors at the Silver Islet docks. The construction phase is nearly completed with the renovations and construction of docks, piers and breakwater. Visiting boaters and charter customers leaving from Silver Islet will now be able to enjoy the lighthouse site while practicing safe-distancing and hand-washing.

Our trail network is now cleared of debris for people to walk and connect with the sounds of the forest, while our interpretive signage is ready to assist visitors' connections to the island's nautical history.

LIGHTHOUSE DISPATCHES

As an added feature, this season will be focusing on the Merritt family's term at the lighthouse from 1947 to 1959. After reviewing dozens of pictures and stories in the winter months, we are excited to be able to share the experiences this family had endured and enjoyed. Charleen Koeppen (née Merritt) as a little girl had many wonderful memories of the island with her older brother Brian. Charleen and Brian would often explore the surroundings as their father Charles would attend to the light and mother Dorothy would prepare a meal. This was at a time when the old lighthouse came down and the new structures such as the keepers dwelling were built; a time of transformation.

Today, we continue to transform, to become caretakers of this historic site and to remind Canadians that relevant history is always underfoot and ready to be explored.

Hoping for fair winds and sunny skies in the weeks to come.

In the lighthouse kitchen, Donny Wabasse creates a rhubarb pie crisp that requires time, skill and concentration.
[Photo: CLLS]

June 22, 2020

Summer brings life to cold rock on Superior

Now, we are experiencing warmer weather at the lighthouse as sunshine brings to life this cold and isolated rock on Superior. Porphyry Island is located 43 kilometres east of the Thunder Bay. If a crow were to take a direct route, she would fly over the chest of the Sleeping Giant to get to us.

When we first arrived three weeks ago, the leaves were just buds and the grass was short and obedient, but now everything is out. It's an exciting transformation that takes place as it fills in the green space. It has been like seeing spring twice, since the big city blooms much earlier.

As Mother Earth changes with the seasons, our pandemic response continues to evolve as we start to receive limited tourists and boats at the harbour. Our new docks accommodate travelers, and the lighthouse road through Porphyry Island Provincial Park Nature Reserve transports visitors through a nature reserve soundscape. It's amazing that, when you are away from the crashing waves, there is a chorus of birds defending their territory, attracting a mate or calling in the flock.

At the light station for nearly 100 years, a flock of chickens could be found near the end of the trail, and still today you can see the henhouse. No Porphyry omelets on offer yet to our host-keepers.

Starting in 1883, the Andrew Dick Diaries held by the Thunder Bay Museum revealed that for 30 years the laying birds' egg-count was always recorded.

As our research continues to uncover lighthouse family history, we find that the Merritt family lived during interesting times just as the facilities were about to be updated. Before the old lighthouse of 1873 was torn down, a new dwelling was built, in 1953. The two-storey, three-bedroom house was standard government issue and it offered spectacular views to all cardinal points of the compass.

Charleen Koeppen (nee Merritt) would be kept awake at night with the constant flash of the light through the window, and she often slept in the bathtub with pillows! The family would also listen to the wireless radio as all lighthouse families were used to the isolation and needed a break. Often, the assistant lighthouse keeper would also drop in and enjoy the serenity.

Today, the smell of fresh-baked pies is wafting on the wind. There's occasional laughter too, as spirits rise to moments in the wilds of Northwestern Ontario. Who knows what our summer season will bring? Maybe respite for battle-hardened, front-line workers. Or a sense of peace and quiet for a mom after home-schooling the kids this spring?

If you're interested in visiting sometime this summer, we are starting Sundays with the *Superior Rocket* charter route weekly from Thunder Bay Marina and possibly with pick-ups from Silver Islet at a later date.

We hope to provide a relief valve for our community while giving visitors an opportunity to relax after practicing good social-distancing and hand-washing. You never know, maybe there's a piece of Porphyry apple pie in the window for you to look at or, if you are very lucky, taste.

With the original Point Porphyry Lighthouse in the background, lightkeeper Charles Merritt, daughter Charleen and son Brian enjoy the sunshine, c.1950.

[Photo: Merritt Family Collection]

Lightkeeper Charles Merritt

The Second World War had just concluded and, for the next fifteen years, Charles Merritt and his family lived at the Point Porphyry light station. The family's history of lightkeeping spanned a total of thirty years, dating back to 1933.

Prior to their arrival at Porphyry Island, the Merritts were stationed at th Angus Island and Trowbridge Island lighthouses, both located near Thunder Bay's entrance. Just six weeks old, Charleen, along with her older brother Brian and their mother, Dorothy, joined Charles at Porphyry Island. The family would spend nine months at a time there, with the children later receiving their education at home on the station.

As the lightkeeper, Charles had numerous responsibilities managing the light and fog alarm, often depending on assistant lightkeepers to help out. Cleaning the light's lens was always a challenge, as the black soot from the kerosene lamps coated the surfaces and reduced and effectiveness of the light.

Charles displayed great bravery, often venturing out in dangerous conditions to rescue sailors in distress. On the shores of Porphyry, remnants of shipwrecks, including the *SS Scotiadoc* from Fort William (now Thunder Bay), have been found. These include a lifebuoy and a ladder which washed ashore and now remain as cherished artifacts.

In the 1950s, radio beacons were established as an aid to navigation for ships and aircraft, with tall antennas erected at the light station. When concrete was poured for the antenna base in 1955, the children left their handprints and footprints, which still can be seen today.

The children enjoyed numerous adventures, especially exploring the island's trails and Rum Bottle Bay, which has became part of island folklore. Former lightkeepers have recounted tales of rum bottles hidden along the shore during the 1920s prohibition era. Today, beachcombers can still discover sea-glass and earthenware from that time.

Whether it was island adventures, shipwrecks, communicating via the ship-to-shore radio, lighthouse maintenance or mending fishing nets, life was never dull. Today, the stories of the lightkeepers continue to resonate with visitors, enriching their experiences on Porphyry Island.

Brian and Charleen are captured holding the life ring from the SS *Scotiadoc* which was wrecked off the shores of Trowbridge Island in 1953.
[Photo: Merritt Family Collection]

LIGHTHOUSE DISPATCHES

July 2, 2020

Visitors unleash energy at Porphyry Harbour

Packing, planning and preparing for any adventure requires energy and focus. It's a surprise now that summer is upon us. How did we get here?

Gratitude is expressed for everyone who practiced social-distancing, and now Northwestern Ontario is temporarily released from the claws of the pandemic; opening opportunities for fresh-air adventures to be experienced.

If this past weekend was an indication of people's desire to get out and do something different, it was certainly proved. Volunteers under Captain Vic Miller and ships' first mate Caroline were able to complete a delivery of work that had been planned many months ago. Curtains, duvets, a chest of drawers and wall hangings, all of which had been assembled by Libby Dahl, were installed with the help of husband Curt.

Dressing the homesteads in 1950's style helps to create the right experience for visitor stays and keeps things in character. Red and white curtains fit nicely, and the colour combination to match the lighthouses reminds us that the two homes were a place for hard-working lightkeepers and their families.

Three-dozen people landed at Porphyry Harbour waiting to explore the island habitat and learn about the role of a keeper. Summer sunshine, sparkling water and sounds of kids splashing in the refreshing waters of Superior announce that things are rolling along.

Dan Adams came to us in his fishing boat to look at the docks and general set up at Porphyry Island after traveling from Silver Islet. In a loud voice, he announced that he had a five-pound lake trout, and if anyone wanted it he'd be happy to provide it filleted. For the new arrivals, host-keepers Claire Belliveau and Gerri Turner, fish dinner was served from the goodness of a neighbourly offering.

Three young families travelled from Amethyst Harbour to enjoy the day and explore the island of volcanic rock. Set free after months of being bound by house rules and safe-distancing, the energy was released in smiles and laughs. Through the eyes of youth, we can reconnect to our own curiosity of things, and change perspective to one of hope.

If this weekend is any indication of what is to come in the short term, we will see a robust season in "staycations" for our community. Whether through the weekly Sunday charter to the island or overnight stays, we always hear the same thing... "I didn't know this was here," or... "you can do that?" Upon arrival, visitors are connected to a unique experience; one not replicated anywhere, and one that continues to evolve.

Take, for instance, the landform known as the Sleeping Giant that separates Thunder Bay from Black Bay. When viewed from the east or from the west, it takes the same form. Who would have known that the first Europeans saw the Giant, not from Thunder Bay but from Black Bay in th 1670s.

For an original perspective on Lake Superior away from Gordon Lightfoot's haunting ballad, "The Wreck of the *Edmund Fitzgerald*", adventurers from the city of Thunder Bay are rewarded with a surprise — a giant that can get out of bed from the other side.

Dan Adams lands a big lake trout and offers it up to the lighthouse keepers and hosts. [Photo: CLLS]

July 7, 2020

Keepers self-isolating on island since 1873

Looking out the window of the lightkeeper's dwelling, the breeze is blowing, the trees are swaying slightly and summer is now well upon us. Point Porphyry, or *Kawagha-mish* in Ojibwe, welcomes the crashing waves as visitors and host-keepers get on with their day. The lighthouse island is located 43 kilometres from Thunder Bay, on Lake Superior, due east over the heart of the Sleeping Giant and across Black Bay.

It's wonderful to hear from people who have done their research, that their expectations are exceeded. One man was so impressed he repeated himself to make sure the point had been made. This is reassuring in changing times to hear some encouragement. Due to the work of a community of volunteers, supportive boaters and mindful visitors, it is difficult to put the experience in a box and say, here it is!

How do you explain... the turquoise water; the challenges faced in a storm by a light keeper; the taste of rhubarb pie made in the kitchen? Maybe some things can't be bottled up and exported for sale? Maybe you have to come and see it for yourself?

Our host-keepers from last week have returned home to Terrace Bay and Rossport and our new keepers are from the city of Thunder Bay. When the host-keepers first arrive we go through an orientation tour about the history of the site, while also talking about safety and what motivates our visitors. Now we've added onto our talk the pandemic precautions and how we are to respond in keeping with health guidelines. We start with the basics such as hand-washing and safe-distancing. This is followed by a demonstration on how to clean the outhouses and keep them fresh. Every step is taken and, considering that the public is only allowed in the open spaces, we are still able to give a comprehensive tour of the site.

Now we are past the second weekend in the summer, and we are continuing to experience many boaters visiting for tours or just to hang out with their family.

Last weekend, we managed to facilitate 11 boats, and had one charter boatload arrive in orange survival suits ready to adventure up the road to the light station. We've also hosted two kayak groups — one from Thunder Bay and the other from Wawa — both having paddled a whole day to start their week-long expeditions across the North Shore archipelago.

With Canada Day celebrations now behind us, and decorations returned to the box, the island is coming alive for another season. It's a place where keepers have been self-isolating since 1873, and even today the practices of yesteryear are still relevant. Now with blue skies and warmer weather, we are ready to provide some respite for visitors to unwind and take in the sights.

Thanks to everyone who supports the cause to conserve and protect our natural resources and provide a place to learn about our dynamic history.

Cleaning, sanitizing and maintaining the keeper's dwelling, host-keepers Heather Conrad and son Alden are thriving in their new surroundings.
[Photo: Heather and Alden Conrad]

LIGHTHOUSE DISPATCHES

July 14, 2020

Uncovering island's past

As the summer moves on, we continue to meet and greet visitors to introduce them to lighthouse living at Porphyry Point light station on a rock in Lake Superior.

Being on an island across Black Bay from the back of the Sleeping Giant, visitors often remark that they have never seen the Giant from an eastern perspective. Changing people's perspectives engages them on a journey of discovery and gives them another impression of our natural beauty.

There is no other Canadian lighthouse operating on Lake Superior that offers programs, home stays and guided history tours. We continue to embrace our nautical history and conservation story.

Our host-keepers, who just finished their week-long stint, Heather and son, Alden, have been super-sleuths uncovering Porphyry's past. During orientation, a list of duties was created as a roadmap for our keepers to stay busy and engaged. One item included discovering an old structure hidden in the woods. A moss-covered chicken coop with trap doors, laying boxes, and window was uncovered behind some old abandoned cars in the forest.

When repeat visitors arrive — those who have already visited the site for decades now — they want to see something new. Clearing brush from the area and removing it to burn, the coop, measuring 15 feet by 20 feet, has been exposed.

While this was going on, Andrew Dick's diaries were being explored further to find references to chicken coops and the lives of the hens. The Dick family lived year-round on the site for 30 years and recorded the daily egg-count along with other hen house challenges. On Aug. 30, 1892, Dick wrote, "A weasel or a mink killed 19 chickens last night; all that was in the house." He wrote on Aug. 31, 1892, "Got the mink that killed the chicks. He went back last night to feed and eat his last meal." These stories help younger visitors imagine how homesteaders survived these harsh realities a century and a half ago. Now we have more to share with our visitors that keep coming.

We have many things to for visitors to explore; the Gordon Graham Gallery, mini-museum and our interpretive story-panels. As boats sail by, fishing boats trawl the depths for fish, and our duty to man the station continues by providing information to our visitors. We are thankful to all the people who support these endeavours as it helps keep things in perspective.

As we continue through these times of pandemic, we again are resolved to provide people with respite and a place to experience the beauty of Lake Superior, and the story of lighthouse living.

The tea kettle is whistling again; better go! There's never a dull moment.

Heather and Alden Conrad clear brush away from the chicken coop that was once used to provide eggs for the keepers.
[Photo: CLLS]

July 21, 2020

Connecting to beauty of light station, waters

Until yesterday, we watched as storms devoured the mainland and travelled north along the shoreline from Porphyry. Then the bad weather set in here. During the week, as we performed our daily chores, the weather has been all around us with bolts of lightening, wind and dark, menacing clouds. On Sunday night, we received 60-kilometre winds, lots of chop on the water with white caps and rollers from the southwest.

Many people are coming to visit, and we are finding that our visitors are excited to see the activities of the people who are here and enjoy the natural setting. Located 43 kilometres on the other side of the Sleeping Giant from Thunder Bay, we have taken care of the light station for the past eight years. The original Point Porphyry Lighthouse was built in 1873 to serve as an aid to navigation.

Our last week's host-keepers, Natalie Vibert and daughters June and Gracie, enjoyed their work-time and time at the beach. Collecting sea-glass from the beach was a favourite pastime, considering it's recycled glass from items keepers discarded years ago, later to be used in art pieces or left sparkling on a window ledge in the keeper's dwelling. The girls did make a significant find — a ketchup bottle with "1932" embossed on its base. Making moments relevant to youth is easier done when the lesson is right in front of them. They are reminded of the fact that glass does not leave the eco-system quickly — it stays around for a long time.

This week also has included moving rocks out of the harbour, and some painting of docks for safety; also, continuing to unearth the chicken coop.

We meet many visitors who are arriving by boat, sailing craft and kayak. Several families are coming out to hear the stories of how the lightkeepers survived on Lake Superior, especially with big storms about. Today, things are much easier, especially when the lighthouse has many friends and, as an example in the past week, some supplies that were needed were delivered right to the dock! It's through these small acts of kindness that help keep things moving and working at the light for the enjoyment of all the visitors.

As our keepers tend to the yard, everyone pulls together to share the experience of Lake Superior living. When people find a moment to stop what they are doing and look at the wonderful, panoramic view, they are often struck by the fact they need more time to explore. Connecting people to the natural beauty of the light station and the exotic turquoise waters surrounding the island is liberating in these changing times.

Next week, we are welcoming the arrival of a research team that is working on an ecological review of the island until the end of September. Until then, we welcome fellow explorers and adventurers to come and join us anytime, and if you don't have a boat, you could consider coming out on a charter some time and enjoy the isolation.

Natalie Vibert, with daughters June and Gracie, work to install striped lines on the docks at Porphyry Island to keep everyone safe.

[Photo: CLLS]

LIGHTHOUSE DISPATCHES

July 28, 2020

Feeling tropical in an island paradise

A visitor last year commented that he felt he was in the Galapagos Islands, and this week we are certainly feeling it. With the turquoise waters splashing up at the point, and people jumping in the water at the boathouse, things feel tropical.

Circling storms menace and thunder is heard across the waters, but our volunteers and helpers keep at their work to ensure a safe visit for everyone. Last week, we ran low on supplies and needed some help, and our newest lighthouse member and friend, Marco, delivered, along with a smile. It's through these moments of isolation that we realize that this is a special place to be, which provides people with an outlet and connection to Lake Superior.

During our regular weekend tour, I shared with several guests who had come by on the *Superior Rocket* from Thunder Bay marina, my understanding of Porphyry Island and its geological significance, starting with the rifting of the floor of Lake Superior millions of years ago, and the formation of the islands and archipelago from magma spewing from far below.

Imagining recent history and the First Nations, I have started to wonder about the significance of the point, considering that it's at the head of the Black Bay Peninsula and a string of islands all the way back to Rossport. Point Porphyry was known by the First Nations as *Kawaghamish*; illustrated on Robert Bell's map of 1869. This map showcases many First Nations names for islands and topographical points of interest in the area. If we imagine back to times long ago, with the view of the Sleeping Giant and Turtle Head on Pie Island, this area might have some further stories to tell.

This week, we are also starting a new program of research and discovery with EcoSuperior and OceanBridge-Direct Action. The project will record baseline data of the environment while also exploring a project on forest therapy. It's exciting to welcome Simon Boudreault and Kelsey Herglotz to Porphyry where they will spend the next two months researching and living on the island.

With lots to explore and new surroundings, it's nice to listen in and hear what other people think of this environment and the history of the light station.

Our programming continues with great results from our volunteer hostkeeper family. It's a joy to hear about their observations and to know that the time has been well spent.

This week, our host-keepers unearthed one of the old ladders from the fog alarm building that had been hidden under the hull of an old wooden boat. Now, we are working on reconditioning the ladder for future display in our little lighthouse museum.

When our host-keepers left, one was heard saying. "You learn a lot about yourself when you are disconnected from the outside world."

We are looking forward to continuing to connect people to the significance of lighthouses on Lake Superior, while also providing some respite.

Next week, we will learn more about the scientific study taking place on the island and hear how things are moving along.

From left, Jayda Nadeau, Pierson Rasmussen, Jacalyn Cop-Rasmussen and Peter Rasmussen spent the morning transporting and stacking the wood pile shown in the background. [Photo: CLLS]

August 4, 2020

Exciting research project underway at island

Summer is well underway and people are getting into the experience of exploring the nature and island lifestyle east of Thunder Bay. Take, for example, Yolanda who is in her 90s, who came out on the *Superior Rocket* to see the sights and panoramic views of Lake Superior.

Standing tall on the point is the Point Porphyry Lighthouse that represents the end of the Black Bay Peninsula, 20 kilometres east of the feet of the Sleeping Giant. A collection point for not only birdlife and other animals, but humans too. They are all seen meandering over the black rocks of this volcanic isle.

To think, we are in Northwestern Ontario where being part of the Canadian Shield is commonplace, but here, there are exotic rock formations with arctic-disjunct plants adhered to them, far away from their arctic cousins but kept cool by Superior's waters lapping nearby.

As the berries fatten up and ripen into a jet-black colour, ideas are already being formulated for the lighthouse kitchen; unbeknownst to the cook. Past lightkeepers relied heavily on the berries that could be found in the area, with several accounts being noted in Andrew Dick's 1880 diary. We know where his favourite spots were; including on other islands nearby.

OceanBridge and EcoSuperior's project is now underway, creating environmental data points on several different aspects of the island's nature. This project will help direct future research towards a better understanding of the Porphyry Island Provincial Park Nature Reserve. Transected by a short, one-kilometre road, the park can be surveyed from many different locations, including shoreline access. The work is exciting because it adds another comprehensive program to a list that includes the host-keeper program, and Mike and Denise Kornell from Sault Ste. Marie, avid outdoors people and explorers, are starting their week with ambition to see that both the conservation and lighthouse history is enhanced.

This week, the lighthouse was visited by a crew from S.A.N.D. Adventures, and the SUNORA regatta, part of the Thunder Bay Yacht Club. At one point during the weekend, the boathouse lawn (with safe-distancing) was filled with people chatting to one another. Now only a snapshot in my mind, people coming together to share in nature during these times, I think, is a healthy escape.

Jim Dyson, a cheerful local fisherman from Silver Islet, brought his family and friends for a visit. Speaking with Jim is cathartic, as his knowledge of the area is filled with the yarns of many fisherman's stories.

Canadian Lighthouses of Lake Superior grounds are well manicured and looked ready for the final half of the summer. For those venturing onto the water, lighthouse volunteers are waiting to show you around the grounds and the new Merritt family exhibit.

Next week, we will learn how our host lightkeeper team did manning the station, and hear more about the tourist trends on this little isle.

Kelsey Herglotz and Simon Boudreault stan beside a weather station recording the maximum and minimum temperature over the last 12-hour period, including precipitation and cloud coverage. [Photo: CLLS]

August 11, 2020

Porphyry Island activity includes weather monitoring

Heavy rains soak the island as the boat rocks and the forest breaths a sigh of relief. Rain has brought resilience and life back after a dry spell. Visitors continue to tour the island, boaters continue to tie up, and the surprises keep coming.

Bill McKay, from a string of light keepers stretching back to the 1920s, returned to the island after a long hiatus. Story after story poured out as echoes of yesterday stream readily forward from his consciousness. McKay shares the location of previous buildings and their use, while sharing with us life on the island back in the late 1960s.

One story reaches back to the closing of the original lighthouse and re-confirms an artifact housed in the mini-museum. The lighthouse ladder from the 1873 light tower shows signs of worn rungs from tending to the light in storms and filling the lantern with whale oil.

This week has also seen lots of hard work by our host-keepers, Denise and Mike Kornell from Sault Ste. Marie. With a long list of duties, they managed to connect to lighthouse living with abandon. Seeking out their next tasks, their sense of adventure was infectious, and also included a visit by their daughter who is working front-gate duty at Sleeping Giant Provincial Park.

The weather station is now on brand new legs and holds a louvered box containing two thermometers — one measuring highs and the other measuring lows.

EcoSuperior's OceanBridge-Direct Action team members, Simon and Kelsey, continue to record weather information as they develop their baseline study of living things on the island. Beach-glass is also collected for a future forest wellness project. It is through their eyes that we can continue to see the role that nature plays around us, while appreciating the panoramic views.

Porphyry Island, located east of the Sleeping Giant across Black Bay, continues to be set against the turquoise waters and blackened skies of passing thunderstorms.

Pleasure boaters and charters continue to arrive, with one boater, Todd Siciliano, sharing his catch of a giant salmon caught in the bay that was gladly devoured by the volunteer crew on the island. Such spirit of sharing from our visitors makes us all feel good as our job is to contribute to helping visitors enjoy their stay.

We are also thankful for Archie's Charters bringing people together to share, not only in the lighthouse experience, but also on the big waters and fish.

On Saturday, August 29, at Porphyry, we'll be holding our first Lighthouse Carnival including, hopefully, the return of the monarch butterflies. The carnival will include food, entertainment, exhibits, tours and a corn roast; an idea shared by the Graham family, previous lightkeepers who entertained boaters many years ago.

This coming week will include a visit by Karen Jones Consultants who are studying the future sustainability and stewardship of Canadian Lighthouses of Lake Superior.

We're looking forward to the weeks ahead as we greet more adventurers who are discovering this area for the first time.

Catching the big one just off Porphyry Island, Todd Siciliano makes a donation of salmon for dinner for the lightkeepers and volunteers.
[Photo: CLLS]

LIGHTHOUSE DISPATCHES

August 18, 2020

Busy week enchants visitors to island

Island life continues to ebb and flow with many people visiting daily; exploring the lighthouse site and beyond. This past week has seen so much going on it's hard to keep up with all of the happenings on the island.

Let's start with the fact that we had three consultants visiting to see what experiences we are providing our visitors and how we can create a sustainable attraction for years to come. Whether around the campfire, in the sauna or attending tours, time flew by for the consultants as so much was packed into their visit that we needed to have extra boats and support for showcasing our area. Not only does this light station merit attention, but so does the Silver Islet Harbour, the Silver Islet General Store, and the Trowbridge Island Lighthouse as they are all components of a plan established many years ago; part of the Lighthouse Trail.

All these areas are in different states of repair, waiting for next season to greet the public. Canadian Lighthouses of Lake Superior (CLLS) provides some oversight in the development of the harbour and has a lease for Trowbridge Island Lighthouse. For the past several years, charters have come from the city of Thunder Bay, and soon, with the opening of the harbour and general store at Silver Islet, visitors are going to have some added opportunities and incentives to use this route.

Located 43 kilometres east of the city, the trip to Porphyry Island by boat is a long one, and sometimes the weather is not too co-operative. You will always find people here at the lighthouse willing to share their story and adventures and, if necessary, keep you safe from the stormy weather.

The Hintikka family fell in love with the island as our host-keepers this past week. Arriving ready to work, they were immediately put to work hauling away brush and developing new areas for visitors to see and understand. For Trisha, the mother, she had been hoping everyday that the Porphyry host-keeping placement would come true, as she has been on the front lines of the pandemic. Happily, she and her family were able to connect with the island in ways some visitors might be envious of. They took long family walks in the forest, through the nature reserve and to the black sand beach to dabble at the water's edge. Abi painted a sign for the head of the trail to invoke some mystery for the visitor. Where did the name *Kawagha-mish* come from?

The Silver Islet Mine

While First Nations peoples had explored and mined copper in the region for millennia, it was in 1868 that Scottish mining engineer, Thomas Macfarlane, made a significant silver discovery on a tiny 50 m² island off the Sibley Peninsula, approximately twenty-five kilometres east of the city of Thunder Bay. This discovery would lead to one of the richest silver mines in the world at the time, yielding two million ounces, valued today at more than $85 million.

The mine featured two vertical shafts, 1,300 feet deep, with a head frame, a blacksmith shop and housing for single men constructed on the island which had been surrounded by wooden breakwaters and expanded to more than ten times its original size. One kilometre away on the mainland, married men resided in the hamlet of Silver Islet which eventually included numerous homes, a church, a jail, a hotel, and a graveyard where many miners were laid to rest. Access to the island was exclusively by boat, and a large wooden wharf was built on the mainland near the general store that still exists today.

Initially owned by the Montreal Mining Company, it was listed on the New York Stock Exchange. One of its officers, Charles Trowbridge, was honoured with an island named after him. The surrounding woods and peninsula were named after Alexander Sibley, who served as president of the Silver Islet Mining Company, the American corporation that took over the operation in 1870.

The greatest challenge facing the miners was keeping Lake Superior from flooding the mine. Two coal-powered steam pumps, transported by ship, were installed. Ultimately, these were the mine's Achilles' heel. When a coal shipment did not arrive in 1884, the mine was inundated and the operation was closed down forever.

Today, the hamlet of Silver Islet is accessible by road and attracts tourists from around the globe, including those arriving by cruise ship. Since the harbour has been updated with government funds, it's now easy for visitors to get on and off the water. This community offers a glimpse into the past; remaining off-grid and, with its historic homesteads still in use, retaining a charm that is rare in modern times. Many visitors explore the surrounding waters by kayak or charter vessel to view the flooded, abandoned mine shafts, prompting reflections on the wealth that this mine once generated for its owners.

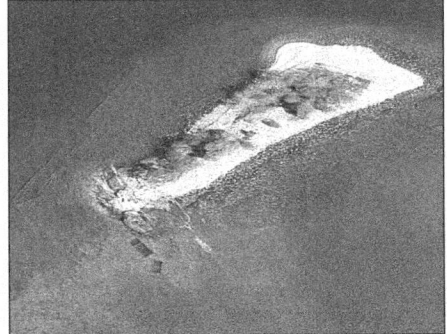

The site of the Silver Islet Mine. The now-submerged mine shaft entrances can be seen off the tip of the island. [Credit: Google Earth, from Landsat / Copernicus, NOAA, Data SIO, U.S. Navy, NGA, GEBCO, Airbus]

Looking at a map of the area by Robert Bell from 1869, we see that Point Porphyry was also called *Kawagha-mish*. The journey of the First Nations is only in our imaginations at this moment as to what it meant for them to see a panoramic view of the Sleeping Giant and Turtle Head on Pie Island.

As the camp-fire is extinguished at end of the day, memories have been made to last a lifetime. Looking towards the dark sky and seeing the stars reminds us of our place in the universe and how fortunate we are to live in this area.

Next week we will tell you more about the upcoming Lighthouse Carnival happening on August 29.

The Hintikka family, Gracie, Patricia, Abi and Shane, hoist a new sign at Porphyry Island. [Photo: CLLS]

August 25, 2020

Get some sea-glass while at the carnival

Discoveries continue to abound as we venture into the woods seeking past stories and happenings on this lighthouse island. Tours and visitors are busy seeking opportunities to discover their own experiences and observations on-shore or from the water.

One visiting couple this week, Don and his wife Suzanne, used the bicycles to reach the lighthouse point to see what was happening with the weather. Don said, "I found myself in the forest alone on the trail enjoying the moment, and thinking that this was just like when I was a kid." These moments of reflection are moments to be remembered and cherished in our busy and changing times.

EcoSuperior/OceanBridge-Direct Action participant Simon Boudreault found himself exploring another part of the island — the beach. "I enjoy picking up sea-glass because it makes me feel like I'm cleaning the beach while gathering small pieces of the history of Porphyry Island," said Boudreault.

Others continue to ask about how the glass arrived on the beach in the first place? We've discovered a picture in our archives that shows a garbage dump by the original 1873 lighthouse. In plain view can be seen a pile of garbage sliding into the water. Once the glass had broken-up, it arrived 450 meters away by Superior's current, polished up and ready for jewelry making or mixed-media artwork.

One of EcoSuperior's projects on the island is to explore the concept of "forest therapy" and seeing how Porphyry Island could become a place to practice this type of meditation.

While venturing through the woods, I came upon an old wooden crank used to draw the lighthouse runabouts up onto the land. It is also situated on the beach just down from the point and is worthy of further exploration.

This weekend will see the Lighthouse Carnival, started when former keeper of the light, Eve Graham and her late husband Gordon, would share time with local boaters by hosting a corn roast. The carnival will include a main event of music with the Scott van Teeffelen Band, fish & chips and a few sideshows. The event is limited to 60 people and includes some 20 visitors who will be arriving from the new Silver Islet Harbour.

For them, the journey will start in Thunder Bay, along the new dual lane highway to the Pass Lake turn off. The group will then venture through the Sleeping Giant Provincial Park forest to historic

Silver Islet. Then, participants will travel with Archie's Charters to Porphyry Island for a day's worth of activities and be returned later. What a trip! Super, new highway; beautiful, green forest, turquoise waters and a community gathering.

We are thankful to Sandra Budd, William Vanderwees and Deb Koivu for their hard work collecting supplies on the mainland for Porphyry Island, located many kilometres to the east across the water.

We hope to share with you next week the event and how the revitalized tradition was received by the boating public and our special guests.

Displaying a hand-made pendant, Simon Boudreault from the EcoSuperior OceanBridge-Direct Action program, works to find ways to repurpose found seaglass in an artistic way.
[Photo: CLLS]

September 1, 2020

First carnival brings entertainment, activities

At 7 a.m., I awoke to my boat rocking because of heavy winds and lots of waves. Overcast with 35 kilometre winds and 30 guests waiting to be transported from Silver Islet, hope hung in the air. Was the weather going to co-operate?

Slowly, the machine of volunteers, supporters and sponsors rallied together for the first-ever Lighthouse Carnival. The weather cleared, the sun came out and a window of opportunity opened up for Archie's Charters to take visitors from Silver Islet to Porphyry Island, some 14 kilometres further east on Lake Superior. With the annual monarch butterfly migration celebration and a corn roast brought forward from the past, visitors were anticipating an interesting event!

Member of Parliament Patty Hajdu, (Liberal MP for Thunder Bay-Superior North) stepped off the vessel to take a tour of Porphyry Island and to hear about new developments on the site. Hajdu has followed the developments of Canadian Lighthouses of Lake Superior (CLLS) for many years now and has been instrumental in reopening Silver Islet Harbour as a safe harbour and public access point.

Guests taking advantage of this event were entertained upon arrival at the lighthouse to watch a 1980s film by CBC television that followed lightkeeper, Gordon Graham. Others chased butterflies, and one visitor commented that they had found two that had perched on the lilac bush and were perfect candidates for picture taking.

Smiles erupted when the Scott van Teeffelen Band performed at the boathouse with cover songs and original tunes. The band brought people together around the campfire to stamp their feet or to sing along. Guests were treated to fish & chips, corn on the cob, caesar salad, and coffee. Everyone was blown away by the quality of the catch and enjoyed the sunshine and warm winds.

CLLS's new "self-isolating since 1873" T-shirts and mugs did brisk sales as people felt it would be a good reminder of the times we find ourselves in.

This past week, we had been busy researching further into the volcanic action that happened 1.1 billion years ago that created this island. As a volcanic island accompanied by turquoise waters, it separates us from the mainland's precambrian shield and the teal blue waters that flow into Thunder Bay from the Kaministiquia River. Maybe this is why people feel like they are in a foreign landscape?

This coming week, we are looking forward to completing some smaller jobs and will again be supported by host-keepers Gerri and Claire.

It is through all of the support of our community that we can continue to bring people closer to nature and the historic lightkeepers' stories.

Already, volunteers and board members are preparing plans for next season to create another event to help sustain the operation and to greet visitors to our shores for years to come.

Next week, we will look a little closer at the data baseline that the EcoSuperior/OceanBridge-Direct Action program is creating.

The Scott van Teeffelen Band provides music late into the night at the first annual Lighthouse Carnival event at the Point Porphyry light station, situated 43 kilometres east of Thunder Bay. From left, Robert Lem, Arden Bruyere (behind Robert), Scott van Teeffelen, Tanner van Teeffelen and James van Teeffelen.

[Photo: CLLS]

September 8, 2020

Every term as host-keeper "different from the last"

Butterflies attempting to make landfall on Porphyry Island have been battling ferocious winds on Black Bay. Watching these little insects in flight reminds us how brittle we can be against the elements, especially here on this little Lake Superior island.

Winds on the water for the last week have been pretty intense due to big weather system upsets from southern hurricanes pushing the jet stream around. Tying everything down for the moment and doing inside work has been the way to adapt — plus, throwing a log on the dwelling's fireplace makes it toasty warm.

This week, a team of participants of the classic OceanBridge program came to learn more about our island habitat and to partake in programming provided by the EcoSuperior citizen scientist and forestry therapy projects. On the trail to the point, the team of eight were able to explore Porphyry Island Provincial Park Nature Reserve. Within the boundaries and on the beach, they were also able to witness how bottles thrown out by past lightkeepers were being cleaned up. Some archived beach-glass became a forest wellness activity by having the group fashion pendants from the historic recycled glass. What better way to clean up the beach and learn a little history along the way? It's expected that the glass will keep coming ashore as it's been in the lake for over 100 years; turning and spinning, smoothing off the rough edges.

Our final host-keeper session was filled by veteran team Gerri Tuner and Claire Belliveau who commented that, "Every term as host-keeper is different from the last." Again we are thankful to these hardworking individuals who work to keep things happening day-to-day at the lighthouse.

Monarch butterflies have returned and, because of the high winds, we have only seen a few clusters gathering on the pine trees. As they soak up the sun and flap their wings, they soon know it's time to migrate towards the south.

In three-week's time, we will be closing up the station for the season and, until then, there are lots of reports to write and stock-taking of a very busy season.

To celebrate the work undertaken this summer, we are having a special charter to Porphyry Island this Saturday from Silver Islet. It will include a lighthouse lunch with the keeper.

For those who came for the carnival a week and a half ago, the memories are still fresh, including those of the new Silver

Islet docks and harbour. If you are looking for a day out, then it's a beautiful morning drive down the Sibley Peninsula to leave for Porphyry. If you haven't seen the volcanic beaches, the turquoise waters and the mysterious plant life Porphyry is known for, then why not consider an adventure back in time? One billion years ago, a 30-kilometre deep volcanic plug was created leaving a unique experience for people to witness on the earth's surface.

My teapot is starting to whistle again. Time for tea, and again to look out at the blue water with the occasional ship coming and going from Thunder Bay, keeping commerce going.

From left, Kaitlin Richard, Brigitte Klassen, Melissa Davidson (sitting), Kirsten Desorcy, Graeme Shaw, Kelsey Herglotz (sitting), Josh DeWitt, Erin Van Breda, Nicole Dupuis and Simon Boudreault strike a pose during their visit to check out Porphyry Island's ecology.

[Photo: CLLS]

September 15, 2020

Moving into final stretch at island

The sound of the axe can be heard in the forest as more wood is split for the cooler mornings and days ahead. Summer is in its final stages and fall is about to come upon us. Yesterday, a poplar tree started to shed its leaves, and ferns are already turning brown.

Plenty of fun around the lighthouse is still happening with our final public charter arriving from Silver Islet last Saturday. Many visitors shared their experience of visiting Silver Islet for the first time and the ease of reaching Porphyry Island while enjoying the view on the water.

Our guests continue to be very inquisitive as they explore the historical amenities and learn more about this island habitat for wildlife. Arriving on a journey from Midland, Ontario, three sailors, Ryan, Nick and Captain Evan, spoke of their adventures. On the high seas of Lake Superior, the trio were delayed in Wawa for eight days; waiting for the weather to clear to make their final leg home to Thunder Bay.

Point Porphyry Lighthouse, which is situated 43 kilometres east of Thunder Bay, provided the crew with continued goodwill as a final night of celebration took place around the campfire. Hearing their stories of how other boaters assisted their journey is reassuring to all of us — we're in this together and working in unison for everyone's safety.

As keepers and caretakers of these lighthouse sites, we cannot thank enough the spirit and assistance provided by our supporters and volunteers. There is a lot to administer and maintain, but the results are there for visitors to comment on, and also to help improve.

Canadian Lighthouses of Lake Superior is in its last phase of a future sustainability plan and roadmap forward. It's exciting to hear from the consultants about their perspective as to how the facilities, programs and events can be rolled out in the future. As the organization finishes analyzing the plan, our Annual General Meeting will be a great opportunity to share some of the findings and new directions.

Slowly, we are starting to close up the facilities for the winter by pulling out some docks, repairing bicycles and doing the odd jobs that have been waiting all summer to be completed. Our garden, tended by Donny Wabasse, continues to see good results, with everyone sharing in the beans, peas, spinach, and I think there is another yield of rhubarb left for a final crumble pie.

As we find time to reflect and take in the site, it's wonderful to reminisce with others about the memories created by families and friends this summer.

Next week, we will be saying goodbye to our EcoSuperior/OceanBridge participants as they leave for the big city to do some final debriefing and analysis on their endeavours this summer.

With changing seasons, the Point Porphyry Lighthouse can be seen on the point, viewed from the old harbour beach by the graveyard.

[Photo: Donny Wabasse]

LIGHTHOUSE DISPATCHES

September 22, 2020

Summer fades at Porphyry Island

Warm winds blow as Indian Summer is now upon us here on this volcanic island 20 kilometres east of the Sleeping Giant.

Boating traffic has tailed off considerably and now we are but two, as our Ocean-Bridge participants left Monday morning for the big city. Simon Boudreault and Kelsey Herglotz will wrap up their time in Northwestern Ontario after making some final deliberations on their experience. Throughout the summer they have made 1,000 observations and have now uploaded the data to an application called iNaturalist, which is an initiative of the National Geographic Society. These observations will be reviewed by the online community to confirm, for example, a name or species while ultimately appearing on a Google map of the island for future reference.

Some wildlife has returned to the light station now that most humans have gone. Sometimes you can smell the animal prior to seeing it, which was the case this morning. A bull moose was taking a leisurely walk down the lighthouse road and, within a few minutes, a bear cub also appeared. The moose has become a nuisance in the garden.

As the lighthouse season is now wrapping up, many thoughts are being digested around the experiences that visitors received while on tour or stopping in for a break from the lake. Through the Karen Jones Consulting study, we heard many positive and constructive results from a survey that 77 people completed: 93% of our visitors were happy with their visit with some feedback for improvement. One respondent said, "It supports history and tourism in the region," while another said, "For the length of time that the organization has existed, and the affordability of the membership, I can't ask for more than the exceptional experiences that we have had at Porphyry." In the next five years, the sustainability plan will be implemented taking into consideration the stakeholders' and community responses made over the last few months.

Now, our attention is turned to closing up the buildings, doing the laundry and removing the water from the cistern before freeze-up. Firewood is being cut daily to cache up depleted stock, with some nice birch being put aside to heat the house in the spring when the lighthouse reopens.

As the nights get longer, more stars are out to view with the glow of the city lights beckoning us to return. In a week's time, *Nina* will venture home across the turquoise waters of Black Bay, but for now, I enjoy some solitude after a record-breaking summer.

September 29, 2020

Season closes on lighthouse

At first, all we could see was a fog-bound coastline, but as the wooden boat *Nina* inched closer, the early-evening lights of the city could be seen; behind us, Black Bay, the Sleeping Giant, Porphyry Island, a hungry bear cub and many memories of a summer like no other.

Our final visitors to the island were the winner's of the "#Tbaycation" contest which included Helen Otterman and seven of her best friends. The prize was a selection of treats from Current River Bakery, a trip on the *Superior Rocket*, a tour of Porphyry, dinner at The Keg and a night at the historic Prince Arthur Hotel. The contest, run by Tourism Thunder Bay, saw 2,000 people enter a picture of their summer "stay-cation" as a way of celebrating Canada's premier outdoor city.

Connecting people to a destination on Lake Superior helps celebrate the historical relevance and wildlife conservation of this lighthouse island. It's a destination that was found this year by 534 people who arrived by boat, 184 who came by charter vessel, and 44 by kayak and helicopter.

To our 20 volunteer host-keepers who maintained the site during the season — with many improvements enjoyed by visitors — thanks for helping keep things rolling. Our volunteer teams who facilitated food and supplies to the island for the past four months took on a challenging logistics job. In addition, many boaters stepped forward; not only to support in material ways, but also to promote this Lake Superior destination.

The Thunder Bay Yacht Club came through with support for destination projects to benefit of the public at Porphyry, Trowbridge, Tee Harbour, Sawyers Bay and Thompson Island. We were happy to receive additional funds from Ontario's Lottery and Gaming Corporation as they continue to support non-profit organizations, as well as many visitor donations.

Our fundraiser carnival on the island was also a way of connecting with the public by providing an opportunity for visitors to experience an annual ritual which had been celebrated in the past by the previous lightkeepers with a corn roast.

All of this support has meant that we can continue our journey to provide a place for people to visit; a place to reconnect to our nature, and a respite from today's challenges.

Thank you goes to our 202 members, many supporters, and enthusiastic volunteers. Without you, we would not have been able to offer a fun, organized attraction.

Through our strategic and sustainability plan, we are optimistic that we can continue to provide our North Shore community with an opportunity to connect to a major part of our existence on this massive lake.

In the near future we hope to have some exciting news as the federal minister for the Department of Fisheries and Oceans, Bernadette Jordan, helps guide our process to obtain other lighthouse facilities for public access.

Slowly, the vessel *Nina* makes her way up the Kaministiquia River to her home port. Memories of the summer are carried aboard, waiting to be unpacked, recorded and to find ways to improve upon for the next season.

Hope to see you next summer to share more from the turquoise waters of Lake Superior on a volcanic lighthouse island teaming with life.

A young bear cub climbs to the top of the mountain ash tree for some succulent red berries at the Point Porphyry Lighthouse.
[Photo: CLLS]

2021

Pandemic Restrictions Relaxed

June 1, 2021

Summer adventure kicks off at lighthouses

The putt-putt sound of the vessel *Hidora*'s engine brought the seagulls out from their roost to investigate. Was this another fishing tug on Lake Superior? No, it's the sound of another summer adventure beginning at the lighthouses this season. As a keeper of the Point Porphyry Lighthouse, located 43 kilometres east of the city of Thunder Bay, and along with many other volunteers, this summer is already starting me off with some much-needed respite from the winter months.

While crossing Thunder Bay and moving closer to the Sleeping Giant, one can see the effects of many sprouting buds that create a lush green sheen below and above the cliffs.

It's thanks to having leases with the Department of Fisheries and Oceans Canada that many lighthouses on the north shore of Lake Superior are accessible to visitors. These isolated places, far from the mainland, have helped get products to market for hundreds of years by guiding ships along their shipping channels. In 2008, the Canadian Government, under the Heritage Lighthouse Protection Act, recognized that there was an opportunity for Canadians to participate in the conservation and protection of heritage lighthouses "... that form an integral part of Canada's identity, culture and heritage." After thousands of hours of volunteer spirit and investment made by Canadian Lighthouses of Lake Superior, three regional lighthouses are now open to the public to experience, explore and live a bit in the wilds.

As *Hidora* passes Silver Islet, the new $3-million investment made to the docks and marina there helps connect tourists to these lighthouse island destinations and create future economic development in the area.

The waters are calm now as we approach Porphyry Island further to the east. The island is gray as the trees have not shown their leaves yet since it's much cooler here surrounded by Lake Superior. The black sand beaches on this volcanic island are exposed more this year as the water level is very low. The forest is dry, and we are not seeing much in our overflowing swamps this season.

The site is still looking good this year, except that our four-foot high dried and stacked pile of birch for the sauna has somehow disappeared over the winter.

The waters remain calm around the island and we are now cutting the grass and getting the site ready for visitors.

When pandemic restrictions are lifted, tours to the lighthouse will come out of Thunder Bay again, but we are also opening up a new route with Archie's Charters from Silver Islet. The benefit of the new departure point on Black Bay is quicker access to Trowbridge Island and Porphyry Island lighthouses instead of traveling across the waters of Thunder Bay.

Our programming on-site will again include host-keepers but, due to the pandemic, our artist-in-residence program has been cancelled for the season. The annual spring cleanup did not take place at our lighthouse sites this season but we are already hearing from boaters that they are willing to help out. It's through this spirit of giving that we learn about the value of what it takes to create an adventure on Lake Superior.

We hope to see visitors from around the area come and commune with nature — no drone of the internet, no home schooling or working at home. We have lots of fresh air in our Superior isolation, just waiting for you to visit!

Hope to see you this summer.

Lighthouses on the north shore of Lake Superior have helped bring products to market for hundreds of years by guiding ships along their routes. [Photo: CLLS]

The Heritage Lighthouse Protection Act

The Heritage Lighthouse Protection Act was passed by Canada's Parliament in 2008, and came into force in 2010. The intention of the legislation was to conserve and protect lighthouses that had significant heritage value to a province, community or group. However, no funds for preservation of these lighthouses was specified in the Act. This was in contrast to the United States Congress which, eight years earlier, had designated 70% of that country's lighthouses as historic and committed grant money to any person or group who took ownership of the lighthouse to preserve it.

Between 2010 and 2015, a process was put in place in Canada for community groups, municipalities and provinces to submit petitions to the federal government to place lighthouses on the list of those eligible to be designated under the Act. Of the 350 petitions sent, to date only 112 lighthouses have received the federal heritage designation. The status of the remaining lighthouses is uncertain.

The Shaganash Lighthouse on Number 10 Island was one of twelve lighthouses originally petitioned for designation by Canadian Lighthouses of Lake Superior (CLLS). After being declared surplus to government requirements, the lighthouse was transferred to CLLS and designated under the Act as a heritage lighthouse in June, 2023. The entire process necessitated many steps including preparing a sound business plan, a site survey, a legal title search, an environmental assessment and lead paint remediation. The heritage designation ultimately took ten years.

The Heritage Lighthouse Protection Act stipulates that any sale or transfer of a heritage lighthouse must provide for the protection of its heritage character. The specific responsibility of the lighthouse group is to preserve the historic, architectural and community values of the light tower. CLLS was fortunate that it received a grant from the Department of Fisheries and Oceans, Canada (DFO). This money will be used to enhance access to Number 10 Island through improved infrastructure and programming opportunities. Plans for the Shaganash site also include research into its history and developing a strategic plan. With the designation and CLLS ownership, there is now potential for leverage of additional resources (for example, from Parks Canada) to develop new infrastructure for boaters, kayakers, and adventurers along the north shore of Lake Superior

Heritage designation plaque which will be placed on the Shaganash Lighthouse.
[Credit: Marc Seguin]

June 8, 2021

Reflecting on being part of nature

Watching my breath in the basement as I dismantle an old Duro water pump from the 1940s is not my idea of fun. Grimy, cold hands and wet feet combined with some colourful words brings success as the house's pressurized water system is operational again. As I worked, I watched the wildlife through the basement window for two hours and was anxious to get outside, warm up, and commune once more with nature.

The island is starting to come alive just one week after landing at Porphyry Island. Flowers are blooming, leaves are unfurling, and monarch butterflies are busy fluttering about. Blue jays and an ear-full of cedar waxwings can be seen foraging for food. In the bay, we see a hawk being chased by two angry seagulls. The chatter of squirrels can be heard, and two rabbits appear on the lightkeeper's front lawn to hop about.

Visitors come and check in with us down at the docks as the Royal Canadian Mounted Police Marine Unit is out doing their patrols. Later, a family comes to spend the night after a successful catch of salmon.

As we are hearing about a big storm in Thunder Bay, the weather closes in on us and we batten down the hatches. There's lots of lightening and loud crashes of thunder, but we are all safe and snug on Porphyry.

Our garden has been tilled to accept the rain and we're ready for another season with spinach already making its debut. Herbs, peas, beets and lettuce are all planted to help feed our volunteer hostkeepers and summer lighthouse navigators.

We are currently working on repairs to the chicken coop because we will have some feathered friends arriving on-site in a couple of weeks. As many have come to understand, sustaining a lightkeeper's family required many small contributions such as a garden, fishing rod, and tending to chickens.

We are not sure what the survival rate for the chicks will be as a wolf arrived on the island during the winter months.

Donny Wabasse, who does much of the cooking and keeps the house in order, has already made a rhubarb pie, which one of our guests tasted and enjoyed.

Our docks are now in place to accept families that are in the same household to stay over. Vic Miller's family came to help out since our lighthouse volunteer activity was cancelled. Vic is a director on the board of Canadian Lighthouses of Lake Superior. His help on bigger jobs such as dock repairs and material management is always an asset to the organization.

Archie Hoogsteen, also on the CLLS board, came to help out by setting up some of the heavy docking that had to be hauled out of storage and back into the water. Through these helping hands, we are getting things ready for the season. Our programming will be limited, but when the restrictions are lifted we are expecting many people to visit Silver Islet and embark on a journey to visit us on the island.

As the fog swirls through the trees and momentarily blocks out the sun, we reflect on what it is to be part of nature. To feel the elements, to see life come back to this isolated location on Lake Superior refreshes the mind and helps reset the balance.

The tea kettle is whistling. Better take a break and await visitors to entertain and educate on our lighthouse experience far from the big city.

Vic Miller shows the new Canadian Lighthouses of Lake Superior pennant that carries the lighthouse logo created last winter.
[Photo: CLLS]

June 15, 2021

New docks coming as island sets up for summer

Lighthouse living is a lifestyle which harkens back to the "good old days" of survival. Getting your provisions ready is only half the journey, as there are lots of unexpected jobs to undertake, and the question is, are you quick and nimble enough to eliminate a problem? Here on this isolated island 43 kilometres east of Thunder Bay, it's about surviving the elements and being prepared for the unexpected.

Canadian Lighthouses of Lake Superior (CLLS) is now in it's eighth year of providing access to the public, and we continue to work to provide a great summer experience for everyone.

We've been experiencing a lot of weather events on the island. I guess it has to do with the fact that the lake is still very cool and the hot air masses circulating around are resulting in thunder and lightening. It's awesome to see the light show far from the mainland, and watch as it follows the coastline towards the north and east. One bolt of lightning touched down nearby, followed by a huge thunder clap.

As many have endured the life of monks during the COVID-19 pandemic, it feels weird to unfurl, unwind and relax a bit after such an ordeal. What a great place to do this — when there are no storms about — as the island again comes to life.

Excitement is building as there are many new projects coming on line and, with our partners, some new opportunities. Silver Islet General Store will be opening soon and the Silver Islet Harbour Association is working on configuring their docks to prepare for the season of visitors.

CLLS has invested in some new commercial docks that are being delivered soon to Porphyry Island. This will help to accommodate the many charter visitors along with more mooring balls for boaters.

Our volunteers are stepping up also to fill in the gaps and help build a great experience for the visiting public. We have one volunteer working hard to round up a flock of chickens to send to the island for the summer. This is to help visitors reflect on how the keepers would have survived in years gone by. During one family's tenure in the early 1960s, they even tried to raise rabbits. To us today, this might all seem odd, but when you are fending for yourself, it's good to have several sources of sustenance to keep you going.

This season, we are opening up the Gordon Graham Gallery at the Point Porphyry Lighthouse to feature local artwork for sale, including Donny Wabasse's photos that are often seen weekly in our Dispatches. Raising funds will be important this summer, as we have lost thousands of dollars due to the shifting sands of the pandemic. These art pieces have been collected over the past few years from our artist-in-residence program that should make a comeback next season.

Admiring the artists' perspectives of our lighthouse island operation helps us to understand what attracts people to the area: the solitude, the silence, the storms and the unforgettable sunset moments captured when the Sleeping Giant has already gone to bed for the night.

This season will be all about returning back to some semblance of normal while looking forward to new horizons and vistas. If you get a chance this summer, stop by and see how lightkeepers lived, worked and played on the biggest freshwater lake in the world.

The tea kettle is whistling again, trying to get my attention, so I better go for now. Next week, I look forward to again sharing my story from the lighthouse.

Butterflies are making a return in abundance to Porphyry Island. They can be found roosting at night in the trees.
[Photo: Donny Wabasse]

June 22, 2021

Snapshot of another week on the island

The vessel *Hidora* rocks and rolls in Porphyry Harbour this morning as winds blows out of the north. Lighting the woodstove provided some warmth from the elements and gave me time to enjoy a morning coffee.

The lighthouse island is being readied with many small jobs to be completed to tailor the site for summer visitors. We've had some visitors who have taken advantage of the sauna and fire pit, with the echoes of laughter reaching deep into the boreal forest. Many are excited to know that a wolf has come to the island during the winter months, and big paw prints can be seen along the beach, plus scat with big deposits of fur making us wonder if the rabbit population has been brought down.

Carlo Franco, a blogger and artist, has come to the island to explore and see what it's like to live here for a week, and to develop content to entice a younger generation to appreciate this historic wilderness setting. It's refreshing watching through the eyes of someone who only discovered Thunder Bay last year when faced with pandemic restrictions.

The art gallery is getting set up for the season to feature not only art, but also a film for interested visitors on the lighthouse in the 1980s.

We have continued to get some rain which has helped move the garden along, and the grass has been cut a couple times and is back under control.

The traffic on the lake has been moderate with the new Silver Islet Harbour Association signing the papers to take on the ownership of the docks and pier, 15 kilometres to our west.

Our gift shop is being setup with the popular self-isolation mugs, t-shirts and, new this year, a pennant for boaters to fly. Thanks to our board of directors and volunteers for helping select and build our new logo and gift offerings to visitors.

It is getting exciting now that the site has evolved back into shape to respect the esthetics of the long history the island provides. On July 1, 1873, Point Porphyry Lighthouse was first lit to warn ships away from two prominent reefs to the south. The original wooden structure stood high over the point. A lightkeeper, Andrew Dick, lived there for 30 years. Starting in 1880, he lived on the island year round. It made him a unique keeper as most left for the mainland during freeze-up.

His family history still ruminates with us today as we walk past the graveyard where his wife, Caroline, is buried. She was an Indigenous North American woman who grew up on Black Bay. Her keys to survival were her fishing and hunting skills, and knowing what medicines were available in the forest. We often reflect on this as a reminder that it takes many skills to survive on this rocky island. It's so cool here that previous keepers would grow their potatoes on the warmer Edward Island that has a larger land mass.

Today, we are receiving our first food delivery from George's Market, and a film crew of local entrepreneurs is helping us share the attraction. It is refreshing to see local creative youth explore local attractions and help tell their own stories. Kasper Wabinski, who owns a local transportation company, is continuing to showcase our region with his own resources. We thank them all for visiting us today and for sharing their experience with others.

Now, time to take a break and enjoy the beautiful scenery while waiting for some kayakers to arrive from Naturally Superior Adventures.

From left, Gangandeep Singh, Chad Kirvan, Curtis Jensen, Wayne Schulz, Anna Sukhoverkhova and Kasper Wabinski are helping to share the Porphyry Island attraction. [Photo: CLLS]

June 29, 2021

Island in bloom as visitors, navigators begin arriving

The lighthouse docks are filling up with enthusiastic boaters and charter boat visitors at Porphyry Island Harbour on Black Bay. The trails are cleared, the grass is cut, and the firewood stacked ready for what we believe is going to be a busy season.

This morning, I took the motor vessel *Hidora* to the new Silver Islet Harbour to collect Canadian Lighthouses of Lake Superior's lighthouse navigators. Kennedy Hamilton and Aleia Ouellette will be our summer students helping to give tours, maintain the site and answer visitors' questions.

CLLS has installed two new floating docks to help facilitate extra traffic to the site this summer. The docks will cater to the powerboats and charter vessels with six feet of draft, or less. The lake level is down by eight inches over last season but, since heavy rains, the levels are back up a bit.

Last evening in the gloaming, we saw a lone wolf on the shoreline, but he was skittish and, when he saw us, retreated back into the forest. In a few weeks, EcoSuperior's summer staff working with the Canadian Wildlife Federation will be interested in learning of the wolf sighting as they record data during their five-week stay.

Four kayakers arrived on their first journey of the season and were on their way to Rossport. Two of the experienced crew were from Wawa's Naturally Superior Adventures; leading tours during the summer in the area.

The island is in full bloom now that the cold waters of Lake Superior are warming up. Some wild strawberries have already produced fruit, with rhubarb being harvested for pies. In days gone by, the lightkeepers would take advantage of what the island had to offer, such as gooseberries, fish and game. With a kitchen garden on-site, it is expected that by early August we can start to harvest some lettuce and other leafy products.

Our chickens will be arriving in mid-July, and we are hoping for a few breakfast omelettes with crunchy vegetables from the garden.

Former lightkeeper, Andrew Dick, would put in his diary from 1880-1910 how many eggs he collected daily, including the day the weasel came to dine, and ate all of the chickens!

Survival on an island far from the mainland can be challenging. Now, the weather continues to get warmer, and we are seeing more fog appear. For a navigating captain, that can create challenges keeping the vessel pointing towards the destination.

We are hoping that visitors will again contribute to the upkeep of the site, which has been developing over the past eight years for public access. It's hoped that people will be again be able to enjoy the experience.

While preparing for breakfast, Donny Wabasse, our cook and house manager, heard a strange noise. Upon investigation, a merganser duck had come down a disused chimney to arrive on the kitchen floor. Somewhat disorientated, the duck was shown the door and returned back into the fog.

In the next week, we are looking forward to visitors for Canada Day while also celebrating the 149th birthday of the Point Porphyry light that has protected mariners from these rocky Superior shores for decades.

Arriving on the kitchen floor at Porphyry Island, a merganser turned out to be a quick surprise visitor.
[Photo: CLLS]

July 6, 2021

Lighthouse offers history lesson in wilderness

As the tour boat came in with its load of passengers, they were in for a huge surprise. Bounding out of the woods came a moose. Frightened by a noise, the beast ran right along the shoreline as the boat positioned itself into the dock. All eyes were on this gangly animal as, with ease, it made for quieter pastures. The group had heard about the wildlife, the panoramic views, and the black sand beaches, but to see such a big animal close up was an amazing sight.

Porphyry Point Lighthouse, located on Porphyry Island in Black Bay, 15 kilometres east of Silver Islet, has again become a busy place with much human activity.

The July 1st celebrations on the island were a family affair, as former light keeper Eve Graham and her son, Kevin, were aboard to help the students orientate to island living while also working on a couple of pet projects.

Eve's history as one of a husband-and-wife lightkeeper team in the early 1980s has given her many fond memories of operating the station years ago. She has continued to show people around and still speaks about life at the station, and the challenges of being far away from town.

Meanwhile, Kevin was busy installing a new shower unit, with tests carried out by willing lighthouse staff member who gave it a thumbs up. Another job, also for creature comforts, was the installation of screened windows around the guest house.

We thank the Graham family for their ongoing support and investment into maintaining this Department of Fisheries and Oceans Canada site for public access. These facilities and other nearby lighthouses are leased by Canadian Lighthouses of Lake Superior to not only maintain these structures, but also to give Canadians and tourists the opportunity to engulf themselves in history in a wilderness setting. This, by far, is not a passive connection to our area but includes many interpretive signs on-site. Our new lighthouse navigators are providing visitors with lots to consider in the one-and-a-half hour tours.

Lighthouses did, and still do, play a role in our society. Firstly, they protect ships from rocky shoals and keep commodities on course, but they also provide an outlet for people to understand how this country of ours was built through shipping.

Our First Nations families and friends can be assured that their history is also interwoven with past settlers who needed help to survive in an unfamiliar setting.

This ebb and flow between people and survival could not have been more apparent when my finger was injured during a simple lift early this week. My pinky finger had been routed by a wayward galvanized nail, and a small trail of blood evidence was left on the beach. When I reached the boatyard, I was happy to be greeted by an inquisitive doctor who just happened to have a suture kit aboard his vessel. Sitting down at the picnic table, I was given a jab to freeze the finger, and then had a close-up view to the art of closing a wound.

Three stitches later with the wound dressed I was ready to go again; mind you, I was quickly reminded to take things slow the rest of that day to let the finger repair itself.

Being in a wilderness setting reminds us of how fragile nature is and how quickly when we need help and reach out to others that they are there for us.

Next week, we are looking forward to more visitors at our docks and hearing about their adventures on Lake Superior. Tea time, it's time to go.

Common Wild Roses can be seen on the black sand beaches near the lighthouse at Porphyry Island Provincial Park Nature Reserve.

[Photo: Donny Wabasse]

Porphyry Island Provincial Park Nature Reserve

Few visitors to Porphyry Island realize that the land ownership of the island is divided into three separate parcels. The Department of Fisheries and Oceans Canada manages the harbour and docks as well as the light station at the point. A small portion of land on Walkers Channel, situated between Edward and Porphyry islands, is privately owned. Ontario Parks is responsible for the majority of the land which surrounds the lighthouse road and harbour.

Covering 106 hectares, Porphyry Island Provincial Park Nature Reserve is characterized by numerous, ancient lava flows alongside quartz and purple-hued feldspar crystals known as porphyries, with the boreal forest featuring white birch and balsam fir, and black spruce thriving in the wetlands. Along the rocky shores, you can find stones adorned with bright orange lichens and several arctic-disjunct plant species. Devil's Club (*Oplopanax horridus*), a plant introduced by First Nations people from western Canada, flourishes on the island and was traditionally used for medicinal purposes, such as treating tuberculosis. Many birds and monarch butterflies travel through these islands along their migratory routes to the south.

When the park was designated as a nature reserve in 1968, it adopted the principle of "take only pictures and leave only footprints." No camping or man-made structures are permitted in the park itself. Researchers interested in conducting scientific work related to biology or geology must register beforehand. In 2020, a local environmental group, EcoSuperior, employed two summer students to identify and catalogue 1,000 plant and animal species found on the island.

Visitors enjoy walking along the shoreline in search of sea-glass and other intriguing finds. A stroll along the island's south shore reveals fascinating examples of the volcanic formation that occurred 1.1 billion years ago. In some areas, volcanic rocks have eroded to create fine sandy beaches that warm in the summer sun, offering views reminiscent of a Hawaiian Island.

In 1983, an archaeological team excavated near the graveyard at the point. Their dig uncovered and analysed 54 human bone fragments, raising questions about the extent of the burial site for First Nations individuals who were laid to rest before the 1870s.

Today, the island remains a tranquil place where visitors can enjoy peaceful walks through the forest.

July 13, 2021

In the swing of summer on the island

The day started out nicely for a group of 15 ladies from the Canada Games Complex who were taking a tour of the Point Porphyry Lighthouse and the Nature Reserve. Susan Lester, the birthday girl, was surprised that her original invitation list grew from six to fifteen people, with everyone bringing a treat for lunch. As the official food taster on the island, I was invited to sample the food and gave the spread two thumbs up.

Keeping active, Jim Heald, our host-keeper, was busy constructing a portable chicken coop with a moss-lined nesting box and two pieces of driftwood for a roost. He was joined by others to complete work on the docks that are opening up to provide more room for visitors' boats.

Attacking a picnic table with a spray of water made for satisfactory fire training in humid temperatures. Summer navigators Aleia Ouellette and Kennedy Hamilton are just finishing up their on-site orientation training and are starting to welcome visitors and providing tours.

The Canada Summer Jobs program provides work placement for summer students returning to school in the fall. It's an opportunity for our lighthouse navigators to work with host-keepers, help with the chores in the homestead and to work on specific projects. Their work has also included a lot of scraping and painting to refresh the site. This reminds us of the adage that a former light keeper once said: "If it moves, oil it; if not, paint it."

A few members of the Thunder Bay Hiking Association joined up for a fun tour around the lighthouse site after disembarking from the charter boat. Not only were they introduced to the volcanic island and fresh, cold, clear water, but they also had the opportunity to meet the many small succulents on Porphyry Point. Arctic-alpine disjunct plants love the cool temperatures and thrive much further south than their cousins up north.

Carlo Franco, the video blogger that was invited to get creative, certainly did. In his 13-minute film showcasing the island, he even developed a made-up Swedish dance around a tree to celebrate the start of summer! You can see this video on Canadian Lighthouses of Lake Superior's Facebook page.

This weekend, more action was taking place at the lighthouse harbour, with a bocce ball tournament; a game that goes back to the Roman empire. The atmosphere was relaxing and enjoyable as everyone played in turn on the lawn. A few loons could be seen quietly swimming in the harbour; birds were singing in the trees, and there was a slight breeze.

Tonight, the lighthouse staff will sit down to a dinner of lake trout caught by Archie Hoogsteen. I am imagining it now, baked in the oven, glazed with toppings, and I'm ready to squeeze the lemon.

We have not seen the wolf now for a couple of weeks but we are still seeing fresh tracks. The rabbit that lives in the swamp has survived the cull and we are happy to see him on our daily walks down the trail.

As we prepare to do a provision run into Thunder Bay to restock on items, we are thankful for all the support shown by the community that allows us to continue our mandate to connect the public to these historic sites.

The Strong Seniors Fitness Group from the Canada Games Complex celebrates a birthday at the Point Porphyry Lighthouse. In front row, Susan Lester, seated in chair, was the birthday girl. [Photo: CLLS]

July 27, 2021

Kayakers, researchers continue adventures

Dipping into the water provides a sense of relief from warm weather as we enter into mid-summer. Watching the sunset glow, amplified by the burning boreal forest fires, I'm left wondering when relief will come?

Living on this volcanic island, 15 kilometres east of Silver Islet on Lake Superior, we are continually met with changing conditions — the relief comes to us in a big storm with lots of lightning and rain.

It's great to sit indoors and watch it all happen as the lightening dances across the sky and long shadows appear in the forest as plants drink up the moisture.

A group of five kayakers headed up by Jim Bailey are spending a week with us; with their base-camp established in the lightkeeper's dwelling. The crew is anxious to get onto the water to explore, and with each day another adventure begins. On the first day, it's around Porphyry Island as a warmup, and the next day it's around Edward Island. The last trip is an overnight trip to the Shaganash Lighthouse further to the east on Number 10 Island.

Through the eyes of these adventurers, we hear about their challenges and smile at their triumphs against the waves and the wind. Each day winds down with a sauna, which is very helpful to warm up the old bones as most of the paddlers are in their seventh decade of life.

EcoSuperior again returns with a team of researchers to the light station to measure climate while continuing to identify species in this magical place.

A landscaping exhibit has been created at the site to address water run-off into a rain garden from the roof's downspout. The purpose is to demonstrate how to slow down and filter water before it is deposited onto the lawn. Beautiful, bright flowers and golden rod are added around the perimeter of the swale as these thirsty plants stand by for the next rainfall.

Each day is a learning experience for Paula Sulston and Rorik Shron who are both taking part in this program supported by the Canadian Wildlife Federation. Last year, you may remember that EcoSuperior had other researchers in the field building up a snapshot of the island's living things. More than 1,000 subjects of interest were captured, reviewed, and confirmed prior to being listed on the internet in an application called iNaturalist.

Jan Starr, a camper from Silver Islet, and her granddaughter, Alina Hoard, and friend Molly Delgati, have come to the lighthouse to participate as junior hostkeepers. The delight in the eyes of the two young ladies reinvigorates everyone to keep things sailing along and to provide the best experience for visitors. Their arrival at the site might have been a first, for they both rode on a tube behind Dad's boat all the way across from Silver Islet. The water temperature has risen to about 18°C, so the experience was not too bone-chilling.

Next week, we will meet another family visiting as host-keepers, and share with you the holiday weekend experience.

Rorik Shron left, and Paula Sulston lay out a transect line to take inventory of plant species on Porphyry Island.
[Photo: CLLS]

August 3, 2021

Porphyry Island on the air

The mid-summer continues to produce dynamic thunderstorms, refreshed island atmosphere and unbridled enthusiasm in our visitors.

Several dozen kayakers have been busy this season, guided by companies taking their clients across the North Shore to Rossport. Enjoying a sauna after a hard paddle from Silver Islet harbour to Porphyry Island, the journey for most won't be forgotten anytime soon. Tents are neatly placed around the harbour and a routine of cooking, cleaning, and planning takes place to prepare for the next leg of the journey. Naturally Superior Adventures from Wawa, and Such A Nice Day Adventures from Rossport, can be proud of the eye-opening experience that they provide, safely, to their clients.

For boaters, it has been a busy weekend as they manage to navigate through the changing seas while calculating their gas consumption. Sailors and power boaters are also arriving for this year's SUNORA regatta, which took the fleet across the North Shore archipelago from Rossport to Porphyry. The annual event wound up with a night of awards and celebrations. The regatta allows new boaters an opportunity to learn about navigating on the North Shore from other experienced boaters.

Our summer student, Kennedy Hamilton, is painting on a concrete slab a huge chart of the local islands stretching from Thunder Bay to Passage Island. This chart helps visitors comprehend the role of light stations on Lake Superior as the lights often have different navigational functions. The Trowbridge Island Lighthouse for instance, near the feet of the Sleeping Giant, helps ships to navigate their way to Thunder Bay, whereas No.10 light (Shaganash Lighthouse) offers assistance to smaller vessels in the North Channel, protecting them from obstructions and the big waters of Superior.

Point Porphyry Lighthouse, 43 kilometres east of Thunder Bay, offers mariners a landmark to the entrance of Black Bay and also helps ward ships off of the nearby shoals. One unlucky vessel, the *Thordoc*, was misdirected in the fog in the 1920s after the captain fell asleep. For many days after, the vessel's cargo of flour was offloaded to refloat the ship. The captain was given a warning after a transportation board investigation, and the local residents had lots of flour for baking.

An afternoon of fun was experienced when a member of the Lakehead Amateur Lighthouse Radio Society, Rob Van Wyck, VE3FLB, monitored the airways for contact with other ham radio operators specific to lighthouses. In activating the Porphyry Point Lighthouse for the first time, Van Wyck was attempting to reach out over the airwaves to one of the 1,665 members of the Amateur Radio Lighthouse Society. "Putting Porphyry Island on the air was a lot of fun," Van Wyck said. "I look forward to a return visit."

The goal of the ARLHS is to promote public awareness of the role that radio and beacons have played in assisting and monitoring mariners' safety at sea.

We did have a bit of excitement on the weekend when the Thunder Bay Raptor Rescue team of Jenn Salo and Ravin Knockaert rescued a juvenile bald eagle from Number 10 Island. A kayaker had called it in and set in motion a rescue to retrieve a bird due to malnutrition. Rehabilitation will take place on the mainland with the bird being returned back to a natural habitat.

Next week we will be welcoming another family to our host-keeper program and look forward to sharing their adventures on the island with you.

Rob Van Wyck has a first-time experience at activating a lighthouse on the radio with other ham radio operators in the vestibule of the keeper's dwelling on Porphyry Island.

[Photo: CLLS]

LIGHTHOUSE DISPATCHES

August 10, 2021

Visitors see improvement — Carnival on the way

Summer living on the lake is upon us as we continue to learn about the beauty of the area we live in. It's through the help of many organizations that we are able to keep providing a connection to Porphyry Island. We received support this year from the Great Lakes Foundation to continue to upgrade landing facilities for the boating public. The Foundation works to connect boaters to destinations on the lake while helping to maintain and sustain the ecology of the area. Having this focus helps us help others to learn the importance of nature and how to protect it.

Boaters, and also our charter services, are already realizing the improvements from the funds with a dock dedicated to commercial service, and an additional mooring ball to facilitate boaters staying in the safe harbour.

Parks Canada, as manager of the National Marine Conservation Area, is also helping with upgrades to provide more picnic areas, information and orientation services on the history and direction to the many who use the island's attractions. It is encouraging to have others help to sustain these isolated attractions for all to enjoy.

This past week, Ben Heywood-MacLeod, a former lighthouse navigator, and his girlfriend, Suraiya, returned to explore the island as host-keepers. Through the many attractions, the young couple were able to canoe around the point to gain another perspective. To hear of their adventures and to see their pictures, we are reminded of the freedom they experience on these waters to investigate the shoreline.

The Post family also visited, and Arthur and Lucy Turk came to make life-long memories of spending time flying a kite across the point. After kite-flying, they met up with Kennedy Hamilton, this year's lighthouse navigator, where she was working on a project to showcase a map of the region's islands.

On a large concrete platform painted white, Hamilton has drawn in Thunder Bay and Black Bay to showcase how the nautical traffic flows in the area. This new teaching tool helps to show how the lighthouses on Lake Superior are lined up and what roles these lights played.

As the lights are still active on the water and are serviced by the Canadian Coast Guard, they still provide support to boating in the area.

People Continuing To Visit Island

All too often we hear of people's phones falling in the water, or that their GPS or compass is not operational;

that's why we still have lights on the lake. One day you never know if you are going to need this assistance to navigate.

The lighthouse group uses the dwellings and outbuildings to help share the story of being a lightkeeper while showing visitors how everything works.

Over the past couple of weekends we continue to see more and more people visiting us and exploring the volcanic island and clear waters of Lake Superior. We are currently gearing up to provide another Lighthouse Carnival event on Aug. 28, to inspire boaters by following a past custom that lightkeepers provided to visitors years ago. We'll have history tours, a film screening, ecology displays and some games to keep everyone engaged; plus entertainment by the Scott van Teeffelen Band.

There are a few seats left on the charters leaving in the morning from Silver Islet, and if you are interested you are welcome to visit our website, or find someone with a boat!

Next week, we will tell you about our new host-keepers and about the work they are completing to keep visitors happy.

Flying a kite on Porphyry Island is one of the activities that Arthur and Lucy Turk enjoyed while visiting. [Photo: CLLS]

August 17, 2021

Island life keeps our eyes wide open

Arriving at the harbour beach, I was surprised to see not one, but three canoes. Three senior couples were out to enjoy the experience but had been, unfortunately, fog-bound for three days on the Sibley Peninsula. After landing at the Point Porphyry Lighthouse, they were able to relax and clean up in the sauna.

The waters are now warmer as we are in the middle of the summer, and the winds are blowing a little stronger also.

Visitors are constantly amazed to meet a friend on the island, learn something or, especially, to see the black sand beaches.

Our host-keeper family from southern Ontario worked to pull up baby pine trees on the trail, building picnic tables and doing some painting. Their eyes are always wide open as the abundant wildlife is ever present with the cedar waxwings eating all the berries and fattening up for the fall.

Being as one with nature is only part of the story as the lighthouse histories and artifacts continue to intrigue and be mulled over. Questions are always being floated about, and this week we are fortunate to have Eve Graham, a former lightkeeper, return to the site as her knowledge is extensive. Her husband, Gordon, now deceased, was the lightkeeper in the 1980s, and left a legacy of images as he loved photography.

These memories and gatherings of boaters and sailors were all part of the lightkeeper story many years ago. These hard-working people who helped move ships and commerce back and forth are again being celebrated at the carnival event on Aug. 28.

The stories of the past are shared, focused around a campfire with corn roasting and everyone having a moment before the end of the season.

EcoSuperior and their team have been busy collecting samples from around the island while also helping visitors with their questions. Rorik Shron and Paula Sulston have been spending several days around the bog that is located in the centre of the island which, from all accounts, is quite a feat to reach. For three days now, they return with their stories and adventures and continue to add more flora and fauna specimens to their digital log.

The rain garden is looking fantastic now that it has been completed with a ton of rounded rocks taking up the centre area helping to slow down any water flow.

Having different projects on-site allows people to explore many facets; not just the geology, but also insects. This season, after planting donated milkweed and watching it being devoured, we are seeing more and more monarch butterflies returning and starting to roost in the treetops. We are hoping that in a few weeks we will again see a resurgence of these insects as we'd seen a few years ago. Two or three trees have managed to capture around 200 monarchs which fluttered about as soon as us animals held down by gravity walk by.

Thanks go to our board of directors who work in the background to help make things work at the light station: Vic Miller, Joe Marcella, John Ongaro, Paul Capon, Deb Koivu, Kevin Graham, Eve Graham, Tony Bossio, Archie Hoogsteen, Elaine Lynch and Carl Pettigrew.

Now, for a walk down to the black sand beach to take in the sights and to relax a little and wait for more visitors to this island on Lake Superior.

Next week, we will share what our team has been up to and how the arrangements are going for the carnival event.

Building picnic tables for the upcoming Lighthouse Carnival are Bob, Lily and Anna, our host-keeping family.
[Photo: CLLS]

August 24, 2021

Tours have tripled to Porphyry Island

The smoke across the sky was fresher and closer to us than ever before, but what was the source? To our south we could see that Isle Royale's northern arm was on fire.

Living on an island, isolated from services and with changing weather patterns, we were a bit concerned about the potential of fire on our own island. Our safety plan on-site was updated, and our new arrivals were given some instruction in the event of fire.

It's been a hot summer, and being out on the lake we still get the fresh breezes, but our peas have shriveled and stopped producing.

Life continues all the same, and the Jellema family of Nick, Ashley, Wyatt and Keir start their journey as host-keepers. The first question they hear upon arrival is, "What would you like to do first? Go on a tour, set up house, or just explore?" After taking the first part of the tour, the family was happy to be staying in the big two-story keeper's dwelling. The two boys checked out all of the rooms, and had a guided tour of the basement with its old water pump and wood-burning stove. It was neat for them to see how the lightkeepers lived years ago, and tonight they'd be having spaghetti dinner prepared by Donny Wabasse.

Out of each rattling window can be seen the heavy wave-action and stormy weather with waves dancing on the Porphyry Reef — a thing that dreams of lighthouses are made of. Are there any ghosts?

Canadian Lighthouses of Lake Superior operates three lighthouses on the waters east of Thunder Bay, and the Porphyry Island destination has been having a very busy summer. Our tours to the island have tripled from last year, meanwhile our visiting boaters have remained the same.

In preparation to draw to a close a hot summer that brought plumes of smoke, heavy storms and busy trails, we are planning for this weekend's Lighthouse Carnival. Entertainment will be by the Scott van Teeffelen Band, and local boaters are helping out by volunteering their time with the fish & chips, and a corn roast. There are tours being organized for new and old visitors, including a screening of a newly released film by Kasper Transportation on his visit to us earlier.

As the community comes together to share in the experience, we must be mindful of all those who spent their lives helping mariners move products by ship to and from market. These lightkeepers toiled away in harsh conditions and lived, in some cases, off the land, or by fishing, to survive. It's through these sacrifices that, when something lands on our table, we give thanks. Thanks to all of our visitors this season who provided us with support and who gave willingly their insight and feedback. Thanks to our boating community for their continued interest and enthusiasm to visit and support our activities.

Yes, life on the lake has its good moments and also its challenges, but it is through these experiences that we learn that every moment is special and if we are fortunate, happy memories will linger for years to come.

Painting rocks for the Lighthouse Carnival event planned for Saturday, Ashley, Nick, Wyatt and Keir Jellema enjoy the refreshing air and creative moment
[Photo: CLLS]

LIGHTHOUSE DISPATCHES

August 31, 2021

Taking mental snapshots of island

The summer continues with some great stormy weather, warm days and waves lapping at the shore. What more could a lightkeeper want than to have some calm days in between storms to catch up on some of the chores?

Our last host-keeping family of the season was busy helping with final preparations for this year's Lighthouse Carnival. Local boaters came together to help support the lighthouse so all the visitors could have a great time. Thirty-three people arrived on-site, with the help of Archie's Charters, to take in a myriad of activities. The events went off with clockwork precision, but we did not see as many butterflies this year as we'd seen in the past.

George's Market provided some corn, and B&B Farms provided the potatoes already cut to go with the fish; which turned out to be a great combination.

The EcoSuperior programming staff who have spent the summer here, facilitated by the lighthouse group, provided tours on some of their ecological and meteorological findings. Their tour included looking at the weather station, reviewing the rain garden and checking out some of the natural observations in the Porphyry Island Provincial Park Nature Reserve.

Local artist, Margaret Mol, had a piece of her artwork auctioned off along with another item. The $300 raised helps to support programming for public access to the lighthouse.

The Scott van Teeffelen Band returned to rave reviews. Their ability to connect with the crowd and share their musical talent kept everyone's toes tapping until late into the night. With the lifting of the fire ban, a bonfire accompanied the night; which was considered a bonus.

Carlo Franco's and Kasper Transportation's short films were screened at the event with lots of chuckles and thoughtful pauses while seeing panoramic views of the sites on this remote island 43 kilometres east of Thunder Bay. Last year's EcoSuperior film about the capture of environmental data and forest therapy was also screened.

It is through the eyes and ears of a young man that we can be reminded of what is important around us. Adam Waxman, son of Al Waxman, who is now deceased and who was the star of "The King of Kensington", a CBC series in the mid 1970s, came to visit with his son. The boy was able to catch a fish on Archie's Charters and have it for dinner in the lighthouse.

After a hectic travel schedule as we all walked together on the forest trail, Waxman asked his son to breathe and take in the sights and sounds of the island. The guidance by a father to his son was beautiful. As tour guides, we ask people to stop and take it in and take a mental snapshot of what they are experiencing.

Our summer continues on with the holiday weekend approaching and still a few more Sunday tours available.

It's nice now that things are starting to quiet down after a busy summer. Tea has just been delivered to me in the light tower, so I'm going to take a break.

See you next week.

A sign goes up to help visitors find their way at this year's lighthouse Carnival. The sign was designed by host-keeper Nick Jellema and family. [Photo: CLLS]

September 7, 2021

More information coming out about island

It seems like today we are offering small animal and bird rescue services, as a baby seagull and a squirrel appeared to have become disorientated in the recent storms. Feeding the small seagull a few cornflakes has energized our feathered friend to pay us back with some signature droppings on the dock.

The lighthouse operation has been busy this week with over 30 visitors coming to look around and learn more about the island and its habitat.

The Porphyry Point Lighthouse is one of three lighthouses currently operated by Canadian Lighthouses of Lake Superior, based in the city of Thunder Bay, Ontario. The non-profit organization, now in its eighth year, serves to connect these government leased lighthouse sites to the general public. Today, the homesteads and outbuildings are no longer needed because of automation. Why not connect tourists with their need for places to visit while creating regional economic development?

The Department of Fisheries and Oceans Canada recently signed a deal with the Silver Islet Harbour Association for the group to take over the operation of the docks that have been there to serve the public since the late 1800s. With the recent re-opening of the Silver Islet General Store, people are now more than ever able to access the history of the area, including the Trowbridge Island Lighthouse close to the toes of the Sleeping Giant.

In William S. Piper's book, *The Eagle of Thunder Cape*, published in 1924 and now available at the Thunder Bay Museum Society gift shop, more details are coming out about Porphyry Island and the area. The book, gifted to our library shelf by Foster Gauley, speaks to times, many years ago, that bring to our minds-eye the opportunity to imagine what life might have been like for our First Nations family.

Imagine being battled every day by the elements of sun, water, wind and waves? Imagine the strain lightkeepers must have felt, since 1873, making sure the shipping channels remained safe and operational.

Our recreational fishermen brave the waters around these Superior islands to catch something for their table. A few weeks ago in Black Bay in an annual occurrence, the water turned "upside down" with cold water coming to the surface while warmer water was sent to the depths below. This causes the fish to migrate to the temperature that keeps them happy, but as the waters of Black Bay reach 65°F, fishermen can now be seen beyond Porphyry Reef, in deeper and cooler waters that are more amenable to our finned friends.

Thanks to Archie Hoogsteen as we are fortunate enough to try out his catch occasionally with lake trout and salmon being served. This helps us as our food rations are starting to dwindle as the season winds down.

Paint pots and brushes are back out to dab worn spots on walkways, paths and steps; all receiving the standard battleship grey, while whitewashing walls and painting the red trim helps freshen things up for next season.

The weather tonight is calm and the boats are settled in at the harbour. It's a time to reflect on the past weeks, continue to digest the summer events, and start to plan for next year's adventures.

See you in a week as we continue to uncover the history, the beauty and the area's gems that many are just finding out about, or some have already explored.

A storm cloud rolls southward across Black Bay with Turtle Head (Pie Island) seen on the horizon.
[Photo: CLLS]

Lighthouse Automation

In a film series produced by CBC Toronto in 1980 titled "Heartland," the central theme revolved around the looming automation of the lighthouses and the loss of the lightkeepers' jobs. For well over a century, lighthouses had been a fixture at sites all across the north shore of Lake Superior, making it hard for the nine keepers in this area to accept that their livelihoods might soon vanish due to technological progress. The keepers were understandably reluctant to lose their income, and the government shared their concerns about potential vandalism.

In 1954, the Shaganash (No.10) Lighthouse, which guarded Superior's North Channel, became the first light to be automated using an alkaline battery. This change was feasible because the light was only needed for short distances to serve local traffic, not for vessels navigating the open lake.

The evolution of lighthouse technology transformed from large machinery, such as generators and pumps, to more compact innovations. For example, in the 1960s, the electricity needed for lighting was supplied by diesel generators, typically three per light station. One generator would deliver power while another remained on standby, with the third serving as backup. This setup highlighted the critical need for navigational aids to be operational around the clock.

Eventually, the Department of Fisheries and Oceans Canada transitioned to solar power for automated lights, having tested this technology for several years. In 1989, at both Porphyry Point and Shaganash, small solar panels were installed alongside heavy-duty rechargeable car batteries. Today, the lights consist of clusters of LEDs with their much lower power consumption and minimal maintenance. In contrast, the more powerful light on Trowbridge Island needed a substantial battery bank. This rotating light was critical for directing traffic into and out of Thunder Bay, and it featured some 30 six-volt batteries housed in the fog alarm building.

Today, all lights along the North Shore are automated. With advancements in technology, such as global positioning satellites, the lighthouses themselves have become less important as aids to navigation. However, they still offer safety and reassurance for mariners on the lake. Equipment malfunctions are commonly experienced by boaters, so the presence of operational lights provides them with peace of mind regarding their location. While the lights themselves are still maintained by the Canadian Coast Guard, it is lighthouse groups like CLLS that preserve these sites, mostly under a lease, for recreation and educational purposes.

September 14, 2021

Taking stock of our time on the island

It's almost automatic, hopping on my bike for a ride to the light station to close off the day. As I coast through the Porphyry Island Provincial Park Nature Reserve on the lighthouse road, my mind is digesting the day's events as tourists keep arriving. Looking up to see that the way is clear, I am met by a startled bear as I round the corner on the pathway. He takes flight and crashes through the forest by leaps and bounds, and then can be seen skirting a big patch of Devil's Club.

Devil's Club is a plant that grows up to six feet high and has sharp spines under its leaves and on its stem. It is believed to have been brought here by First Nations people from western Canada as a remedy for arthritis, cancer, fever and tuberculosis.

Now, regaining my composure, I continue up the path to the keeper's dwelling, a two-storey house built in 1948. As the nights start to get longer, the generator is energized to provide light to the homestead, which adds a degree of comfort after being bombarded by the elements all summer long.

As we take stock of our time on the island this summer, it's nice to remember the many visitors' smiling faces and inquisitiveness, and that support that volunteers provided.

Lake Superior has many interesting stories to share, but also as a lightkeeper there is so much to just observe on the water. The frequency of ships steaming past has increased, and we can just see the big wave that these ships push ahead of their bows.

In the old fog alarm building, built in 1908 to help ward ships off the reefs with a sound-making device, there was also an observation room. From this room, weather statistics, facts and figures were kept, while a record of passing vessels seen in the shipping lanes was recorded.

Names such as *Thordoc*, *Scotiadoc*, *Alexander Henry*, *Nokomis* and the tug *James Whalen*, were all part of the shipping story in this area from days gone by.

The job of these lighthouses remains to help keep commerce going and build a stronger country by creating a healthy trade surplus; grain being one of the most noted commodities to pass these shores. But, in the past, the Silver Islet Mine created its own bonanza in the 1860s.

Local sailor from Silver Islet, Ted Duke dropped by to share his memories of the Porphyry site over the years. He did this as he ate some freshly grilled lake trout hooked by Archie Hoogsteen. Many years ago, boaters would rendezvous for a social night at the Porphyry boathouse and also convene work parties to repair vandalized buildings. It's through the support of many people from Silver Islet over the years that gave Canadian Lighthouses of Lake Superior a better opportunity to sustain its operation in the early years.

If you are interested in coming out this season, our last charter leaves on Sunday September 19 from Silver Islet and can be booked at www.clls.ca.

Next week will be the last of this season's Lighthouse Dispatches, and I'm looking forward to summing up the summer with you.

Until then, have a good day!

As the sun sets, the light tower and keeper's dwelling are illuminated from within, and I'm ready for a night of reading and relaxation.
[Photo: CLLS]

September 21, 2021

More visitors explore island amid tough season

Beautiful weather has played out most of the month, making wrapping up the Porphyry Island site and season even more enjoyable. Tonight, we are expecting to see the harvest moon in all its glory as our final epitaph to a busy and successful season. Over the past few nights, the water has been painted by the moon's reflection; which also draws out the contours of the living landscape.

As our tours are now winding down, we had seen an influx of inquisitive visitors over the season with a threefold increase. Some may argue that this takes away from the experience, but lighthouses are Canadian assets that we all own, so why not take advantage of them and learn a bit?

The boating public also explores this beautiful gem of a lake that we all are privileged to have in our midst; with just under 1,000 people coming to explore and engage on these lands leased from the Department of Fisheries and Oceans Canada.

Porphyry, Trowbridge and No.10 lights helped Canadians and visitors to understand the role these important sentinels of the lake once provided, and still provide today. Added interpretive displays this year also helped.

Our host-keepers and summer students aided visitors to connect with the beautiful environment and water. This year, a map was painted on one of the disused concrete pads to illustrate the highlights of the area seen from Point Porphyry.

The season also offered some challenges due to COVID restrictions whereby Canadian Lighthouses of Lake Superior (CLLS), a not-for-profit organization, lost some 350 volunteer hours in the startup to the season, which were never recovered.

CLLS also experienced some growing pains as the organization continues to build towards being a fully sustainable operation.

Our partners such as Parks Canada National Marine Conservation Area, the Great Lakes Cruising Club and Superior Shores Gaming Association all contributed funds to building on-site infrastructure such as docking, mooring balls and other visitor amenities. Our boating volunteers who helped to facilitate our annual Lighthouse Carnival and who exemplified community spirit, showed a sense of respect by sharing with others.

CLLS also saw participation from other groups and organizations such as the Thunder Bay Yacht Club's annual SUNORA event and, more recently, with Sail Superior's learn-to-sail program; which saw five students pass through the area last week.

The Silver Islet Harbour Association that is made up of representatives from CLLS, the Silver Islet Campers Association and the Yacht Club, facilitated access to the lake for many travellers this season.

Upon returning from their charter trip to the lighthouse, people were welcomed into the Silver Islet General Store for ice cream. The location offers an authentic experience as the history is present and has not been eradicated by time.

This season has been a real learning experience because of changing times due to the pandemic. The desire of the local population to explore their own backyard, and their thirst for knowledge and history has been exhilarating. To have the opportunity to connect people back to our land, back to our history and back to the environment has been a privilege.

Next season, I hope we can continue to connect even more people while, of course, respecting our environment, our First Nations people and these lighthouse icons that help us understand our culture, commerce and past.

"Painted skies and contrasting terrain leave us with a sense of awe and wonderment that we should be so privileged to witness the Sleeping Giant in this light," says Lighthouse Dispatches columnist Paul Morralee.
[Photo: Donny Wabasse]

LIGHTHOUSE
DISPATCHES

2022

Visitors From Around the World

LIGHTHOUSE DISPATCHES

May 31, 2022

Island still waking up from long cold winter

As the Sleeping Giant grew closer, a light-green glow could be seen on the treetops. Spring is starting to take root surrounded by these cool waters of Lake Superior. Cruising in my classic 32-foot wooden vessel, I'm taking in the sights and feeling a burden lift from my shoulders. I am now back in the elements of my "summer" experience.

Getting back to the light station on Porphyry Island, located some 43 kilometres east of the city of Thunder Bay, the waters are calm and fairly flat. As we make our way around the feet of the Giant, Silver Islet is our first port of call, where the Viking Cruise Ship *Octantis* will be stopping in on her maiden voyage to our lake.

Tourism to these isolated areas helps to fund services and the building of infrastructure for visitors and guests to enjoy. In the past, it had been forestry, fishing and minerals that provided this area with commerce. Now, tourism takes to the stage.

The Silver Islet General Store is ready to serve, along with the members of the non-profit Silver Islet Harbour Association. I'd recommend a cinnamon bun with tea for now; hold the ice cream for your next visit.

Canadian Lighthouses of Lake Superior representatives were on board to meet Viking visitors and officials to continue to drum up excitement about all things nautical; with lighthouses included! The mood of the international visitors streaming off the motor launch was electric, as you could well understand since the area has lots for them to see and do.

My next goal was to continue on my journey, another fifteen kilometres east, to set things up for the following day's visit of over thirty-five volunteers to Porphyry Island! The annual spring cleanup sets us up for the coming season. With lots of helping hands, the site is massaged into shape. We all need some respite from the recent past, and getting your hands dirty is a good recipe for feeling good and connecting back to Mother Earth.

New prospector-sized tents are erected, latrine pits dug, houses spring-cleaned, trails and yards raked, and docks assembled in the harbour. Our volunteers have come to respect the value that they bring to the activity. They understand that their efforts help the on-site programs, and allow the boating community, kayakers, and charter visitors to enjoy the landscape and attractions. Each step made by our hard-working volunteers is a step towards providing a safe, enjoyable visit while elevating the history of the area.

The island is still waking up from a cold and long winter. Some ice and snow are still on the islands with the water temperature around 44°F, or in Celsius it's just as cold at 6°C. Porphyry Island is a little grey at the moment, with buds pushing through and the grass starting to turn green. The rabbits are hopping about — the population has rebounded after last year's wolves had their way. Some species of bird life can be seen migrating through. Most birds, I believe, must think they have reached the North Pole. It's bone-chilling cold.

Our summer programs are coming along with good response for the host-keeping and artist-in-residence programs for July and August. Our newest program, Builders On Superior Shores (BOSS), a program for young women between the ages of 14 and 18, continues to attract participants for the four-day session at Porphyry Island. BOSS provides some hands-on carpentry and lighthouse work during their stay.

If you are interested in seeing how the site has transformed over the years, you will like the slide show by former resident at Porphyry, Bill McKay. He will be sharing his pictures on June 15th, 7pm at the Delta Hotel, Falls Room, for Canadian Lighthouses of Lake Superior's Annual General Meeting.

Summer charter tours are going to start June 19th, every Thursday and Sunday from Silver Islet, leaving at 9 and 11 in the morning.

The kettle is whistling to me again, so it's time to take a break and figure next steps for getting the lighthouse ready for visitors.

People enjoy the view after a day of volunteering at the Porphyry Island overlooking Black Bay. [Photo: Cody Angus]

June 7, 2022

Connecting people to heritage on the big lake

As the temperature attempts to warm up, nature is making slow progress with some buds starting to unfurl on Porphyry Island. There is a sense of hope with the greenery returning as the landscape is starting to infill back to living things.

The domestic travel on the lake is down, as we have not seen many people out fishing or exploring. Across the lighthouse site, many projects are starting to take shape. With the help of many volunteers during the cleanup, a lot of big jobs were completed.

Inside the new spacious bell tents, visitors will find a small, wood-fired stove to keep them warm at night and to knock the edge off of the dampness. The tents give an added opportunity for visitors to stay overnight while each accommodating five to six people. The more accessible the island is to accommodating visitors, the better.

Other work includes the lighthouse road that connects the harbour with the light. The work planned is to cut down the brush to give visitors a better view of the forest. Often, in the winter months, trees are blown down across the trail requiring some labour to remove them.

Our summer staff, Abigail Beatty and Annie Ross, arrived today and were excited to see the site and their new summer accommodations. Also accompanying the students is Julie Rosenthal, a professor at Lakehead University's School of Tourism, Outdoor Recreation and Parks. She also serves as a director on the board of Canadian Lighthouses of Lake Superior. Rosenthal will be volunteering her time to assist in the preparation for the summer term and some programming aspects for visitors.

It is because of many hard working volunteers that we can continue to provide a service of connecting people to some of our heritage on the big lake. As we ramp up for the season, volunteers are generous with their time; getting propane, delivering food and giving a helping hand.

This week, we welcomed several people working for Parks Canada visitor services with the National Marine Conservation Area of Lake Superior. They were here to do a familiarization tour of the property and to learn how we interpret our landscape, the living biosphere and lighthouse history. To wrap up their tour, they went to the famous black sand beach to experience another perspective. From the island's southeast side, you can see Passage Island and Isle Royale, both in American waters, between which the shipping channel passes.

Our garden has been well tilled, and the planting has been completed. The radishes are starting to sprout and so are the cucumbers. The rhubarb wants to take the whole garden over, but it is already being eyed up for the next pie.

Both homesteads on-site have their cisterns filled with Lake Superior water, beds all made up and compost toilets primed and ready to go. In two week's time we will be running our first regular charter for the summer that operates on Thursdays and Sundays.

If you're interested in visiting us some time this summer, you are welcome to check out our website at clls.ca.

Time to get back to getting things ready for the summer and take a moment's pause to enjoy the incredible beauty the area has to offer.

Visitors from Parks Canada who are on a familiarization tour of the Lake Superior National Marine Conservation Area enjoy an afternoon at the lighthouse. From left, Paul Morralee, managing director of Canadian Lighthouses of Lake Superior, Liam Giffin, Mirabai Alexander, Marlene McBrien, Hafi Sayed, Abbi Buckley, Trevor Waytowich, Nicole Eckert, Annie Ross, Abigail Beatty, Svenja Hansen, Colin Crowell, Manon Cuthbertson. [Photo: Julie Rosenthal]

LIGHTHOUSE DISPATCHES

June 14, 2022

Summer is approaching

Budding leaves are starting to unfurl on the island, giving us some hope that a thing called summer is approaching. With below-normal temperatures, it's been wonderful to feel the heat from the wood-fired furnace in the keeper's dwelling.

Canadian Lighthouses of Lake Superior, at the Porphyry Island site 15 kilometres east of Silver Islet, hosted a three-day visit for a private school from Woodstock, Ontario. Each morning, as a routine, we were up early to make sure that the fire was lit to start their day. Once energized, but still a little sore from hiking up the Sleeping Giant the day before, the group took in a guided tour of the lighthouse site. This included the main lighthouse features and other key points such as the geology of the black sands, an introduction to the living forest, and capturing the essence of the majestic surrounding waters of Superior.

Thanks to our Canada Summer Jobs funding through Member of Parliament Patty Hajdu's office, we were able to realize two students for this summer! While receiving their on-site orientation, they were also able to provide an afternoon learning session to the school.

Through collecting sea-glass from the beach, students were able to fashion some new Porphyry jewelry. The source of the sea-glass is from glass bottles disposed of in the late 1800s and early 1900s from the back of the lighthouse.

We were happy to have with us last week one of our board directors, Julie Rosenthal, who is the students' supervisor, orientating them to some of the summer's tasks. Rosenthal is a professor of Lakehead's School of Outdoor Recreation, Parks and Tourism, and is helping our non-profit organization focus on developing connections to the community over the season.

This past weekend, we had another team of volunteers come together to work on the docks that were damaged during the winter. Six volunteers labouring with cold feet and hands showed determination! The crew was able to complete 80% of the work, leaving the docks in much better shape. As a bonus, the summer students cooked up an apple-rhubarb crumble pie that was presented to the workers as a thank you!

On Sunday, I started my journey home to prepare for our Annual General Meeting. Passing by Silver Islet, I was met by a flotilla of Thunder Bay Yacht Club members enjoying a planned race back to Thunder Bay. Set against the Sleeping Giant, it was a sight to see — people enjoying the outdoors and using the wind, which was gently blowing, to travel home.

The purpose of my trip to the mainland is to assist with the customary rollout of reports at the AGM that's taking place in the new Delta Hotel on Wednesday at 7pm.

The first half-hour is the formal part, followed by an informal talk by a former lightkeeper who will be sharing his experiences from a time when the site was in transition from the original lighthouse to what we see today. The photos he'll be showing are interesting vintage slides with lots of local colour, including the Canadian Coast Guard Ship *Alexander Henry* when it was painted black instead of red!

If you are interested in coming to visit us during the summer, please check in at clls.ca and we can then connect you to this wonderful resource on Lake Superior for you to discover.

Students were pleased to find and collect sea-glass from the black sand beach. They were visiting from The Oxford School in Woodstock, Ontario.

[Photo: CLLS]

June 21, 2022

Atmosphere buoyant on island

Two loons were making their haunting call as I looked across the calm Superior waters towards the Sleeping Giant and the city of Thunder Bay beyond. It's great to be back on the island to take in the panoramic view and also to reconnect with nature.

Pounded by the elements of a harsh wind and ice cold water at 34°F, survival is your main focus! Fog is starting to roll around near the shoreline as the mainland heats up and the cool waters slowly abate.

Communing with nature is a great way to give yourself some balance in your life, but for our visitors on Sunday, they certainly felt the elements. Dodging between rainstorms reflected in our Environment Canada radar information, we were able to get our first visitors into the gallery for a viewing of a history film. Then, the skies opened and it became more of a hit-and-miss game as to who got wet or not.

On Friday night, we had some other guests who had rented the main house for the weekend. With a warm woodstove keeping the place toasty, to their surprise they were obliged to entertain a few more people. The guided tour group needed to be warmed up, so a timid knock on the front door was immediately met by a hearty response.

The atmosphere was buoyant, especially when visitors met others from different parts of North America, and the conversation became effortless. Once warmed up and with an earlier departure back to Thunder Bay, everyone was in high spirits.

Our summer students have returned after their orientation on the island a week earlier followed by a short stay in the city. Their job is to do some chores, work on some projects and also meet and greet the lighthouse guests.

This week has been about learning about the lighthouse history; which has also included meeting a former lightkeeping family, the Grahams. The students also attended the Canadian Lighthouses of Lake Superior Annual General Meeting where they had the opportunity to meet a member of the McKay family and hear about the period when the lighthouse was under great change. From these exchanges and experiences, it's hoped that when visitors come to the island we may be able to share some further insights into what it must have been like to live here!

These lighthouse-keeping experiences go back to a time in the 1870s when the light was turned by gears and weights, and the light source was whale oil. Today, there's a simple solar panel, a car battery, and an LED light; with a visit every second year by a Coast Guard maintenance crew.

This season will see the return of the popular Lighthouse Carnival on July 16th, that includes food, entertainment and on-site tours. Each year, boaters get together to help organize an event that the public can attend by taking the charter boat from Silver Islet. The Scott van Teeffelen Band will again return for another year!

If you'd like to get a good grip on what it's like to visit a volcanic island on Lake Superior, this is certainly a day to consider, otherwise we have our regular Thursday and Sunday tours. Don't forget that if you'd like to come and stay overnight, you'll be able to claim a 20% "staycation" rebate from the government.

As the summer is fast approaching, we are ready for visitors to explore and to discover new vistas. Time for a cup of tea before I get back to my chores around the light station.

Guests enjoy soup and sandwich lunch after a wet, blustery tour of the Point Porphyry Lighthouse.
[Photo: CLLS]

LIGHTHOUSE DISPATCHES

June 28, 2022

Lighthouse gearing up for Canada Day

Thundering waves cast themselves against the island for another day giving me a moment to pause and connect with nature at Porphyry Island. On the barren, hard volcanic rocks, the wind carries the spray far and wide at the point, giving the arctic-alpine disjunct plants a good watering. These black rocks are also covered by richly coloured orange lichens that seem out of place with the blues of the water and sky.

This place is just 43 kilometres east of the city of Thunder Bay and it's where you can relax after the lighthouse chores are done, and you can let your mind become free of all the deadlines.

Visiting the city last week, I am reminded to be careful near traffic. However, being in the bush, there are other threats, like lightning or the appearance of a bear. The purpose of my visit was to see the installation of the new Thunder Bay Main Lighthouse kiosk in marina park. The reaction to the completion of the project has been positive — there being a great sense of pride coming from the Hammarskjold High School student-builders. With proud teachers watching on, students helped put on the finishing touches as the large scale-model lighthouse was lowered into place. The kiosk will help visitors and locals connect with community groups that offer activities on the waterfront, while also providing some tourism opportunities on the north shore of Lake Superior. Considering our waterfront is predominately made up of trans-shipment infrastructure, it's nice to know that there are places to visit beyond the grain dust and clamoring trains.

At the Point Porphyry Lighthouse this week, the weather has continued to be slightly cool for this time of year. It might sound odd, but when the wind blows over the water, things can get very frosty. The water temperature is coming up a little, but it's still cool, and our lilac bushes are getting ready to bloom after city bushes have been blooming for weeks now.

Our summer students, Abby and Annie, are settling into the routine with lots of chores, projects and programs. Their main responsibility is to give a lift to the Builders On Superior Shores (BOSS) program, which is for young women who might like to get a job in the trades or just enjoy a summer camp experience. Their program has a few more spaces available.

We are preparing for Canada Day celebrations, which is also the day when the Point Porphyry Lighthouse became operational in 1873, 149 years ago! Decorations will be going up and our summer programming will begin!

This year, our tours are operating on Thursdays and Sundays, and feature a guided or self-guided tour, optional lunch or bring your own picnic, and a chance to explore the island with your partner or friends.

Our annual carnival is also coming up where we serve up some tasty fish & chips, have entertainment provided along with an ecological tour and a film screening. The date is July 16th, and it's thanks to local boaters who are volunteering their time to make the event fun and enjoyable.

Preparing for the summer has been a slow and methodical process to ensure that everything is looking good and the site is clean and ready for visitors. Our team of volunteers are working on a few other projects to help amplify some of the local history. We are going to be building a mini exhibit to help visitors understand the journey of sea-glass that people flock to discover on our beaches. It's always exciting to see what people find along the water's edge, and we try to help them understand the origin of the glass.

Living on the island, there are many opportunities to explore the beautiful landscape and enjoy the view of the Sleeping Giant across Black Bay. Now, it's time for a walk to the harbour to check on my boat.

Footsteps return to the lighthouse on the black sand beach at Porphyry Island. [Photo: CLLS]

LIGHTHOUSE DISPATCHES

July 5, 2022

BOSS program underway in earnest

Summer is finally with us, or so I had thought. Enticed by a previous warm Saturday, we are back to running for firewood to stay warm. Aboard my motor vessel *Hidora*, moored at the Porphyry Island Harbour, 43 kilometres east of Thunder Bay, I am stoking up the woodstove with the kettle gently warming up. There are other boaters here doing the same thing — trying to keep warm. The water temperatures are still very cool, in and around 6°C range, which is great because you can keep the beer cold in the boat's hold.

Beyond weather, we are all working hard to keep the light station operational for our visitors. Yesterday saw the arrival of our first participants in the BOSS program. Builders On Superior Shores started with an unveiling of the compass rose to celebrate the group's arrival to participate in this summer's program.

BOSS participants will learn new carpentry skills, and how a lighthouse operates as a tourist attraction. Many events have been prepared for the young ladies, and they are already enjoying the experience and taking on the challenge. Yesterday, this included a polar swim — minus having to cut any ice!

Years ago when the public started to visit the island, who would have thought that there would be a summer experience program specifically for women to learn about working in the trades?

Boaters this weekend arrived in droves along with some kayakers from the USA. All were out exploring the unique climate and wildlife habitats while enjoying the serenity of the waves lapping at the shore and having hot, black sands run between their toes. We've also had three sailboats visiting us with one boat having sailed all the way from Parry Sound. It's great to hear about their adventures on the lake and about the places that they visited along the way. We are hearing that the number of people on the lake is a little low, but it is picking up.

Our lilac tree is starting to flower now so you can see that our weather is a little different from the mainland; slowing the growth. When you are on a rocky island, the surrounding cold water makes the growing season start a little later.

On Saturday, our first host-keepers of the season arrived to start working on a list of chores and minor repairs. It's lovely to have an extra pair of hands to help keep the place looking good. Gordon and Karin Mackenzie from Nipigon, are here for the week and are already well into their second day of work!

Mackenzie brought his 1947 steel trawler down the Nipigon Straits to Lake Superior, which took a couple of days to arrive at the lighthouse. The vessel really fits the lighthouse island experience, as many of the lightkeepers would have their own boats about to make some extra income from logging and fishing.

To wrap up the Canada Day celebration, boaters dispensed with their old and outdated flares, which was our light show for the evening. Returning to the bonfire, stories continued into the night, and laughter echoed through the trees. Not only was it a celebration for Canada, but it was also Point Porphyry's birthday — 149 years since its construction!

Unveiling the compass rose at the Porphyry Harbour, from left, Builders On Superior Shores (BOSS) program coordinator, Abby Beatty, BOSS participants Paige DeProphetis, Joelle Nolast, Kaia DeProphetis and Mackenna Coulson, as well as program coordinator Annie Ross, are excited about this week's events. [Photo: CLLS]

July 12, 2022

Visitors enjoy ecology, geology of island — Carnival on the way

Cycling up the hill towards the lighthouse, fog had enveloped the trail. This comes as a bit of a surprise because it was sunny moments earlier. Fog always arrives and departs silently, like a ghost. Turning back the pages in the McKay Lighthouse Diaries from the 1920s, the fog was far more prevalent then than it is today!

The light station is looking good now after our first visiting host-keepers having left their mark. Gordon and Karin Mackenzie, visiting from Nipigon, worked hard to plant donated milkweed and complete a shopping list of other chores. It's great how, with everyone's input and help, we can continue to build and to grow. Our charter visitors are now returning with families and friends in tow on Thursdays and Sundays. It's always a pleasure to amplify their experience by adding in local context, with a dash of history.

Our visitors are enjoying the ecology and geology of the island as they begin to understand the role that lighthouses play in the trans-shipment story that Thunder Bay is known for. The island's information panels and guides help to bring the big picture together. It's interesting to meet new people who have never witnessed the breadth and scope of Lake Superior. Renate Dittmann from Germany is in Canada to visit friends and also fill in as host-keeper for the week. Dittmann said, "The size of Canada, and the views from the lighthouse are humbling, and I am glad I get a chance to experience this!"

With the diversity of landscapes, activities and events, this week will be busy as the Lighthouse Carnival is happening on Saturday. Moved to earlier in the summer, there will be history and ecology tours, a film screening, games, entertainment, and fish & chips; or you can just sit back and take in the view. Only a few tickets are left if you are interested in coming by charter boat from Silver Islet.

Today, we saw two more intrepid travellers arriving from Silver Islet in bright red canoes that are closed in over the gunwales with a skirt made of canvas. For the two gentlemen whose journey will end in Rossport, they were happy to reach shore, use the sauna, and pitch their tents.

This week, we have had a couple of families tenting out and exploring the island. We've seen some people from Scotland and are starting to see a few more American boaters returning to our shores.

Following the Lighthouse Carnival we are having a book tour on-site, on Saturday July 23, with Jean E. Pendziwol, author of *The Lightkeeper's Daughters*. The Thunder Bay Yacht Club is sponsoring this activity following its mandate since 1945 to promote boating on Lake Superior. Canadian Lighthouses of Lake Superior has some seats available if you'd like to partake.

Our lilac bush is ready to bloom; which is a week later than usual, and our vegetable garden is very slow with only a few beans and peas popping up. The rhubarb has taken over, and it's getting a bit unruly and may need to be cut back.

Listening to the waves lapping up on the shore with a gentle breeze in the trees, I hear thunder rumbling in the background! Better finish up now and get indoors before the rain comes.

Preparing for the Lighthouse Carnival this weekend, Renate Dittman assembles the final parts of the information sign. [Photo: CLLS]

LIGHTHOUSE DISPATCHES

July 19, 2022

Host-keeper hitches ride with band

A magical morning at the lighthouse started the day as a moose stood for her Facebook pose before returning to harvest plants back in the Porphyry swamp. Having flown over the Atlantic Ocean from Germany, it's moments like this that our host-keeper, Renate Dittmann, will always remember.

Interpretive displays keep visitors engaged, and Dittmann had a project she wanted to complete. This year's annual Lighthouse Carnival guests were thrilled to see a new lightkeepers' timeline. Drawn on the wall of the diesel-spill containment berm, lightkeepers were named, and the dates they served were displayed. Lightkeepers, from 1873 until the light was decommissioned, are featured along with some other important dates.

Point Porphyry Lighthouse, just east of Silver Islet on Lake Superior, will again be hosting a book tour with author Jean E. Pendziwol, this Saturday. If you've read *The Lightkeeper's Daughters* book, check out www.clls.ca for details on this excursion which still has a few seats open.

Our first artist-in-residence since pausing the program due to the pandemic arrived on Sunday. Emily Read will be drawing wildlife characters on our trailer and museum to freshen up the look and provide more learning opportunities for youth. It's through this program and others that we continue to take input from volunteers to help elevate the history and beauty of the area. Her partner, Ale Hidalgo, a professional photographer, will also be enhancing our picture portfolio.

The other day, I took in the silence at the point — no wave action, just a flat and calm lake, which is nice as it doesn't happen too often in the summer. The lilac bush is now in full bloom with a wonderful fragrance which now freshens-up the rooms in the house that are often rented in the summer.

On the weekend, this year's carnival went off without a hitch and was well attended. Headlining was the Scott van Teeffelen Band which has made the annual pilgrimage and is always thankful for the opportunity to perform out on the lake. Some boaters on Edward Island could also hear the tunes. Guests were treated to a fish & chip dinner put on by local boaters from the marina. Around six hundred boaters and their friends each year appreciate and use the facilities. The exchange of goodwill was palpable as the guests and boaters mix into the evening. Later on around the fire, stories were exchanged as the music closes off the warm summer night.

The annual fundraising event, including history and ecology tours, is a way to share. Canadian Lighthouses of Lake Superior brings some historical substance and opportunity for the general public to understand the role that shipping has played in the area.

The host-keeper made friends with the band members and managed to hitch a ride back to town to catch her flight home, after her husband was unable to travel from Germany to meet her. It's moments like this when people find solutions and, in the end, everyone wins.

On Sunday, I steamed home to the mainland to celebrate the 60th anniversary of the Canadian Coast Guard, hosted aboard the *Alexander Henry* Museum Ship docked at pool six. The Lakehead Transportation Museum Society (later renamed the Transportation Museum of Thunder Bay) brought together many stakeholders and friends to share in a ceremony that included the Pipes and Drums of Thunder Bay, dignitaries and guests. A tasty BBQ followed, sponsored by the Thunder Bay Port Authority, with a huge birthday cake to close the celebrations. It made me ponder for a moment... "Look how this organization of volunteers has reconnected us to our nautical history in eight short years!"

Thank You!

A group of boaters assembled in the morning fog to partake of some yoga moves on the helipad on Porphyry Island. [Photo: CLLS]

The Porphyry Helipad

Visitors to Porphyry Island often inquire about the red and white targeted concrete platform located near the lighthouse at the point. This platform allows Canadian Coast Guard helicopters to land technicians safely landing to do their maintenance and inspections.

In the past, lightkeepers, their families, and belongings primarily arrived by ship. For instance, the tugboat *James Whalen* provided support at many light stations on Lake Superior from 1905 to 1960, and significant changes occurred later with the arrival of the Canadian Coast Guard vessel, the *Alexander Henry*. For years, tugboats and Coast Guard vessels would drop off lightkeepers in early spring when ice still surrounded the islands. Crews had to rely on sheer manpower to transport supplies and belongings across the ice to the lighthouses and the keepers' homes. This process was fraught with danger. There's also a story of the Merritt family's children's blankets becoming encased in ice in the 1950s due to the frigid spray. Offloading families was a time-consuming task as each lighthouse crew disembarked at their assigned island for the season.

Recognizing the access challenges faced by keepers and crew in the spring, the Canadian Coast Guard constructed a heliport on the stern of the *Alexander Henry*. A small Bell helicopter, with its large bubble window, would transport belongings to the island through multiple short trips, significantly expediting the offloading process and eliminating the need to navigate the spring ice.

The helipad has also served additional purposes since the lights were automated. For instance, technicians arrive every second year to inspect the light, or consultants come to assess the condition of the building infrastructure. This season, after requesting access from *Ornge* Air Ambulance for emergencies, the Porphyry helipad was surveyed and is now officially designated as a landing zone, allowing access to deal with any emergency in the area.

Every three years, the helipad's concrete surface undergoes a thorough scraping, cleaning, and repainting, requiring six person-days to complete. The original target, or bull's eye, was painted with just two rings; later, a third ring was added for branding purposes. Volunteers were easily motivated to paint the platform as they were drawn by the breathtaking 260° panoramic view of Lake Superior and the surrounding islands and bays. Today, the landing pad hosts many yoga sessions which take advantage of the fresh air and tranquil setting.

July 26, 2022

Interpreting serenity in words, art, photos

Lighthouse living continues with a full compliment of artists, host-keepers, summer students and programming. It's been a week filled with activities, community involvement and some discoveries along the way.

Our artist-in-residence, Emily Read and partner Ale Hidalgo, have been very active helping to promote the area through art and photographs. The results of their work in different fields will help our non-profit organization build educational opportunities for visitors.

Host-keeper, Pamela Cain, has been busy helping keep the site up and running with a mix of disciplines required; from planting milkweed to helping with meal preparations and interpretive participation.

Local author Jean E. Pendziwol also made an appearance as part of an annual Rendezvous-on-the-Water by the Thunder Bay Yacht Club. Gathered around the fire, Pendziwol gave some background on her inspiration for writing her book *The Lightkeeper's Daughters*. Her father, Craig McDonald, was also present, helping fill in more details about sailing on Lake Superior.

It always amazes me to see the depth and beauty this island has to offer visitors and how, captured in words, art and photos, they interpret the serenity of these moments.

No sooner had Read put her painted rocks up for sale, half of them were sold. This gives our guests a future reminder of these moments in the wilds out on a Lake Superior island. Located 15 kilometres east of Silver Islet on Black Bay, the breadth and scope of what's on offer is enormous. I am sure that a lifetime out here would still not satisfy a human for all the wildlife, exotic geology and beautiful fauna offered up.

Hidalgo could comprehend our biodiversity, volcanoes and beaches as these features area similar to those in his homeland of Costa Rica. With his photographic eye and camera in hand, and his gentle approach to visitors, many engaging images were captured; especially at the start of the charter trip when guests get to see the Silver Islet Mine shaft and hear Captain Archie's narrative.

On Sunday afternoon after experiencing a traffic jam at Silver Islet and possibly reminiscent from days gone by when tourism was a big thing in the area, two families left for Rossport on kayaks. Stopping in at Porphyry, the families made a meal over the fire, and some took a moment to visit and learn more about the light station.

Watching the childrens' eyes light up was really exciting because this is when indelible memories are made and kept for life. Early next morning, the routine that would be repeated another five times was begun. Tents were whipped to get moisture off, and kayaks were packed to balance the load. What an adventure on the waters of Superior!

On Sunday, we also greeted our second group of Builders On Superior Shores, who were all excited to be part of learning more about jobs in the trades and get an education on how a light station operates. The students will be building a new picnic table and have already measured and marked the boards; ready for the first cut.

Like the Hammarskjold High School students who built the Thunder Bay Main Lighthouse kiosk to provide a service to visitors, there comes a great sense of satisfaction of doing something! We're all fortunate at the lighthouse to have the opportunity to witness change and be part of a progressive experience.

Posing in front of a new photo booth, painter and artist-in-residence, Emily Read (right) and host-keeper Pamela Cain are surrounded by animals and birds.

[Photo: Ale Hidalgo]

August 2, 2022

Waves of visitors reach island

Tie-dyed t-shirts hanging on the clothesline reminded me of a tourism commercial for Newfoundland & Labrador. This is not the sixties, nor are we on the East Coast, but we are living on an island that reminds some of an east coast light station.

Each day that passes, the girls from the Builders On Superior Shores program are reminded of their isolation away from home. Through stormy weather, bright sunshine and the smell of a canvas tent, the girls experienced many new activities, including building a picnic table!

Later in the week, twelve kayakers venturing east towards Rossport stopped in and created their own tent village; adding more colour to the site. As with any first-day adventure, the paddlers were ironing out some of the kinks and taking stock of being out on the water for a six-day excursion. Naturally Superior Adventures of Wawa have two trips currently traveling in opposite directions on the North Shore.

To think, our First Nations peoples had taken to the water in their birch bark canoes, not only to fish and hunt, but to move with the seasons and gather supplies for winter. Visitors now can enjoy a charter trip with ease across the mouth of Black Bay on Thursdays and Sundays, and turn around to see the Sleeping Giant and Turtle Head (part of Pie Island) sitting on the horizon.

Many who visited over the previous long-weekend came to unwind with family and friends. One young couple that have been exploring the North Shore for years and finally after visited Porphyry Island, decided already that next year the island would be base camp for future fishing expeditions.

Fifteen kilometres east of the Sleeping Giant and Silver Islet, some families have been exploring this island for fifty years or more. One family coined one of the beaches "black beard beach" because it's so dark. It's amazing that, with all the volcanic action 1.1 billion years ago, the burnt-out volcanoes can still be seen today and the sands still remain hot — but that's from the midday sun.

"Therapy sand" is how one guest put it. Wiggle your toes in the hot sands and relieve sore feet. Some sailors just finishing the final leg of the SUNORA greeted the island as a short respite before returning home. The Thunder Bay Yacht Club's annual regatta helps new boaters navigate the wonders of the North Shore that so many, one-day, dream to see.

Vic Miller, a director on the board of Canadian Lighthouses of Lake Superior

(CLLS), was also out to see the improvements to the site, to visit with his family and to help out with some small tasks. It takes many hands and minds to keep the operation going, and it's with the attitude of "every little bit helps" that the grounds are kept tidy, inviting and ready for the next visitor. Chuck and Christine Sandford also helped out with repairs to the dock after it was cast ashore and damaged last November. With a can-do attitude, each little step ends with goals reached. CLLS thanks everyone who helps us build better facilities as this amplifies and shares the story of lighthouses with others and fulfills the lighthouse group's mandate.

Today, the forest is lush and green, the wild roses are pink and glowing, and the buttercups are in full bloom. Time to sit back and watch the ships pass by on their way to Thunder Bay, and enjoy the height of summer.

Builders On Superior Shores program participants Olivia Kingston, Katrina Vanderwees, Sarafin Fedorus, Rachel Perzan and Dani Duquette enjoy a moment of satisfaction after planning, cutting and assembling a picnic table at Porphyry Island.

[Photo: CLLS]

August 9, 2022

Well-rounded adventures keep rolling for everyone

Summer winds continue to pick up the cooler-than-normal Superior waters making some visitors happy to escape the heat from down south. Our American boater traffic has increased slightly after seeing little of it over the past two seasons. It's a pleasant change.

With the lighthouse site in full swing, tourists are arriving all the time, especially on the weekly charters that allow visitors to enjoy the rich environment. Many, of course, come for the lighthouse attraction but are quickly diverted to the outstanding natural beauty surrounding the island and its inhabitants.

Point Porphyry is not only the point of the island, but it also signals the start of an archipelago of islands stretching 100 kilometres to the east across the North Shore.

Families are returning with kites in hand to test the winds of the lake and get a memorable snapshot of "going to fly a kite". The MacLean and deBakker families spent an overnight in the main keeper's dwelling with six kids, a dog and four grown-ups. Like the week before, the lawn turned into a tent city, with little ones bedding down under the stars, periodically interrupted by the flashing light from the tower.

As the keeper of the light and managing director for Canadian Lighthouses of Lake Superior, I am thankful for our visiting host-keepers and artist-in-residence with the roles that they play enhancing the activities on the island.

Host-keeper Rose Hansmeyer was on duty painting anything that required a dash of red paint, and she inadvertently put a thread of red in her own hair! Not necessarily the type of souvenir that you'd like to come home with, but maybe a rite of passage?

Marlene Coffey, our artist-in-residence, was busy creating painted fridge-magnets. Visitors were invited to make a donation and take home a hand crafted memento. How special is your day when you bring something home that was actually created by an island artisan?

This week, while visiting the Trowbridge Island Lighthouse, I managed to see some beautiful white roses and arctic-alpine disjunct plants on the grounds. From the island, you could see vessels transiting from Thunder Bay towards Passage Island; possibly venturing as far as the Atlantic Ocean and beyond. Also, just off of Silver Islet, I could see the majestic Viking Cruise Lines ship with its "tentacles" reaching out as different expeditions took to the water. Many visitors ventured to the mainland and thought that the hamlet was just an island. In talking with tour guides Tom and Todd who take people down Silver Islet Avenue and up to the Sea Lion rock, the reaction to the area has been very respectful, with lots of questions and interest. These visitors are looking deeper into the significance of the area and exploring one of the more popular destinations on their itinerary.

The girls from the Builders On Superior Shores convened once again on the island for a final session of the season. This time around, the girls will be building a bench for hikers to stop and take a rest. Last night, the girls travelled around the site looking for some clues so that they could complete a scavenger hunt. It was fun to watch them unravel the clues and to reach the end of their challenge.

Animation of the lighthouse grounds and site has always been an ambition which would reconnect people to their surroundings. Having visiting families, boaters, artists and children makes for a well rounded adventure for everyone.

Sails filled with wind, laughter and good times; how fortunate we are to share in these nautical experiences and to live on one of the largest freshwater lakes in the world! Time to get back to some lighthouse chores and split some more wood for tonight's campfire.

Working in the artist-in-residence's studio, Marlene Coffey paints souvenirs for visitors to the Porphyry Island surroundings.
[Photo: CLLS]

August 16, 2022

More to life than electricity, luxuries

At last, warmer weather is upon us as big, fluffy clouds pass us by on this isolated island 43 kilometres east of Thunder Bay. Visiting guests have now returned with the warmer weather, and many power and sail boaters are tying up to stay the night. Some have been sharing their experience from the "Live from the Rock" Folk Festival, saying they've enjoyed their time and how nice it is to get back to "normal" after pandemic restrictions.

It's through informal boaters' communications that we hear about what's happing on the north shore of Superior. Surprisingly, not much slips past. You could imagine in the old lightkeepers' day how important it was to know what was going on around you. The advent of the radio-telephone turned into a party-line of chat among husbands, wives and friends sharing their lighthouse experiences over the airwaves.

Eve Graham, a former assistant lightkeeper, shared her thoughts of being on an isolated island when, in 1980, the CBC series "Heartland", presented by Sylvia Tyson, showcased the Graham family. Today, it is less lonely, but some still come for the isolation.

Nancy Wallace turned 75 years young this past week and invited her friends to visit the island and have lunch. An American family, also visiting and forgetting their lunch, joined in as there was lots to go around. There's something magical about being in the lightkeeper's dwelling; sharing conversation while looking out the window as the world goes by. A family from Colorado later took up residence over the weekend in the keeper's dwelling, and they were impressed with the scenery and the cooler Lake Superior nights.

Abby Beatty, who has just finished her summer work-term, said, "Before coming to Porphyry, I was very dependent on electricity and luxury items, but now after living on the island, I have realized that making memories and new friends is way more important than having electricity and luxury items." Colleague Annie Ross said, "Since coming to Porphyry Island, I have learned a lot about what it takes to be a lightkeeper, and have come to appreciate the challenges and commitment given by those who were past lightkeepers."

These two young women not only greeted six hundred guests, but also facilitated the Builders On Superior Shores program with great success. As each moment of the program was well orchestrated, the participants had lots to keep them active, including building benches, picnic tables and Adirondack chairs. The bench construction, now complete, has been pressed into immediate service as a rest spot, and it marks the halfway point on the 1.3 kilometre road allowance through the forest.

Up at the lighthouse point, the gooseberries, strawberries and raspberries are starting to fatten up. I'm looking forward to some more pies before the season comes to a close.

I'd better get going as there is another boat arriving at the dock and I also need to welcome in our new artist-in-residence.

After completing their wood working project and making tie-dyed shirts, the Builders On Superior Shores, Abby Beatty, Lara Garcia-Lebuis, Char Ailey, Keanu Psenicnik and Annie Ross, finish a very satisfying experience on Porphyry Island. The visitor experience exhibit they are hosting is to demonstrate the process of how glass breaks up to arrive as seaglass on the black sand beach.
[Photo: CLLS]

August 22, 2022

Freshwater mermaid?

Searching for a moment alone, Penelope Smart, our artist-in-residence, traveled along the coastal path to a secluded beach. Upon arrival, and dabbling in the water with her emerald green, one-piece swimsuit, an armada of powerboats descended along the southern shoreline of Porphyry Island. Struck by the sheer numbers, Ms. Smart timidly waved, expecting the episode to simply pass. The boaters were curious though. Had they seen a freshwater mermaid? Landing on a beach nearby, the shore-party crashed through the woods, along with a bounding dog, to take a closer look.

Later on when the group of five boats landed at Porphyry's harbour, dogs, children and parents were ready to discover further their new find. Blair, Keri, and Maddy said of their visit in the guest book, "What an incredible gem, on the most beautiful lake in the world! Bucket list checked."

When you read comments like this, you come to realize that Canadian Lighthouses of Lake Superior is providing people with an outlet to become better acquainted with our Superior environment. Porphyry Island, located 15 kilometres east of Silver Islet on Black Bay, continues to draw interesting people.

Anna Buske, Susan Dykstra and Linda Ryma enjoyed a photographer's retreat in the main keeper's dwelling. Ryma mentioned that she experienced, "Perfect weather for photography. It was a great weekend." Whereas Dykstra focused on, "...the morning fog, sun, Northern Lights, Milky Way," and concluded by saying, "You can see it all here." And Anna Buske confessed that there's "...a lot of variety, from astrophotography, landscapes, macro(shots), ferns, mushrooms and foliage" to capture.

Ms. Smart also found time to assist in our gallery on the island by changing up the displays and also helping to draft new interpretive signs for next season. It's always wonderful for our lighthouse group to receive such valuable assistance from experienced people in the arts field.

The site continues to be busy with weekend traffic of boaters and fishermen. It was nice to hear that fishermen Todd and John shared their catch with visitors to give them a real taste of Lake Superior. Of course, they did not let out where their secret fishing spot was — that is just not done. But sharing the catch heightens the experience for the inland boaters who were visiting.

This week saw the third and possibly the final visit from my parents from Southern Ontario. Over the past eight years, they have witnessed the transformation that has come about because of many volunteer hours, sponsor's dollars and local supporters. They were happy to again experience the pleasure of beautiful panoramic views and nice summer weather. My mother took to picking several containers of gooseberries that had ripened nicely. For the next four days, we had gooseberry and apple crumble for desert. Life continues on the island, and with Mum's cooking, what could be better?

History tours to the island are still available on Thursdays and Sundays from Silver Islet until third week of September.

Twinkling starlight and the Milky Way guides photographers on an inter-galactic voyage into the darkened skies over the Point Porphyry Lighthouse.
[Photo: Anna Buske]

August 30, 2022

Time stopped for artist on island

Freelance travel-writer, Jim Bamboulis of the Travel Mammal, said, "Going to the black sand beach is not a typical thing. In the moment, I lost my sense of location." Others have gone so far as to express their ideas such as, "It's like sitting on a Hawaiian beach surrounded by turquoise water with an oceanside view to the horizon."

Situated on the east side of Black Bay, the Point Porphyry Lighthouse offers an opportunity to experience the lives of previous lightkeepers. Bamboulis, invited by Tourism Thunder Bay to see the sights and experience things around the area, was impressed with the excursion and overnight stay on the island. His partner, Brie, came along and celebrated her birthday.

Visitors can now experience a new time-line showcasing the site since 1873. Next year, we'll see the sesquicentennial year for Point Porphyry Lighthouse on July 1st, 2023.

Lightkeepers were often challenged by these waters. It's not hard to fathom what First Nations people might have felt when they faced Lake Superior in their birch bark canoes, long before the white man's arrival. Understanding perspectives was captured through the sketch work of our most recent artist-in-residence. Bea Martin brought lots of passion and experience to the game and was found, day and night, sketching scenes around Porphyry Island. Martin said, "Porphyry Island is a paradise. Time simply stopped for me from day one. Not only was I able to sketch non-stop, but also I could relax, recharge and disconnect from everything."

Her attitude was refreshing as she took time to capture the landscapes. Not only did she proceed with her work, but she also took time to help out at the light station as we've recently been invaded by a family of Canada geese. Laying their "calling cards" on the lawn, Bea helped distribute next year's fertilizer for our gooseberries with a quick flick of her wrist from the shovel. Now that's dedication!

Our most recent host-keeper from Thunder Bay, who resides at Silver Islet in the summer months, Timothy Langille, spent his time reducing a shopping list of jobs. From dressing up the bell tents with new camp cots, to chopping wood for sailors and kayakers needing wood for the sauna, Tim brought us many great moments as he managed to get lots done to make the place look clean and tidy.

Monarch butterflies are starting to return now and, with over two hundred milkweed planted around the site, we are hoping this will keep them happy. Overall, monarch traffic is down over last year, but we are hoping to see a surge in the coming days.

With the routine of helping to dock visiting tour boats every Thursday and Sunday, I was bemused to hear a tourist say to me, "be careful," as the charter moored dockside. Looking up from tethering the boat with a mystified look on my face, I was surprised to see my twin-brother on board with a crew of laughing guests. It was quite the surprise for sure, but the laughter quickly died away as my brother was set into the yoke of lighthouse keeping.

Having an identical twin on-site made me think of my own ideas of a show like "Just For Laughs" as we had a moment like that once... but that's a whole other story.

On reflection, it's wonderful to have family about when we've all experienced the isolation that the pandemic presented us.

Donny, keeper of the household, has just boiled up a pot of tea, so it's time to relax and watch the effect of gathering winds as waves and ships go by to destinations around the world.

Sitting within the fuel berm wall, Paul Morralee (centre) demonstrates a new visitor experience exhibit on the timeline of lightkeepers and their families. [Photo: David Morralee]

September 6, 2022

Many visitors experience long-weekend on island

Last week, 50 kilometre-an-hour winds hit the island from the northwest for several days, allowing many chores to get completed as pleasure boats were nowhere to be seen.

Living on an island for the summer is an exercise in adjusting to changing times and seasons. There is a sense of peace through it all as you watch wildlife continuing to thrive and prosper with the abundance of berries. The annual migration of a bear to our island is now complete as we see paw prints in the black sands along with a friendly mink swimming between the docks.

Working gently to close up parts of the facility used for programming, we are preparing for next season with more interpretive venues and opportunities.

The long-weekend at the lighthouse island, situated on the east side of Black Bay some 43 kilometres away from the city, saw many visitors. Sailboats, motor cruisers and fishing vessels all showed up with around fifty people in tow. This included local tourists from the regular charter who had an opportunity to see another tourist attraction, the Viking Cruise Lines vessel.

During the weekend, many of the visitors were busy taking in a sauna, sunbathing on the black sand beach or walking the trails around the island. It's through these experiences that people come to commune with nature, explore new territory and relax.

For one crew from the sailboat *Bella*, they all set to work collecting firewood on Sunday morning. One team felled the tree, and another team were the cutters and stackers. They spent a couple of hours making sure that cut wood was available to other boaters and visitors. When you witness this sort of support for the island, it makes everything worthwhile. The acknowledgment of effort required to keep a place like this open for visitors is appreciated; especially for the people who come next.

The reward for their labour was a huge display of Northern Lights that slipped their way over the tops of the forest and took more and more of the sky as the night went on. Pictures of the boats moored in the harbour with the dancing lightshow made for exciting campfire talk.

As the season starts to close, it's wonderful to look at some of the things that were created this year; such as a new picnic table and benches for visitors. These furnishings help visitors sit and enjoy a picnic lunch. Gail Palko and her crew had a wonderful picnic lunch at the boathouse.

I managed try some of their Thunder Oak cheese, which was a treat they brought from the mainland. They had come to enjoy the long-weekend, and met many other people. The sail boaters had set up a tournament with wooden spittles called Mölkky, a game from Finland. Like lawn bowling but with a few twists, it was easy to pick up and fun to play.

Now that the weekend has finished and the beach and grounds are tidied up, we are ready for other adventurers. This week will take advantage of the calm weather to get more chores done, and we expect to see more visitors on Thursday and Sunday with the charter boat.

Time to enjoy the warm breeze, the quiet solitude and the beautiful vistas that Porphyry Island provides.

Cooler nights bring on the Northern Lights that brighten up Porphyry Harbour and add to the exciting chat around the fire pit.

[Photo: Cam McWhirter]

September 13, 2022

Work remains as island winds down

My journey on Lake Superior began many years ago on *Nina*, a wooden cruiser that was built at Fort William in the 1950s. She was the first vessel from which I explored Superior and the lighthouses twenty years ago.

Now, I was on a trip to return to Porphyry Island with *Nina* and supplies, but first, I wanted to stop to visit a special lighthouse enthusiast, Maureen Robertson, who was visiting the Trowbridge Island Lighthouse.

The Trowbridge light tower, made of reinforced concrete and erected in 1924, was fashioned in the same style and layout as the Peggy's Point lighthouse at Peggy's Cove, Nova Scotia, near Halifax, but that lighthouse is a little shorter. The Trowbridge light is situated near the feet of the Sleeping Giant and can be seen from Silver Islet. Its 3rd-order Fresnel lens has directed vessel traffic to and from Thunder Bay for nearly one hundred years!

Robertson, who had been a volunteer keeper at Trowbridge, was returning to take another look after an absence of many years. Speaking with her, she was thrilled to be back for a visit, but was concerned about the future of the station. Over the past ten years, Canadian Lighthouses of Lake Superior, after acquiring a lease to operate the site, has been challenged with access, as you can only approach the island in calm weather.

Motoring another 20 kilometres east, I arrived at Porphyry Island where we experienced a monumental moment. A touring visitor announced during lunch that Queen Elizabeth II had died! Not the type of news anyone wants to hear, but we fell into silence to personally reflect on her reign. After lunch, I lowered the station's flag to remember her contribution to our country, and the world for that matter.

Our weather has matched a bit of the solemn mood — torrential rains into the night. We stoked the fire and lit a candle to complete the day. Chores still remain as we continue to receive guests during some amazing weather this past weekend.

We saw one boater return twice to Porphyry with a new crowd, ready to explore. Many from the Thunder Bay Yacht club are also cramming in another weekend prior to haul-out. The Kim family's destination, decided by the children, was a complete success.

Other work continues as we start to wind things down on the island. Cleaning the cistern was one of the jobs. The cistern is like a giant swimming pool that takes up half the basement and is a storage vessel for the building's water supply. Pumping the water from the lake up into the cistern and then sweeping the walls and floors made it ready for next year.

Researcher Sallie Bishop-Legowski, who had completed a thesis on "Thermal Regime of Two Talus Slopes in Northwestern Ontario" from Carleton University, visited the island to look for permafrost heaves in the bogs and marshes of Porphyry. It was so interesting to hear about Bishop-Legowski's research and fascination with permafrost and how it forms. Bog cranberry (*vaccinium oxycoccos*) was also seen, which was a complete surprise.

As the weather continues to be warm, calm and pleasant, it is now the time when we see the birds start their migration south. Soon, it will be my time to migrate back to the mainland; but for now, there is still work to be done.

The Trowbridge Island Lighthouse, situated by the feet of the Sleeping Giant, is viewed by Maureen Robertson, a lighthouse enthusiast and volunteer.
[Photo: CLLS]

The Trowbridge Island Lighthouse [Courtesy of Marc Seguin, with notes from Kraig Anderson.]

Seventeen kilometres west of Point Porphyry, Trowbridge Island is situated at the edge of the main Thunder Bay shipping route, just off the end of the Sibley Peninsula. The steamer *Theano* was wrecked on the island in 1906, but it took another eighteen years before the government built a lighthouse there.

Construction was started on an octagonal reinforced concrete tower in August, 1923, and the lighthouse, a duplex dwelling to house the lightkeeper and his assistant, and a fog alarm building were completed in 1924. The thirty-nine foot tall tower was located on the island's highest point and was topped with an iron lantern which housed a 3rd-order Fresnel lens with an oil-vapour lamp.

Between 1924 and 1988, there was a succession of eight head lightkeepers at the Trowbridge Island Lighthouse. Among them was Gordon Graham who kept the light there from 1965 to 1979 before taking on the keeper's job at the Point Porphyry Lighthouse for the next nine years. The Trowbridge light was automated in 1988 when the last keeper, Orton Rumley, left the island.

Starting in 1997, the Canadian Coast Guard leased the keeper's dwelling on Trowbridge Island to Maureen Robertson, who used the house as a summer home for fourteen years. After her departure, Diane Berube and her son Ben spent a couple of summers on the island.

Canadian Lighthouses of Lake Superior secured a lease to the island in 2016, and the group is now making plans to restore the lightkeeper's dwelling and the other buildings that are part of the Trowbridge Island light station.

Trowbridge Island showing the lighthouse, lightkeeper's dwelling and fog alarm building, c.1930.
[Photo: Library and Archives Canada, NPC1975-387]

September 20, 2022

Island bringing unexpected pleasures

Since the end of the COVID-19 pandemic, the ebb and flow of travelers has returned to regular levels as we start to close up the light station. A visitor from 2018, Tom Harries from Minnesota, appeared at our docks prior to some nasty weather that was heading our way. It is through the eyes of the traveler that we can see more and experience other perspectives that Porphyry Island has to offer. Harries took advantage of the Paterson Foundation's sauna to break the cycle of cool, inclement Superior weather.

On an island many kilometres east of Thunder Bay on Lake Superior, Harries was invited to a dinner of bannock bread and a sweet potato beef stew. With steamed-up windows from the bubbling medley and howling winds outside, dinner was served. The meal was completed with a sweet oatmeal-apple crisp, which was enjoyed by all.

When the weather comes and the wave action builds, the island becomes a fortress of sorts. Nobody arrives or leaves. All must wait for calmer waters and future connections with mainlanders. This is the time when planned inside work that has is accomplished. As we prepare for the shut down, windows are closed, screens put away, laundry done and the site is then prepared for the following season.

Two of our big tents, used to house the Builders On Superior Shores summer program for young women, were taken down. It's with thanks to Parks Canada's Lake Superior National Marine Conservation Area that has helped Canadian Lighthouses of Lake Superior meet visitor service expectations that enabled us to purchase the tents. Several years ago, I was invited to visit another National Marine Conservation Area — Fathom Five on Lake Huron. This is where I was able to see several yurts and visitor experience amenities to help welcome visitors to the national park. So, it's now with some satisfaction that visitors have similar amenities to enjoy here.

Slowly, the work is being completed and our second-to-last work party arrived for some Sunday afternoon hauling and moving of docks and such. It was interesting as we had three Pauls and two Andrews working in the crew. It left for some amusing interactions, but was quickly remedied by, for example, "Andrew One" and "Andrew Two". Had we all worked longer together, I am sure we would have come up with some interesting nicknames.

This time of year on the island is magic, as you get to experience lots of unexpected pleasures; squirrels stopping to visit inside the boathouse; an earful of cedar waxwings flying over head; a party of blue jays making noise, and raft of loons floating past; all keeping us entertained in the fading days of summer.

And in these days, and as we have completed our last tour of the season, I am often reminded of how this island plays an important role outside that of history and lighthouses. It is also a place of respite from the day-to-day, and an opportunity to reconnect and rejuvenate. In my former days as a local filmmaker, I had the opportunity to work closely with the NorWest Community Centres in regional health projects. It was a privilege to be able to give a tour to a group of seven health workers who I am sure gave much of their time keeping us all safe. Thank you for visiting.

And to the other 900 island visitors, we are hoping to see you all again next year. One more week to go until it will be my time to return to the mainland.

Taking time to recharge and reconnect to Porphyry Island Provincial Park Nature Reserve and the light station. Staff from the NorWest Community Health Centres enjoyed a day of respite. From left to right, Dr. Ray Balec, Dr. Jennifer Lawson, Allison Anderson, Kelsey Hoogsteen, April Pilon, Dr. Berit Dool and Ashley Aitken.

[Photo: CLLS]

LIGHTHOUSE DISPATCHES

September 27, 2022

Light station winds down — Next year in sights

Laying in bed an extra thirty minutes, I reflected upon my last day of the season on Porphyry Island. With continuing fair seas and warm temperatures, it was a good day to be leaving.

After seeing off seven host-keepers, four artists-in-residence, two Canada Summer Jobs students and thirteen Builders On Superior Shores participants, I could empathize with how it feels to leave — happy, but sad, for the season is now coming to a close. Porphyry had over 900 visitors exploring, learning and making a step towards understanding how shipping operates on the largest freshwater lake in the world.

The colder spring, higher gas prices and two-years of delay of out-of-town family events, made for a slower start this year. As the summer progressed, numbers improved, and so did the weather. Considering that Canadian Lighthouses of Lake Superior (CLLS) is one of the only market-ready experiences in the Lake Superior National Marine Conservation Area, it was a pleasure to meet visitors from around North America and the world.

Our annual fundraiser in July was well attended with lots of help from local businesses such as George's Market and 99.9 FM providing support. Many boaters also volunteered their time to help support the lighthouse. Members from the Thunder Bay Yacht Club held their annual North Shore Regatta awards night on the island in August, providing a venue for boaters and sailors.

Porphyry Island, situated on the east side of Black Bay across from Silver Islet, played host to other groups who came for photo opportunities, environmental studies, geological research, or to delve into exploring family history.

Many thanks to all our partners such as Silver Islet Harbour Association, Thunder Bay Yacht Club, Canadian Coast Guard Thunder Bay SAR Base, Lakehead Transportation Museum Society, Ontario Parks, Tourism Thunder Bay and the Department of Fisheries and Oceans Canada. Without the support of these partners, we would not be able to flourish.

CLLS is also thankful for support from the Canada Summer Jobs program and MP Patty Hajdu's Thunder Bay-Superior North office, Thunder Bay Community Foundations and the many donations we received from visitors and members and the general public. Our summer staff, Abby Beatty and Annie Ross, were exceptional in hosting visitors and coordinating the new BOSS program.

With this collective approach, everyone brings something to the table. It's through these actions that we can continue to provide an outlet for our region, province and country to share in our history. Volunteers, board of directors and members all make their contribution, providing time, resources, knowledge and finance.

Next season will see some more changes with expanded services. Also in 2023, Porphyry Island will be celebrating its 150th anniversary! Festivities are being planned.

During the winter months, CLLS will be providing a speakers' series on lighthouse history in the area. There will also be our annual fundraising dinner in the early spring, and applications will open in late February or early March for host-keepers, artists-in-residence and a summer student.

It is with thanks that I acknowledge the opportunity provided by the *Chronicle-Journal* newspaper to share the stories from Porphyry Island this summer. Now that the light station is wrapped up for the season, I can change gears and prepare for next year.

Until then, enjoy your winter!

Taking a final look at the keeper's dwelling, Donny Wabasse spent the last four months taking pictures and cooking up a storm while living on the island.

[Photo: CLLS]

LIGHTHOUSE DISPATCHES

2023

150 Years of Lightkeeping

LIGHTHOUSE DISPATCHES

May 30, 2023

Island's season to see anniversary, carnival, new beer

Another season of lighthouse exploration and engagement begins on the north shore of Lake Superior, with some amazing upcoming events, programs and activities for everyone to participate in.

Tourism and economic development are augmented in small steps with the help of dedicated volunteers and supporters of Canadian Lighthouses of Lake Superior (CLLS) who operate three lighthouses on the North Shore as a non-profit charitable organization.

Situated some 43 kilometres east of Thunder Bay, beyond the Sleeping Giant, is Black Bay and the Point Porphyry light station. Each year, nearly one thousand people attend activities at the lighthouse, including excursions, host-keeper programs and artist-in-residence programs.

This season, CLLS will celebrate the establishment of a lighthouse on Porphyry Island 150 years ago, in 1873. On Canada Day a replica of the original light, constructed by Hammarskjold High School woodworking students, will be unveiled. Everyone wins when working with high school students who are active in securing future job careers in the trades, and with other students who are taking the program as an elective.

From the city of Thunder Bay, nestled behind and blocked from the water by the Lakehead's port infrastructure, visitors are allowed a small window of opportunity to jump aboard a charter boat to the island to experience the area's natural beauty and nautical history.

Arriving at the island nearly a week ago, it's like going backwards in time as the climate is still very cold — the leaves are ready to unfurl at the first burst of heat. Inside the keeper's dwelling, we've got the fireplace keeping things warm in the evenings as we pursue the steps required to open for the season.

Thanks to volunteers who helped the lighthouse group on the annual cleanup on Saturday to help give the lighthouse a spring cleaning, we had many volunteers, including members of the Thunder Bay Hiking Association. The TransCanada Trails Care grant also contributed some funds for the activity with participants receiving a Columbia t-shirt and baseball cap for their help. Not only were all the trails given a clearing up, but the houses, and tents were set up for this season's visitors.

Island life is starting again with the seasons turning and the lake ready for its annual acrobatics. Watching the little birds return and seeing the Canada geese flying north is a pleasure to behold. The island is waking up from its winter sleep. A few monarch butterflies are visiting too, along with some sparrows and blue jays.

The water is extremely cold, with it measuring around 38° Fahrenheit (3.3°C) which was a challenge for our dock crew. Andrew St. Claire, Paul Rooney, and Archie Hoogsteen all took their turn replacing floats, adjusting docks and setting anchors so visitors have a place to land at the island. The enthusiastic attitude of the entire volunteer crew was a wonderful and helpful start to the season.

Our lighthouse group again would like to thank the Thunder Bay Hiking Association for providing 18 volunteers who all came with rakes, shovels and snips to tail back the overgrowth.

This season is shaping up well with the 150th anniversary celebrations, the annual Lighthouse Carnival in August and, soon, an announcement regarding the launch of a new beer to celebrate 150 years to be presented by the Lakehead Beer Company and Thunder Bay Yacht Club.

The tea kettle is whistling in the background, so its time for me to take a break. Thanks for joining me for another summer of fun and activity.

Island Waking Up From Winter Sleep: Many volunteers make light work of it as they attend the annual cleanup at the Point Porphyry Lighthouse.

L-R, front to back: Lucy Palermo-White, Suzanne Allain, Viviana Nardo, Marie Cowley; Middle Row, Joyce Carlson, Heather Williams, Gerry White, Frank Martin, Renee Martin, Lorna MacAskill, Helen DeFranceschi, Bonnie Portelance, David Portelance, Bruce Holmes, Ti King; Back Row, Charlie Johnson, David Smith, Jeff Williamson, Heather Conrad, Claudio DeFranceschi, Cathy Schroede, Scott MacAskill, Archie Hoogsteen, Corrine Hoogsteen, Harriet McMillan, Doug McMillan. Missing from the Pictures Anne Santarossa, Betty Radbourne, Raija Zatti, Bill Boyce, Hilda Postenka, Paul Buckley, Glenda, Norm and Luke Giroux, Andrew St. Claire & Paul Rooney. [Photo: CLLS]

LIGHTHOUSE DISPATCHES

June 6, 2023

Change springs up on island like a light switch

The laughter was coming from the beach as a dozen Grade 8 students were exploring for sea-glass. This is the third time students from the Oxford School in Woodstock, Ontario, have taken a trip to Thunder Bay, which also included stops at the Port Authority and Fort William Historic Park.

As pockets full of sea-glass came back to the keeper's dwelling, the significance of the material was revealed. Its source was possibly an empty wine bottle tipped into the water years ago, or perhaps a broken dinner plate. Touched decades earlier by the lightkeeper's hand — now cleaned up off the beach — the students were rewarded with a lasting memory of a personally-crafted piece of jewelry they made!

The weather here on the island had left the living things in a dormant state; stuck in neutral between winter and summer. Everything was so grey. The fog was rolling in and the wind blew nonstop from the east bringing with it the chilling cold. I split more firewood to feed the hungry stove and, by candlelight, read the night away.

Then, like a light switch the next day, things changed. The buds that had been on standby, all of a sudden burst open. Sweaters and jackets were removed and, with a sigh of relief, the fight to survive lessened.

Monarch butterflies now fly abundantly about the point wondering where their milkweed is? Last season, we had a donor bring in 200 new plants, but again things are slow to get moving on the island as we are three weeks behind the mainlanders' climate.

Another hearty crew of adventurers stopped for a tour and moored at the dock overnight. Porphyry Island, located about 43 kilometres east of the city of Thunder Bay, on Black Bay, offers a great playground for outdoor enthusiasts. Lakehead University's School of Outdoor Recreation, Tourism & Parks crew with Captain Swatton aboard Sail Superior's *Frodo* took in the sights and learned more about the relevance of history and the role lighthouses played in keeping shipping safe. Annie Ross, a Canadian Lighthouses of Lake Superior (CLLS) summer employee from last summer, led the crew on an interpretive tour of the island and light station.

This summer is shaping up to be a big celebration — 150 years of Point Porphyry Lighthouse's existence. Back in the 1860s, Thomas Dick wrote to the government demanding that safe passage be provided to immigrants aboard ships leaving Collingwood, Ontario, and passing through Sault Ste. Marie to the Lakehead and further west. There was no Highway 17; no airplane, and no railroad at that time. Part of the celebration will include a new brew from Lakehead Beer Company, called Porphyry! I might miss my cup of tea on that day and test it out on June 27th at the launch.

Another date to keep in mind is the lighthouse's Annual General Meeting on June 14 with guest speaker Rick Oldale talking about "Shipwrecks at No.10 Lighthouse". Located 53 kilometres east of Thunder Bay, Number 10 Island signifies the start of the North Channel which was formed behind the islands by the mid-continental rift 1.1 billion years ago. This lighthouse, officially known as the Shaganash Lighthouse, has been divested by Fisheries and Oceans Canada, and designated as a heritage lighthouse under the federal Heritage Lighthouse Protection Act. CLLS will be the new owner once it clears the public announcement process. Not only will CLLS own and operate its own light, but will be able to create new programs, products and offers to the public.

If you are looking to come visit us this summer; to explore the volcanic beaches, panoramic views and keepers' stories, jump on the Silver Islet charter on Sundays and Thursdays. Come for the solitude; put your feet in the sand, and lose yourself in thought as you stare at the turquoise waters and shimmering sunlight. Porphyry now offers respite, not just for shipwrecked crews, but also for overstimulated minds.

Staff and students enjoy their visit to Northwestern Ontario as they stand in front of one of the tents at the Point Porphyry light station.   [Photo: CLLS]

LIGHTHOUSE DISPATCHES

June 13, 2023

Weekend of discovery, work

Things are starting to settle down now that most of the start-up chores are completed at the Porphyry Island light station; ready for guest tours in a couple of weeks. The weather has become much nicer with the cool winds at last abating.

It's wonderful to take a moment to watch the monarch butterflies investigating many flowering plants on the lighthouse point while fluttering so effortlessly. It seems that every lighthouse island has been domesticated with its patch of rhubarb, gooseberry bushes, lilacs and forget-me-nots.

The walking trails on Porphyry are looking great and it is with much gratitude that Canadian Lighthouses of Lake Superior (CLLS) acknowledges over fifty volunteers who have been helping out over the past couple of weeks.

This weekend, a band of volunteers jumped aboard Archie's Charter boat for the 10-minute ride from Silver Islet to Trowbridge Island. The wind was brisk from the north, but with only a short fetch for the waves to gather, we were able to dock against this sparse rocky island.

Trowbridge Island, located near to the feet of the Sleeping Giant, directs up-bound traffic along the shipping lanes from Isle Royale to Thunder Bay. Built high on a craggy cliff, the concrete light tower with its iron lantern is almost an exact replica of the Peggy's Point Lighthouse at Peggy's Cove near Halifax, Nova Scotia. The light was built after SS *Theano* was wrecked at Trowbridge in 1906.

Volunteers started with a tour and a safety orientation prior to getting a chance to clear the yard of brush. Everyone came together for lunch on the veranda of the keeper's dwelling, while watching the swallows swoop down to eat their lunch too.

Upon completion, and with a little effort, the vessel was untethered from the island and made it back to Silver Islet. What a great day, and a great experience of discovery, including seeing a 3rd-order Fresnel lens up-close; the only one on the North Shore.

On Sunday, we had another crew out to Porphyry to work on the docks and move a boat back into the water. What a wonderful day it was as the island was immune from the wind, and the sun shone bright.

Tomorrow at 7p.m., in partnership with the Transportation Museum of Thunder Bay (formerly the Lakehead Transportation Museum Society), CLLS will hold its Annual General Meeting on the *Alexander Henry*. The event starts with a short business meeting to catch members and friends up on the current state of the organization, followed by a guest speaker.

LIGHTHOUSE DISPATCHES

This year, CLLS is honoured to have Rick Oldale speaking about "Shipwrecks at No.10 Lighthouse". Oldale is an avid scuba diver with lots of interesting research behind him, and he'll be showing a 20-minute video of underwater footage of two wrecks, the *St. Andrews* and the *Emerson*. Oldale will speak about the history of these vessels and the search he undertook to find them. He will also share some other stories he heard, first-hand, from the lightkeepers of years past.

In two weeks time, there will be another opportunity for friends of the lighthouse to unite as a new beer has been commissioned. Lakehead Beer Company and the Thunder Bay Yacht Club have teamed up to commemorate the 150th Anniversary of Point Porphyry light station. On Tuesday June 27, at 7p.m., come down to the brewery on Park Avenue and enjoy a clean, crisp beer. A percentage of the funds raised through the sales will be donated to the lighthouse. Cheers!

Standing in front of the 3rd-order Fresnel lens at the Trowbridge Island Lighthouse, volunteers get a close look at the glass and brass that made up the light. (Left to Right) front row, Julie Rosenthal, Nancy Allen, Chancy Atwood; back row, Paul Capon, Michel Dumont. [Photo: CLLS]

June 20, 2023

Meeting noteworthy, model offers a resource

Lowering the model of the Thunder Bay Main Lighthouse back into place on Prince Arthur's Landing near the Delta Hotel gives me a good feeling. Watching volunteers working together to move, deliver and anchor the structure shows how people can help connect visitors to our history and community.

Lighthouses have always been used by mariners as a tool to find their way safely. To landlubbers, the model light gives them a way to find things to do that might interest them. The model includes a map of the marina that connects visitors to several community groups that are volunteering their time to share our collective history.

Take for example Bob Scarcello, a volunteer with the Thunder Bay Railway Historical Society who, when I arrived at the caboose by the roundabout, opened the door and said, "Welcome." To see the restoration inside the caboose, and to hear the stories of some of the artifacts within, riveted my interest. These are selfless acts of building community; one person and one step at a time.

The Transportation Museum of Thunder Bay also is part of the community on the waterfront, and this year Canadian Lighthouses of Lake Superior held its Annual General Meeting on the *Alexander Henry*. Not only was the crew's mess overflowing with interest to hear the guest speaker, but also excess visitors were managed by opening up the door to the adjoining galley.

Rick Oldale spoke of the Shipwrecks around No.10 (Shaganash) Lighthouse located 15 kilometres east of Black Bay. He showed films from his dives in the mid-1980s when technology was still in its infancy to collect video images underwater. He captured everyone's imagination that night as the video showed the bones of two ships. Brad, a local artist from SVDcompany, also showed his wares and connected his art with the nautical theme of the evening, presenting some of his No.10 Lighthouse canvases.

To expand further on last week's column, in 1953, near to the Trowbridge Island Lighthouse, the freighter *Scotiadoc* was rammed by the freighter *Burlington* in a fog. The *Scotiadoc* is now the deepest wreck on Lake Superior: 259 meters (850 feet) below the surface.

Meanwhile, topside, preparations are underway to celebrate the 150th Anniversary at Point Porphyry on July 1st. Jim Dyson, a well-known fisherman from Silver Islet, collected parts of the 1873 Point Porphyry Lighthouse replica. The model will be shipped across Black Bay later in the week to be re-assembled at the point.

Dyson said that "...he's had a lot of inquiries as to what the building is for!" He just told them that they could see it assembled at Porphyry this summer, which should perpetuate the mystery and excitement further. The Hammarskjold High School which undertook the construction of the replica is sending representatives to be present at the unveiling on July 1st. White bed sheets have been donated to hide the replica until the right moment.

The season is well under way with tours starting this Thursday and Sunday with a charter running from Silver Islet to the lighthouse. The tour of Porphyry Island showcases the volcanic beaches, exotic plant life, and includes the history of the keepers of the light. The lighthouse is situated in a location where you can see the reverse of the Sleeping Giant to the west, the USA's Isle Royale to the south, and Black Bay to the north.

We have a family of host-keepers coming this Sunday, and we are looking forward to getting them underway with some projects. One task will be to bake the cake for the July 1st celebrations, and we've been talking about how to build a three-layer cake to represent the structure of the lighthouse. I've been politely told to stay out of the kitchen.

Next week we'll share the preparations for the festivities and let you know about who's visiting us.

Dive Back In Time. Aboard the former Coast Guard Ship *Alexander Henry*, Rick Oldale takes us on a deep dive back in time to see two wrecks close to the No.10 Lighthouse, 54 kilometres east of Thunder Bay on Lake Superior. Oldale kept everyone engaged as he showcased his work from the late 1980s using some innovative underwater videotaping.
[Photo: CLLS]

LIGHTHOUSE DISPATCHES

June 27, 2023

Pristine area of island amazes visitors

Now that the flowers are blooming and the temperatures have warmed up, we're happy to be on the island with life surrounding us. Through the eyes of our visitors, we are reminded how fortunate we are to live in this area. We've had people from all over the US this week, including as far away as Florida. They are all amazed at the pristine environment and wildlife on the island including rabbits, squirrels and our resident pine marten.

Since the pandemic, we are happy to see the return of the Voyageur Outward Bound School group from Ely, Minnesota. The kayaking group came across the archipelago of islands from Rossport; stopping overnight at Porphyry on a week-long tour. As is often the case on these trips, they volunteer their time to give back to community groups. From cutting wood and stacking the lumber pile to raking the beaches, it was all-hands-on-deck.

What a pleasure it is to work with youths and to see their enthusiasm for making things better for the next visitor. Once introduced to the sauna and some swimming, a meal around the picnic tables rounded things up nicely. Their next stop was Sand Island, near to Silver Islet, where they would finish their trip the next day.

Canadian Lighthouses of Lake Superior also had the opportunity to share the story of the lighthouses with other community-minded groups such as the Transportation Museum of Thunder Bay, Science North, and Parks Canada. The purpose of the tour was to introduce tour guides and others who work in the public sphere to see what the lighthouse history tour looks like as a tourist. Lunch included hot yam soup, sandwiches, and rhubarb-apple pie. This was followed by a Parks Canada activity.

Twenty easels, paint trays and seats were set up on the front lawn of the keeper's dwelling dwarfed by the light tower. Participants were given some direction how to get started in the process of painting. The "Painting Superior" program offered by Parks Canada is a way to introduce visitors to develop an appreciation of art through nature. A dozen participants painted for an hour, with great results and a great reminder of the day. On Canada Day, this event will again be offered.

The next day, we had a group arrive from the Lakehead Nurse Practitioner-Led Clinic. What a joy to take these healthcare workers around the island as a way of respite and fun. The group had a picnic lunch and went about exploring the island located 43 kilometres east of Thunder Bay on Black Bay. Sea-glass captured everyone's imagination, and I found a flint arrowhead. What a thrill that was! To hold this artifact in my hand led me to wonder who had chipped the flint away to form the pointy end. Did this arrowhead bring down a moose?

This week, we welcome two host-keeping groups to help us out on the island; Dawn Lumina accompanied by her mother and son, and a couple from the United States. First off Monday morning, we held our health and safety orientation. Then, they set out painting and dabbing paint to spruce up the place. This weekend will see the 150th Anniversary of the Point Porphyry Lighthouse, and there is expected to be around 60 guests. The tour boat is fully booked, and many local boaters are making their way over for the festivities. The event will include the unveiling of the Hammarskjold-built 1873 Point Porphyry Lighthouse replica, and Parks Canada will run its "Painting Superior" program.

Today, if you are feeling thirsty, please drop by Lakehead Beer Company on Park Avenue in Thunder Bay as they will be releasing a light rice beer called Porphyry. Come try the new brew, and support the Thunder Bay Yacht Club's initiative to raise funds for the 150th Anniversary of the Point Porphyry Lighthouse. Beer is available in cans so you can share this once-in-a-lifetime brew with family and friends. Thanks to all of our supporters and volunteers helping us maintain our mandate to educate the public on lighthouses and keep them relevant.

I must get going as there are more chores to complete prior to the events.

Surrounded by forget-me-nots, Brenda and Rebecca journey for the first time to the lightkeeper's dwelling where they will spend the next week helping out. The host-keeper and artist-in-residence programs help people engage in the story of lighthouses on the north shore of Lake Superior. [Photo: CLLS]

Lake Superior Islands

The north shore of Lake Superior in Canada extends east from the Pigeon River international boundary all the way to Marathon, Ontario, beyond the town of Nipigon. This shoreline was part of the mid-continental rift system which formed about 1.1 billion years ago, shaping the Lake Superior basin. The rift, which spanned 2,000 kilometres in an inverted "U" shape, with Nipigon situated at the bend of the U, played a significant role in the geology of the region.

Post-glaciation, the water level of Lake Superior was approximately 500 feet (160 meters) higher than its current level. Porphyry Island, positioned at the tip of the Black Bay Peninsula, marks the western end of a chain of islands that extends 100 kilometres to the Battle Island Lighthouse and the town of Rossport. These islands emerged around 5,000 years ago when the water levels receded, unveiling the volcanic remnants of the rift from a billion years earlier.

Isle Royale, on the American side of the lake, was once a site for extensive copper mining along its shores and inland mines. This mining activity sparked a rush during the 1800s as prospectors sought out other valuable ore. In 1868, Silver Islet became a leading silver producer globally, and the quest for precious metals continued on various islands like Edward Island, adjacent to Porphyry.

Located in a region characterized by high cliffs, some of these islands are part of a geologic dike system that has pushed up layers of bedrock which are now exposed. One example of this is Porphyry's neighbouring island, Hardscrabble. Porphyry Island itself showcases something different with its pools of cooled volcanic rock prominently seen flowing outward to create its shoreline. Moreover, the island boasts black sand beaches formed from eroded basalt, which constitutes a significant portion of its shoreline landscape.

Due to the lack of fertile topsoil and the inherently cold climate influenced by Lake Superior, these islands posed challenges for early settlers. Porphyry Island thwarted several agricultural efforts. In contrast, Edward Island, situated nearby, offered slightly warmer soils, and this is where Porphyry's lightkeepers successfully cultivated potatoes.

The boreal forest enveloping these islands is dense with balsam trees, interspersed with Old Man's Beard, a lichen known to hang from branches. Traditionally, First Nations people utilized this lichen for various medicinal purposes, addressing conditions such as lung, intestinal, throat, and sinus ailments. Between Porphyry and Edward islands, in the middle of Walkers Channel, there is an unnamed island. In the past, there was a rock formation on the island which, before it collapsed during a storm in 1948, looked like a human face. This is where ritual offerings were dedicated to "Shaminitou" (the Child Saviour). This unique rock structure was acknowledged by First Nations peoples as far away as British Columbia, potentially explaining the presence of a plant called Devil's Club (*Oplopanax horridus*), which is native on the Pacific coast but appears on only a few Lake Superior Islands.

July 4, 2023

Lighthouses, new and old, on 150th anniversary

Surrounded by swirling fog, frothy seas and a cool Superior climate, the sauna was being kept well-stocked with firewood. Later, kayakers, boaters and sailors would all take turns warming up and cleaning up.

In the serenity of the island, the flowers are in full bloom and the lilac bush is ready to provide the smells of summer. Wild roses on the black sand beaches are starting to open, providing a burst of colour.

Under this beautiful canopy of colour came lots of action by volunteers to make the upcoming anniversary event shine. There were five exceptional host-keepers who had spent a week readying the site. Dawn, Stella, Brenda, Paul and Rebecca all dug in to give it their best. Upon completion of the new outhouse pit, tourists even dropped by to see what was going on there!

As fortune would have it, the sun shone bright at the right moment as the Canada Day festivities for Porphyry Island's unveiling of the newly-built replica of the original 1873 lighthouse took place. Standing at one-sixth its original height, the old Point Porphyry Lighthouse was proudly on display again after the original lighthouse had been demolished in 1960. Saturday marks the 150th year of operation of the light station, which has helped thousands and thousands of ships navigate all these years past the point situated 43 kilometres east of the port of Thunder Bay on the other side of the Sleeping Giant.

Many rounds of applause were heard as introductions and salutations were made. The gathered masses included charter boat visitors, local boaters and political representatives; all out to celebrate our connection to trans-shipment. Not only has the lighthouse provided Thunder Bay with a prosperous role assisting in trade for 150 years, but it also signifies that tourism is now playing a bigger role.

Jim Dyson from Camp Bay beside Silver Islet, played an integral role in arranging transportation and men to move the model to the island. Garry Dawson was on hand with Thunder Bay Tug Services to ferry the final part of the model lighthouse to the island. Carefully moving the all-terrain vehicle and trailer off of the drawbridged vessel and up onto dry land was smoothly planned and executed. Slowly, under watchful eyes, the body of the lighthouse was taken up McKay Drive (named after a former lightkeeper) to be connected with the other parts of the model for the first time.

On the point, pausing in the moment, we think of all the men and women who served to make this country prosperous by being lightkeepers. Every small step by

Canadian Lighthouses of Lake Superior and its volunteers helps to bring the keepers' stories forward for all to share.

It's wonderful when we see community partners step up to assist a charitable organization whose mandate is to connect people to our nautical history. Thanks to Lakehead Motors, the Port of Thunder Bay, Parks Canada, Lakehead Beer Company and Archie's Fishing Charters & Lighthouse Tours for their support. And a special mention to the woodworking students at Hammarskjold High School for completing such a wonderful replica lighthouse model for people to enjoy for years to come.

A cake, decorated by our host-keepers, a donated raffle item from one of our volunteers, and a local artist with his wares were all on hand to mark this momentous event. Some 67 people attended with all accommodations booked; there was no room to spare. As everyone chatted and explored the island and the beautiful location on Lake Superior, sweet memories were formed.

Now, standing firmly in place for all to see, the lighthouse group is forever grateful and thankful to all of the volunteers who took on the challenge to let the light shine bright.

These volunteers played a role in making the Pt. Porphyry Lighthouse model a reality on Porphyry Island. They are, from left, Dawn Luomala, Jim Dyson, Garry Dawson, Master Jack Cooke, Les Legace, Paul Luomala, Mark Sokolowski, Brenda Johnson, and Stella Boutilier. [Photo: CLLS]

July 11, 2023

Porphyry Island is a sanctuary for many

Swallows circling over the lighthouse grounds are looking to feed their babies in the red and white birdhouse. It's a pleasure to watch as the mother and father take turns tending to the little ones in the nest.

Now, a couple of weeks into the summer, we are continuing to experience rolling fog along the shoreline. Coming and going as it does, it's nice to see the constantly changing view as it can surprise you — one moment fog, and the next, clear sailing.

Our tours are starting to pick up with everyone enjoying the new lighthouse model exhibit that was enthusiastically completed by the Hammarskjold High School students. As time goes on, it's rewarding to hear how visitors see the lighthouses and the questions they bring forward. One question is often asked, "Is this the original site where the 1873 lighthouse once stood?" The answer is yes. Reviewing a survey done early in the 1900s, we were able to establish the location of the original lighthouse against the other building footprints.

Host-keeper Chris Eby, who's recently returned to his hometown of Thunder Bay, was enthusiastic to take on the adventures of lighthouse living. Completion of an outhouse was undertaken, with the roof being shingled and some final framing of the timbers completed. Eby worked hard to provide a comfortable setting for all visitors to the island, while working on providing the amenities necessary.

One family on Sunday's charter who had originally come from Ukraine and now resides in Mississauga, Ontario, was ecstatic with the natural beauty of the place. Three-year-old Caroline and her dolly, Sheepy, explored most of the island. Lost in the moment, Sheepy and Caroline became separated, and a search party for Sheepy was launched. The mother took on the duties of consoling the young one while father went into search mode. From the boathouse to the keeper's dwelling, everywhere was searched. After a third scout was sent out to look, Sheepy was found hanging on the back of the washroom door. Disaster was averted when Caroline embraced her dolly and life returned back to normal.

Porphyry is a sanctuary for many visitors who visit us over the summer months. With the black volcanic sands and interesting rock structures underfoot, it's no wonder visitors are so fascinated. Walking the beach this week, I was able to look at the rocks and follow them under the clean, clear water. One thin sliver of quartz could be seen and it reminded me of the Silver Islet Mine sunk deep below the waters on the other side of Black Bay.

Porphyry Island offers its guests an interesting selection of weather. Visitors to the island ask, "What should I wear?" Windbreaker, sweater, t-shirt is my answer, as all day long I am taking articles of clothing off only to put them all back on with the shifting winds.

This week, the lighthouse group has an artist-in-residence, Pamela Cain, who is already creating art! Last season Cain had come to the island to work as a host-keeper and, while here, she developed some themes she is currently undertaking in her art. It's exciting to see how art can transform our view of the real to the surreal, and draw us in to discover what the artist is trying to communicate.

Parks Canada's history team from the National Marine Conservation Area is continuing to work on collecting some information on the historical sites around the western end of the park. Covering over 88,000 square kilometres and running from the feet of the Sleeping Giant, east to Bottle Point near Terrace Bay, this playground slowly opens up to future visitors.

Writing from the tower, the wind is whistling and the sound of crashing waves can be heard. It is relaxing to be part of the view, the sounds and the sunshine. Now, to get a cup of tea and take a break.

Squaring up the boards before pounding in the final nails, Chris Eby host-keeper, enjoyed his stay on the island for the past week. [Photo: CLLS]

July 18, 2023

Survival at an island lighthouse

Weather this summer continues to play a role in keeping everyone on their toes. With many using the sauna at Porphyry Island, Superior water is still pretty cool at 8°C. To think, last week, a kayaker who stopped over for a short break at the Point Porphyry Lighthouse later found himself in distress on Black Bay and was rescued after three hours in the water!

Survival is what the island has been all about since the beginning of lightkeeping on the North Shore one hundred and fifty years ago. In November 1929, the *SS Thordoc*, a Paterson-owned vessel, struck the reef off the point due to a magnetic disturbance that the area is known for. From a newspaper report, we read that a fair maiden and other guests travelling aboard the ship were lowered in a lifeboat over the side of the stricken vessel only to have themselves pitched into the water. Since the water over the reef was only a few feet deep, the women noted that, as they waded ashore, when looking up they could see the light, only one hundred feet away! They stayed in the lighthouse overnight; warming up after the ordeal.

Today, life is a lot easier because of the hard work of many people to provide more comfort to visitors. Take for instance, Gordon and Karin Mackenzie, host-keepers who travelled from Nipigon by boat and who took to the work at hand. Many of their projects focused on finishing touches with new signage and a reworking of the gift shop. They both were great hosts to the many visitors who came to the island this past week and weekend.

The tours continue to bring in enthusiastic adventure-seekers looking to learn more about the lives of keepers on Lake Superior. Leaving from Silver Islet on Thursday's and Sunday's charter boat, visitors get a chance to see the Silver Islet Mine shimmering below the surface, and arrive at Porphyry some 15 minutes later. Porphyry Island sits on the eastern side of the mouth of Black Bay, about 43 kilometres east of Thunder Bay.

Overhead, we've had two nesting sparrows looking to feed their young — great entertainment for the visitors to watch. Visitors are also seeing lots of monarch butterflies and adventuring to the black sand beach to collect sea-glass.

Next month, on August 5th, is the Annual Lighthouse Carnival fundraiser, which will include live music, history tours, and fish & chips. Volunteers from the boating community come together to host tourists arriving on the charter who are anxious to explore the island and learn more. Tickets can be purchased on line at clls.ca .

One of the most favourable places to visit is the black sand beach located on the southern shoreline of the island. Not only is this beach alluring, but it also provides solace from today's woes. The lighthouse group leases parts of the island, with Porphyry Island Provincial Park Nature Reserve taking up the rest. The island is also surrounded by the Lake Superior National Marine Conservation Area, making it a great place to share in protecting the environment for all to enjoy.

Pamela Cain, last week's artist-in-residence, produced some acrylic wall art of several canvases combined together to give a sense of the scope and scale of these North Shore islands. Against seafoam green and blue-shaded wall in the living room, a painting was donated for all to share. The painting shows both Black Bay and Thunder Bay.

We thank our volunteers who work hard to make the place shine. This includes our Board of Directors who work each day on completing errands to keep things running smoothing on the island. This past weekend Michelle Sinclair celebrated her birthday, which filled all the tents and houses for a weekend of yoga, games, great food and family time. When we are afforded the opportunity to see people enjoying some time to recharge, it is again with thanks that we have so many people behind the scenes helping make it work!

Time now for a cup of tea and to look out the window as more rain in expected in the next hour.

Exploring the island and expressing it though arts helps people in their understanding of the role that art takes in sharing a lighthouse. Gordon and Karin Mackenzie, hold up a painting made by artist-in-residence, Pamela Cain.

[Photo: CLLS]

July 25, 2023

Tranquil life continues on island

The calm waters that are slowly warming up invite many to go swimming to enjoy the tranquil setting of this unique island on Lake Superior.

Visitors who first arrive at Porphyry Island feel like they are somewhere different and, yes, they are! For this is the site of the youngest volcanic activity that attempted to calf off another continent 1.1 billion years ago.

Not only do people from Canadian Shield country get turned around, but so do people from Thunder Bay who discover that, from Black Bay, the Sleeping Giant appears in the west.

Our visitors are very happy since the Voyageur Outward Bound group toured through on kayaks and dug a new latrine pit. The expedition has been out in the environment for forty days and counting, and they still have another ten days to complete. This group of five young men are with three leaders who teach them how to work together as a team; somewhat like our host-keeper, artist-in-residence and staff do while attending to the lighthouse site and its many guests.

Last week, we said goodbye to artist Lee Angold who completed some very detailed art depicting, among other things, Old Man's Beard lichen and orange lichen. This week, we welcome back Katelyn Jefford, former summer student, as she turns out poems. The lighthouse team is already reading her work — three poems hot off the press today.

As for host-keeping, we are happy to have Tor Laine and Zack Cetz-Huchim tackle the spoils of a very busy weekend with sauna buckets to fill, wood to arrange, and firepits to set to ready mode.

Meanwhile, managing the households, Donny Wabasse is keeping the station running smoothly. This Saturday, he managed to greet over thirty-two visitors including eight kayakers, several small fishing boats and some bigger craft. The house and tents were filled, with everyone having a good time.

It was a joy to watch one young family with three toddlers being introduced to the light station. Just think of the experiences that they received as they cycled down the path for a swim. Some say that the beach is a lot like being in Hawaii with its very black sand!

The songbirds are singing their songs in the forest but, with the mosquitos around, you have to make a run for it! Considering the mosquitos came early this year, let's hope they leave just as soon.

Tours are running on Thursdays and Sundays, and are starting to fill up quickly. The annual Lighthouse Carnival that acts as an annual fundraiser has two-thirds of the seats already booked. On Saturday, August 5th, if you want a memorable lighthouse experience, come for a tour, listen to some live entertainment and devour some fish & chips to conclude a busy day. This year, the Scott van Teeffelen Band will be playing in the afternoon and will cater to many tastes of music.

It so nice to have support in the community to bring these activities to life. Parks Canada, Ontario Parks and the Silver Islet Harbour Association all do their part to make the lighthouse experience work. Our tents, programs, houses and amenities are all being used so that people can commune and connect with nature.

Next week, we will be also preparing to meet the SUNORA sailing regatta as they return from Rossport! Until then, I think I am going to find a quiet place and watch the world go by, for a moment!

Discovering the Lake Superior National Marine Conservation Area, Zaqueo Cetz-Huchim, points towards the east across Black Bay from the Trowbridge light tower. [Photo: CLLS]

August 1, 2023

Always something to do on Porphyry Island

In the build up to the Lighthouse Carnival event this weekend, volunteers are working hard to prepare, both on the mainland and at the light station.

Our visitors this season continue to explore the island, with more coming this year from the United States than before because of the relaxing of pandemic restrictions. It's wonderful to hear about their adventures on the North Shore; about who they have visited and what they have seen. The perspective from the eyes of our visitors is always fresh and new. For our host-keepers and artist-in-residence, each day is a new experience that they reflect upon and share. This expression of experiences is helpful to identify what it is that people are looking for in a visit to the lighthouse.

Four years ago, our current artist-in-residence was a Canada Summer Jobs student at the light station. Katelyn Jefford said, "It was in that summer that I gained new skills and met many people." Delving into poetry on this adventure, Jefford was able to inspire visitors with her work and inject another facet into their visit. The artist animates the site in many ways that help connect visitors to this beautiful volcanic island.

Meanwhile, in the host-keeping department, Tor Laine was enjoying every moment completing the tasks on a list, and connecting with visitors. As a quick study, Laine was able to help visitors enjoy the experience by helping direct them to interesting facts about the area. The change of scenery, I am sure, was as good as a rest for our volunteers.

The weather has been playing a little role at night with flashes of lightning and booming of thunder. I can imagine our guests checking off the boxes to say they have seen or experienced some stormy weather on Lake Superior.

With fresh green grass, bright flowers, and strawberries mixed in the front lawn, everyone is relaxing, even the baby squirrels. Each day I watch as the gooseberries slowly ripen.

At the light station, there is little time to relax because something is always about to break down, or a little problem is about to occur. Last week, the wheel went flat on the cart used for provisions, and the basement water pump had a split in the pipe. Each little challenge reminds us that we are so fortunate to be surrounded by the beauty of the area and tranquil setting.

This weekend, Canadian Lighthouses of Lake Superior will hold its 4th Annual Lighthouse Carnival fundraiser. Live entertainment will be provided by the Scott van Teeffelen Band along with lighthouse and ecology tours, a fish & chip meal and many places to go hiking and swimming. If you are looking for something to do on this holiday weekend, there are six seats left, and you can sign up at clls.ca. The event takes place at Porphyry Island, located 15 kilometres east of Silver Islet, where you catch the charter boat.

Now that our new host-keepers have arrived — two couples, one from Minnesota and the other from Dryden, Ontario — we are all working together to get the site ready. Three new picnic tables are to be constructed. Our outhouses have new pits dug. The place is looking good and smelling nice!

Thanks to all the people who volunteer their time to keep this site open and available to visitors, and to our supporters and sponsors who provide us with additional funds to help keep activities and opportunities open.

As the waves gently lap on the shore, another group of kayakers have arrived from Rossport. They are excited to see the site and are staying in the guesthouse, a fitting way to conclude their trip across the North Shore before shipping out to Silver Islet tomorrow.

Another few guests have just arrived. Time to show them around the light station, museum and art gallery. Then, I will take a moment to look at the water and enjoy watching the rolling fog go in and out.

Host-keepers Tor Laine (left) and Zaqueo Cetz-Huchim measure twice and cut once while assembling picnic tables for this weekend's Lighthouse Carnival. by charter boat.

[Photo: CLLS]

August 8, 2023

Carnival showcases many qualities of area

The calm, sweetwater seas of Lake Superior greeted many visitors this past weekend for the Annual Lighthouse Carnival fundraiser. Situated east of Thunder Bay on Black Bay, Porphyry Island attracted over 80 participants for the event. Boaters from the area came together to host part of the event, with a fish & chip dinner. Volunteering to help raise funds, the visitors get to meet people who are out enjoying the wildlife.

This year saw participation from the Thunder Bay Yacht Club's SUNORA Regatta that finished their excursion at the light station after traveling across the North Shore. Another group arrived in two charter boats from Silver Islet to partake in the festivities. Now in its fourth year, each time, the festival gets better, especially with a motivated set of volunteers. The history and ecology tours, and screening of the 1980s film about Gordon Graham being a lightkeeper with his family, were well received by visitors.

The event showcases many qualities of the area including the volcanic sands, the beautiful boreal forest and Superior's clean cold waters. Both of the bell tents were rented out, as was the keeper's dwelling. There were, at one time, 15 boats in the harbour. We had four hostkeepers who worked all week to prepare for the event — building some picnic tables and raking the beaches.

Over 30 volunteers helped to make the event happen, with some even venturing onto the helipad for a morning yoga session. With the grounds ready for the activities, wildlife was also on stage. Our resident pine marten was up a tree, and running across the lawn was a string of baby squirrels following mom's orders. Not many monarch butterflies around at the moment, but we expect more in three weeks with the cooler weather.

The replica Point Porphyry Lighthouse exhibit, built by Hammarskjold High School students, received many great reviews and comments relating to civic pride and the raising up of history from the past for all to enjoy.

Our weather continues to be different from that of the city of Thunder Bay, with some cool breezes and lots of sunshine. Inhabitants of the island watch as the thunderstorms pass to the north towards Dorion. We are in our own weather cycle here, surrounded by the cool waters of Lake Superior.

The routine of life on the island is now here as most of the major projects are completed for the season. The day-to-day running of the station takes a concentrated effort to maintain the site for visitors to enjoy. The fire pits are stocked up and maintained and the toilets now are all sitting above newly dug pits; so everyone is happy.

As the season has another month to play out, we are encouraging people to come and explore this area of the world. Surrounded by the volcanic sands, many visitors are thrilled by this novel view of the results of geologic activity some 1.1 billion years ago. If you're interested, tours from Silver Islet are filling up for Thursdays and Sundays.

This week, we also started our annual yard and grounds upkeep at Shaganash Lighthouse (aka No.10 Lighthouse) which is situated another 15 kilometres east of Black Bay. The 34-foot wooden tower, built after a fire in 1922, stands looking towards the west and north as it provides local mariners with guidance through the North Channel. Many boaters duck behind Shaganash Island to stay out of the bigger weather that Superior is known for.

The Shaganash Lighthouse on Number 10 Island.
[Photo: CLLS]

The Boreal Forest

Exploring the plant life on an island in Lake Superior is truly captivating; from the towering trees in the forest to the delicate arctic-alpine succulents that line the shore.

Porphyry Island's larger plant inhabitants, the trees, include balsam fir, white spruce, white birch, aspen, and mountain ash. These trees form a dense and diverse forest within a cool climate, often shrouded in fog. They compete for nutrients in shallow soil while contending with cold temperatures, fluctuating precipitation, and the effects of global warming, including rising water temperatures.

Draped along many tree branches, Old Man's Beard lichen (*Usnea florida*) thrives by capturing moisture from drifting fog, giving the trees a stunning appearance adorned with water droplets. Indigenous peoples utilized this fungus to treat respiratory issues and sore throats, while today it serves as a fire starter and as a picturesque feature of the majestic forest.

Additionally, Devil's Club (*Oplopanax horridus*) can be found in abundance on a few local Lake Superior Islands. This formidable plant can grow up to 14 feet tall and boasts spines on its stem and the undersides of its leaves. Its large leaves support clusters of red berries that appear toward the end of summer. The plant was introduced by First Nations people for its antibacterial and antifungal properties, having traveled from British Columbia on Canada's west coast. Those who venture into the forest quickly learn to keep a safe distance from these plants, as they can cause painful scratches.

Succulents, like the Saxifraga often referred to as Hens & Chicks (*Jovibarba globifera*), thrive in the volcanic rocks and cool climate. This alpine plant, found in regions like Iceland, Greenland, and along the north shore of Lake Superior, grows close to the ground on Porphyry's point and shoreline, particularly in sunny spots. Visitors are encouraged to tread carefully around these small plants, which bloom from late May to early June.

White birch is also abundant on Porphyry Island, and it adapts well to the environment. This tree has supplied Indigenous peoples with a key material for constructing canoes. When soaked and molded around cedar ribs, birch bark creates a flexible yet sturdy hull, essential for navigating around the densely overgrown boreal forest, which posed challenges for transporting goods.

The forest offers warmth, shelter, sustenance, and survival amid the harsh winter conditions. Today, a 1.2 kilometre trail allows visitors to Porphyry to immerse themselves in the beauty of the wildlife and the serene embrace of the forest.

This week, the station invites two new host-keepers and an artist-in-residence. Mary Espinosa is working with oil-based and water-based paints to tease out details from the rocks and forest of the island. She has already entertained ten guests who came today from Silver Islet. It's exciting to see the art being created right before your eyes while also seeing what areas catch the artist's eye. Today, it was a ridge to the south that holds all the blueberries. That's going to be for the bear when he returns in the next few weeks. Berries ripen later here as the spring is delayed a couple of weeks — the lake remains ice cold until mid-June.

Time to go and tend to the chores on-site as the weekend event has left a lot of cleaning and preparing for our next guests.

A fish & chip meal is served by many hands. Over 80 people arrived on-site for the Lighthouse Carnival and activities.

[Photo: CLLS]

August 15, 2023

Gift received where magic always remains

After we dried off from the storm, the summer weather returned. Living on isolated Porphyry Island, some 43 kilometres east of Thunder Bay, comes with its challenges; predominately, the weather. One moment, wet and miserable; the next moment, dry and happy. Dressing for all weather conditions is the only solution to get through the chores and provide for the many visitors to the island this week.

Lauren Dalicandro and Phil Luckai, as host-keepers, scoured out a place on terra firma to put *Nina*, an old Lake Superior wooden boat, "on the hard" for the winter months. *Nina* has plied these waters for over sixty years, and she will become a display for visitors and a little "bunky" for stranded overnight guests. She will be restored over the next few years. Already attracting attention, her pumps gave out and she delicately pressed her hull to the floor of the lake to rest for a few hours, until being resurrected and repairs made!

Meanwhile, the forest has quieted down since our host-keeper from Mexico returned home. Zaqueo Cetz-Huchim was often heard singing out loud as he completed his work at the boat yard. Some visiting boaters wondered if someone had left their radio on? Happiness in the forest has no bounds, and everyone enjoyed some entertainment in Spanish, and occasionally in the Mayan language.

Part of the host-keeper experience is to caper to new summits, network with other travellers and explore the unknown. Travelling east 15 kilometres to the Shaganash Lighthouse on Number 10 Island, a work party cleared the island trail and removed brush from around the foundation of the old lighthouse that burnt down in 1921. Replaced with the 36-foot wooden tower seen today, a new lock has been installed on the door after the building was vandalized last season. The site will become another Canadian Lighthouses of Lake Superior (CLLS) destination for boaters and kayakers in the years to come, and will emulate some of the programming that Porphyry has become known for over the years.

It's been interesting to see visitors come and go over the summer, and to hear about other lighthouses in the area. It's amazing that we also hear "through the grapevine" that Porphyry Island has become too busy to visit! This certainly is not the case; in fact, our numbers are intentionally restricted to give the organization the ability to retain the ecology of the island and maintain the services for visitors.

This week, we did receive a very special gift. The Van Dellen family, descendants of Charles Merritt, arrived from western Canada to celebrate the history their family has with the island. Merritt had operated the Point Porphyry Lighthouse for several years in the mid-1940s, and over those years, many stories were formed and gathered. For example, bootleggers once lost a load of rum in the harbour and the family searched for remnants of it in Rum Bottle Bay in the 1920-1933 era. Nothing was found.

Corresponding with CLLS over the past five years, the family has contributed many family photos to help us build a better understanding of what life was like back then. Renting the keeper's dwelling for four days, they enjoyed the experience; swimming, star gazing and watching big storm action out of the many windows of the house. They were also very appreciative of all the volunteers, the CLLS Board of Directors and supporters for keeping their history alive.

From this beautiful island on Lake Superior, visitors continue to be fascinated by the history, ecology, and natural beauty during their time here. Soon, the weather will turn again, and cooler nights will prevail, but the magic will remain.

Using oil-based paints, artist-in-residence Mary Espinosa revelled in the beauty and awesome power of Superior. Her art reflects a time back in the 1960s, prior to the original lighthouse on Porphyry Island being demolished and the current tower being erected. [Photo: CLLS]

LIGHTHOUSE DISPATCHES

After a day's work at No.10 Lighthouse, located 54 kilometres east of Thunder Bay, host-keepers Lauren Dalicandro and Phil Luckai enjoy the cool summer breeze. As host-keepers, the week-long experience provides them with some insight living as a lightkeeper on Lake Superior. [Photo: CLLS]

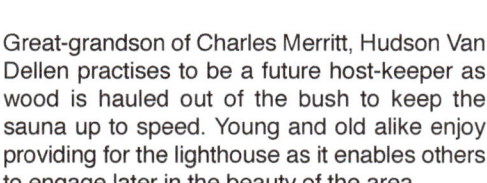

Great-grandson of Charles Merritt, Hudson Van Dellen practises to be a future host-keeper as wood is hauled out of the bush to keep the sauna up to speed. Young and old alike enjoy providing for the lighthouse as it enables others to engage later in the beauty of the area.

[Photo: CLLS]

LIGHTHOUSE DISPATCHES

August 22, 2023

Visitors astounded

As summer marches on, more visitors arrive at the light station to learn about the history and importance of the work undertaken by lightkeepers. Enticed by the illusion of a quiet getaway, my two brothers, David and Steven, arrived to find more abundance of chores and work to undertake than they ever expected. Slowly, as they eased into the work, they began to enjoy the surroundings and to see how the system operates to engage visitors.

The Point Porphyry Lighthouse, celebrating 150 years, has become a great place to learn about the significance of shipping and the movement of products on the Great Lakes, to and from the Lakehead. Situated on the east side of Black Bay, visitors are astounded to find themselves standing on lava from 1.1 billion years ago! As visitors arrive, the first thing we share is what's under foot. Understanding the geology helps to form the opinion that things here are different from the nearby Canadian Shield. With the black sand beaches, and the fact the Sleeping Giant is seen around the other way as compared to the view from Thunder Bay, the double-takes are interesting to witness. What is that?

Climbing the 25-meter light tower, looking down at the ancient billowing lava flow underwater against the turquoise lake is thought provoking; then, in the next moment, turning the eye skyward to see a bald eagle drift by as a visitor with a long lens captures the sensation and magic of the moment.

As brothers David and Steven created and crafted an outhouse, we all take a moment to pause and realize how lucky we are to share in this work in such a beautiful location.

Sailor John Keetch and his wife Lucy enjoyed an extended visit to the island. Keetch joined in the building of the outhouse because he wanted to do something to help maintain the site for the next visitors. We thank all volunteers, sponsors and supporters for their help! People like this help keep the place operational and ready for visitors who sometimes just come for a walk to stretch their legs or use the facilities such as the sauna.

This week, 80 people appeared at the Sleeping Giant Provincial Park visitor centre for a lecture on Canadian Lighthouses of Lake Superior and our mandate to connect people to the lighthouses' history. The lighthearted introduction helps visitors understand the context of the surrounding waters, and it engages them to come and take another look.

Several mentioned the *Edmund Fitzgerald* and its last, disastrous journey across these waters. With a few well-placed examples, more people are able to see that you need to pick the time you travel on Lake Superior.

Many visitors were from southern Ontario; enjoying a visit to the park, and it's wonderful to hear statements about how inspiring the area is. These words helps to reinforce a better understanding of where we live through the eyes of others.

The sea-glass on the beach continues to capture the imagination of visiting children, two of whom also helped collect firewood and sweep off the docks. By starting children on these chores early, their future may be filled with more giving, and an opportunity for them to network and make new friends.

A group of five kayakers spent their first night on Porphyry Island as they start a two-week journey to the east — to Rossport and beyond. These adventurous souls arrived to take advantage of a hot sauna and a chat around the fire. Sharing these times with visitors helps again to give us a greater appreciation of where we live and why people are attracted to visit these offshore islands in Lake Superior.

Next week, we will again see tours arriving; hoping for clear skies and flat seas to enjoy the last few weeks of summer.

Outhouse: Completing another job at the lighthouse is always satisfying. The No.10 (Shaganash) Lighthouse will soon be receiving its own outhouse. John Keetch, along with David Morralee and his brothers, Paul and Steven, pose by their creation. [Photo: CLLS]

Lunch: Visitors enjoy soup and a sandwich at the lightkeeper's table after their tour of the island.
[Photo: David Morralee]

Point Porphyry Lighthouse: Standing on the point, a replica completed by the woodworking class from Hammarskjold High School, is bathed in the light of the sunset glow. [Photo: CLLS]

August 30, 2023

Full boats continue to arrive at island

The weather at the lighthouse keeps reminding us that the summer is moving along and that, soon, fall will arrive. With this in mind, our activity is focused on making a list to prepare for the seasonal closure of the light station on Porphyry Island in one month's time.

Whether at the point or working down in the boathouse, it's always with a feeling of gratitude that we are surrounded by this amazing beauty and panoramic view. The birds and ducks are starting to flock together, with cedar waxwings and loons congregating on their patch. Flying in formation, the cedar waxwings are seen from the top of the tower sitting in the treetops, ready to glide to another destination.

Recently, a bear was sighted on the island, but humans need not worry as there's a good crop of gooseberries, raspberries and blueberries to keep him occupied. We can see that the bear is very clever. He starts on the mainland where berries ripen first. He then carries on to this cold Lake Superior island where berries ripen later. By swimming the gap from Magnet Point on the end of the Black Bay Peninsula to Edward Island and then across to Porphyry, he's able to arrive all cleaned up and ready to go berry-picking.

Our tours on the island continue to bring in full boat loads as the summer comes to a close. Early in September, we still have some tours open as many people are returning to school or a job after the summer. This coming long-weekend, there are some openings. This is a memory-making experience. Memories are made from moments that stand out and make us think about our time on Earth.

We've been having a lot of boaters visit the docks recently, and one boater asked about the newly constructed outhouse. He asked, "Where is it going?" and I said, "Number 10." He then questioned me further, a bit fuzzy about my answer, he said, "I know about going number 1 and number 2 in the outhouse, but what is number 10?" I said, "It's one of the lighthouses that Canadian Lighthouses of Lake Superior maintains for visitors." The laugh continued as the story was retold over and over again. There's always lots of chatter on the island.

This week after several weeks of waiting for parts, I was able to get my wooden vessel, *Hidora*, operational again. The points had failed and, after repairs, I cranked the boat over a few times. To my dismay, it wouldn't start! Happily, I found that I had left out the rotor, so no spark was being delivered to the engine. Thanks to other boaters, I was able to complete the repair.

LIGHTHOUSE DISPATCHES

Out here, you need to work together to get things done. Knowledge isn't something that can always be downloaded off of the internet. Wisdom comes from the many travellers that pass this point and who are willing to share.

Nina, another wooden vessel, is being retired at Porphyry this year. She is set up for visitors to learn more about boating in the last part of the last century. Like a baby, the boat is going to be placed in a cradle and, once secured, hauled up the beach, out of the water to stay "on the hard".

Bringing people together to help out on these projects is all part of the visitor experience. Through hard work, many volunteers keep the site ready for boaters, kayakers, and tourists to enjoy this part of Northwestern Ontario. What a joy to be able to help people interpret their surroundings, share the story of trans-shipment and nation-building through lighthouses. Our First Nations community also shares in that story too, as we pay homage to 10,000 years of survival in these harsh but beautiful lands.

As the southwest swell laps on our shore, and the clouds are ready to dispense of their cargo, I better get the washing in off the line and get a hot cup of tea underway.

Black Sands Tree: (L to R) Jorma Halonen, Marvin Vantaa, Gerry Vantaa and Elaine Bagdon explore the black sand volcanic beach of Porphyry Island while posing beside a tree that cracks rocks to get to water below. [Photo: CLLS]

LIGHTHOUSE DISPATCHES

Coral Wave Sailors: Kristina Pulkki and Aaron Tator, with deckhand Suki the cat, sit enjoying the solitude, a sauna and a Porphyry beer crafted by Lakehead Beer Company to commemorate 150 years of lighthouse living. [Photo: CLLS]

Tower picture from above: Visitors enjoy the view afforded them as they capture a moment from the light tower at the Point Porphyry Lighthouse located 15 kilometres east of Silver Islet. [Photo: CLLS]

September 5, 2023

Lightkeeper life ongoing ahead of winter

The sweetwater sea is glistening in the sun as boaters, fishermen and sailors take in the last of the season's warmth. Summer time marches on as migrating birds are enjoying their last adventure together prior to departing the island for southern climes.

Visitors have been on the lookout for migrating monarch butterflies, but so far only a half-dozen have been seen, which reflects a downturn over last year. Our skies are filled instead with smoky air and, because the mainland is warm and Lake Superior's waters are cool, fog appears along the shoreline.

The Sleeping Giant comes into and out of view because of the fog... or is it an illusion? For some Silver Islet charter visitors this week, they never looked back during the crossing and were surprised when they turned around to see a reverse of the Giant!

The long-weekend visitors and guests from Sail Superior came to explore the island, and some came to play bocce ball or take a sauna. The black sand beach also had visitors amazed to find just how hot the sands could get, and they beat a retreat to the shade.

Life as the lightkeeper continues with preparations for wintertime; also making sure the facilities are looking fresh for the next season. It's always nice to have visitors provide support and recognition for the work required to keep things operational. Our volunteers this summer did an amazing job keeping the facilities looking good so that everyone could enjoy themselves.

Visitors this week made donations in the box, which helps to keep things going. Overall, our donations are down over last season. This has been a nationwide trend since the pandemic.

The number of visitors this season is equal to the number of visitors from last year; which is wonderful to see. Fulfilling the mandate of Canadian Lighthouses of Lake Superior is all about connecting people to the history of our area. Although the history of our nation is young in comparison to other countries, now is the time to continue to support organizations that give us civic pride.

The *Alexander Henry* Museum Ship is an example; built by proud men and women of Fort William and Port Arthur in the late 1950s. This former Coast Guard ship, along with the tug *James Whalen*, owned by an industrialist, serviced lighthouses from 1905 until the 1980s. These former working ships supported the lighthouse story for three quarters of a century with brave souls aboard keeping the shipping lanes open.

When visitors come to see the lighthouse, they can see the many displays depicting the roles these ships played, including helping in the many modifications made in 1960 at Porphyry.

As the season winds down, the tents purchased a few years ago with funds from Lake Superior's National Marine Conservation Area, are taken down for safe winter storage. Some of the docks have received some further upgrades and are detailed with red and white stripes — Coast Guard colours.

The great thing about working at the lighthouse is that you get a wonderful view as to what's happening for miles around. Every little noise requires scanning the horizon to seek out the source and to see what's going on.

Big vessel traffic on the way to and from the Lakehead passes by Point Porphyry about 43 kilometres east of Thunder Bay. This ebb and flow reminds us of the city's importance to shipping.

This week, we look forward to our second-last scheduled tour and a rental of the keeper's dwelling on the point.

How I love to gaze out the windows during a stormy night and imagine the keeper and his family warming up by the fire and listening to the radio. Although those days are long gone, the flicker of a candle can still be seen nightly.

Interrupted by the whistle of the teapot, it's time to take a moment to relax prior to going back to doing some more painting.

Moon Rise: Lighting up the lawn and casting shadows everywhere, the super moon rises over Lake Superior between the birch trees on the point at Porphyry Island. [Photo: CLLS]

Sunset: As the sun sets in the west just behind Hardscrabble Island, another day is done. "Red sky at night... a sailor's delight." [Photo: CLLS]

Sail Superior Departs: Donning high visibility survival suits, visitors depart Porphyry Island located 15 kilometres east of Silver Islet. Visitors come to see the black sand beaches, tour the sea-glass beach, and commune with nature. The *Superior Rocket* travels quickly over the water. [Photo: CLLS]

Lake Superior National Marine Conservation Area

Sitting on Parks Canada's red Adirondack chairs at Point Porphyry and gazing at the Sleeping Giant across Black Bay reminds us of the vastness of this land and waterscape. Thanks to the dedication of former Member of Parliament Bruce Hyer, who garnered support for the conservation area across all parties, Prime Minister Stephen Harper announced a plan in 2007 to establish a new National Marine Conservation Area (NMCA) on Lake Superior. Established in 2015, the Lake Superior NMCA was designed to safeguard over 10,000 square kilometres of land and water. Parks Canada prioritizes environmental protection and conservation while offering visitors an experience that also honours our history.

In Canada, there are four other National Marine Conservation Areas working collaboratively with local communities to enrich the narrative of our history while preserving these regions for future generations. Parks Canada has supported Canadian Lighthouses of Lake Superior's leased lighthouse properties and related programs in many ways. In 2016, research was conducted to create visitor experience signage focusing on local shipwrecks, the island's flora and fauna, the history of the lightkeepers, their survival stories, and the First Nations' connection to the area. CLLS has received funds from the federal agency, making various aspects of the site accessible to visitors for educational purposes.

In the early days, volunteers from the Thunder Bay Yacht Club constructed floating docks funded by Parks Canada to accommodate the growing interest in the island. Additional amenities for boaters, sailors, and kayakers were sought to fulfill the need for overnight accommodations through large bell tents. Recently, efforts have shifted to the Trowbridge Island site, focusing on accessibility and the interpretation of the lightkeepers' stories.

Today, Parks Canada hosts annual programming on-site to help visitors connect with the environment. Recently, the "Painting Superior" program was launched, where participants learn beginner painting techniques. The lawn in front of the keeper's dwelling has become a gathering place for budding artists eager to capture the beauty of the landscape on canvas.

Currently in the interim management planning stage, the NMCA is addressing land use with First Nations while also considering programming needs for an influx of over twenty cruise ships. CLLS continues to collaborate closely with Parks Canada to continue supporting visitors' experiences through education and understanding of the area's rich history, ecology and environment.

September 12, 2023

Awe of island remains in full force

As the sun was setting a few nights ago, a new constellation of lights appeared on the horizon next to the Sleeping Giant. What was it? I could see the blink of the Trowbridge Island light nearby. The object, just south of Silver Islet, supported a string of lights and was not moving. After some investigation, it was confirmed that it was the 205-meter *Viking Polaris* at anchor in Perry Bay for the night. What an adventure for visitors to be on Lake Superior, especially after some of the weather we have recently been experiencing.

A week ago, we watched from Porphyry Island as a huge storm made its way north and east along the mainland. From many kilometres away, we could hear the clap of thunder that took over thirty seconds to reach us. You can instantly understand why they call it Thunder Bay!

At the light station on Porphyry Island, preparations were made because of the storm — windows were shut, clothes taken off the line and everything battened down.

In the wind, we could smell smoke from a nearby forest fire and, with some concern, we checked our own island for any lightning strikes. Everything calmed down later, but the light show was fantastic, with huge strikes seen all the way around. The winds we experienced that evening were around 35 kilometres an hour, but no major trees fell and no other damage was experienced.

The wildlife seems to take it all in without any fuss. Again, we are seeing the birds gathering prior to traveling south to warmer climes. Our monarch butterflies have yet to return. So far, we have seen only a few.

Over the weekend, we had a few boaters in to use the sauna and take the children for a walk to the lighthouse. It's great to see people using these facilities that the Department of Fisheries & Oceans Canada leases to us. Canadian Lighthouses of Lake Superior has a mandate to connect the lighthouse story to the public. Each time another sign is put up or more information is gathered, it offers the visitor more context and understanding of the area that they can later share.

Thrown over the cliff's edge, a lot of artifacts are still being washed up on the shore. The sea-glass continues to hold the attention of youth. Finding a piece of glass represents history thrown from the lightkeeper's hand a century ago, and it could soon be fashioned as a piece of jewelry!

Our last two tours of the season were nearly full, with lots of excitement when they finally come ashore. Each tour consists of a walk to the black sand beach, a tour of the light station, and sometimes a taste of Donny Wabasse's cooking.

This summer, Donny has been tantalizing visitors with recipes that he's gathered from visiting volunteers. This past week, we had some Queen Elizabeth cake. The recipe apparently appeared sometime prior to the Queen's coronation, but today we remember that it was only a year ago that she passed on. The cake quickly left the plate when presented to guests — everyone was satisfied with the date and coconut ingredients.

This week, we had Nancy Ringham and her family and friends visit. Some of Ringham's friends were doing a three-week

A group rests after the tour around the lighthouse point and grounds. Front row, left to right: Ruth & Bruce Wilcox with Ella, Nancy Ringham with Arlo & Bill Ringham. Back row, left to right: Carol Besignano, Paul Morralee, and Kasey Etreni.
[Photo: CLLS]

counter clock-wise tour of Lake Superior. Their experience was, as they said, "Magical everyday."

Supporting the Porphyry experience, Gordon and Karin Mackenzie raised three hundred dollars selling 'friendship knots' and lighthouse cookies during Nipigon's Blueberry Festival. The Mackenzies had stayed at the lighthouse and volunteered for a week this summer as host-keepers. Now, to see them raise more awareness and funds is heart-warming, and helpful. THANK YOU!

As the site slowly shuts down, there is lots of work that needs to be undertaken; from putting picnic tables away to taking down signage and ring buoys. With many people visiting this past summer, a list is created from suggestions made by our visitors. There is always room for improvement, and finding new ways to engage people is the goal.

The waves continue to lap against the shore. The wind continues to swirl, and the sun, well, it's hiding right now. Must dash now to the other end of the island to complete another project prior to dinner. Tea time will have to wait.

A man and his dog on the helipad and other visitors explore the point at Porphyry Island on an overcast day as summer fades. [Photo: CLLS]

LIGHTHOUSE DISPATCHES

September 19, 2023

Lighthouse sees record number of visitors

The incredible summer weather continues with calm seas and warm days as the station prepares for a winter break from all the action. With sunny skies, it's a pleasure to work at closing things down, especially knowing that, this summer, the lighthouse received its highest number of visitors ever.

Over the summer, Porphyry Island had 187 visiting boats, which transported 922 visitors to the island, including another 41 people who paddled Lake Superior in their kayaks. Boating traffic is now slowing down, but we are still seeing many fishing boats trying their luck on Black Bay.

Canadian Lighthouses of Lake Superior dedicated this season to celebrating the 150th anniversary of the Porphyry Island light station, but it was not done alone.

Lakehead Beer Company gave us some added support this summer through their Porphyry beer sales, made from rice. They provided the lighthouse group with excellent exposure, but also a donation to offset the cost to build the 1873 Porphyry Lighthouse model. The beer company helped to generate community spirit, which was inspired by the Thunder Bay Yacht Club's social committee.

Sitting on the Parks Canada Red Chairs at the point, and looking towards the Sleeping Giant, it's reassuring to have the help from the city and area to support the on-site programs. Next month, the lighthouse group will have a small installation at the Thunder Bay Museum to share the 150th anniversary with people who were unable to visit the island this season.

The lighthouse group now operates three light stations on Lake Superior with Porphyry being the main attraction. Over the weekend, lots of the jobs were completed; from pulling out some of the docks and mooring balls, to moving things inside for storage.

Today, I saw a flock of blue jays around the lighthouse while the squirrels are up in trees raining down pine cones everywhere. The deciduous tree leaves are starting to yellow along with the shrubs, and our moose has returned, leaving tracks down the lighthouse path.

Four teenage girls enjoyed the weekend exploring the island, collecting sea-glass and taking in a campfire with s'mores. Hearing the laughter and seeing the use of the facilities is great as many volunteer contributions and donations keep the site up and running.

Later that evening, I sat indoors just watching the big fluffy clouds passing by with a book in hand; being grateful to have the opportunity to take in the view, thinking of the many hardships that lightkeepers had to endure over the years maintaining the machinery, and the effort to keep the light illuminated.

Beside the fog alarm building, I have my own project to remind me of a lightkeeper's hardships, as the generator's carburetor has become plugged and is not operating. With a headlamp and tools, I removed the carburetor to try to clear the jets on my makeshift work table. The work is without satisfaction, and now we use a backup generator as it's only a few more days until the close-up.

Preparing for the next season has included cutting down some deadfall and splitting it to dry over winter. Everything

From the window of the Porphyry Island lightkeepers' dwelling, clouds form over Lake Superior creating moments of reflection. The weather this summer has not been without some big storms and giant thunder bolts.   [Photo: CLLS]

done now will help set the tone for next season. With less than a week to go until departure, I am making more time to enjoy the experience of being near Superior's awesome beauty.

To think, you can look out of any window and see for miles and miles, and even see the United States! It's so calming and enjoyable to just "be", and not always "do"!

Next week I will share some more highlights of this summer and ways you can get involved over the winter months with the lighthouse group. 🚨

Sage Carlson (left) and Teagan Hansen point out a spot on the horizon where two extinct volcanoes from the mid-continental rift can be seen. The rift, from 1.1 billion years ago, created several other volcanoes on the Black Bay Peninsula, and helped form the basin in which Superior now sits.

[Photo: CLLS]

LIGHTHOUSE DISPATCHES

September 26, 2023

Island guests had sense of discovery

As seasons change, so do our perspectives. Fall is now upon us. The leaves are starting to fall on the island as preparations are completed to close up the facilities for the season.

On Friday last, two souls were transported aboard my wooden motor vessel *Hidora*, built at Thunder Bay in 1963, as I returned her to home port. My passenger, Donny Wabasse, had helped as site manager, cooking and coordinating the dwelling visitors and guests and, after not leaving the island once for three months, I am sure he is happy to be home!

As with any story about what these lights on Superior offer, it is difficult to put it into a neat little box and say, "This is what the summer was like." Meeting 1,000 people in the summer and hearing about how they found the lighthouse interesting was really an awesome experience. Many of the guests have a sense of discovery as they'd heard through word-of-mouth about this unique destination on Superior and ventured, sometimes, into the unknown.

Half of all Canadian Lighthouses of Lake Superior's visitors came by charter boat or through an outdoor adventure company or organization. The Thunder Bay Yacht Club, Voyageur Outward Bound group, Naturally Superior Adventures, and Such A Nice Day Adventures all took advantage of renting houses and tents on the island for their expeditions; while Sail Superior and Archie's Charters did the main lifting with around 50 boat-loads landing on the shores for full interpretive tours, nature walks and forest bathing.

The Thunder Bay Hiking Association worked hard with other volunteers to maintain on-site trails at Porphyry Island during the spring cleanup. There were also 2,000 volunteer hours invested by host-keepers, artists-in-residence and local power boaters, all to fulfill our organization's mandate to connect the public to Lake Superior's nautical history and nature. Outhouses, picnic tables and dock works were some of the improvements made on-site in the summer, while a local school engaged woodworking students to build a replica of the original 1873 Point Porphyry Lighthouse.

Sharing with local dignitaries, guests, volunteers, sponsors, and visitors, the replica light built by Hammerskjold High School students was unveiled July 1st, marking 150 years of history. To see the pride the community has taken to share history on this little island 43 kilometres east of Thunder Bay was a humbling moment. Memories tie back to other local stories of the 1905 tug *James Whalen* or the 1960s icebreaker and lighthouse supply vessel *Alexander Henry* Both vessels can still be seen dockside in the city of Thunder Bay.

This season, the Transportation Museum of Thunder Bay, Science North, Parks Canada and Ontario Parks all connected in some fashion with Porphyry to entice visitors and facilitate their choices in Superior Country. Ontario Parks' Sleeping Giant Provincial Park accommodated CLLS with two presentation times to allow us to share with their visitors the attractions at Porphyry Island Provincial Nature Reserve and Trowbridge Island.

The Lake Superior National Marine Conservation Area, Great Lakes Cruising Club & Foundation, Thunder Bay Museum and others all made substantial contributions and assisted in telling the

The light station situated on Porphyry Island on Black Bay awaits new and returning visitors for next season to explore the rich geological, environmental and historical stories. The two keepers' dwellings and light tower make up part of the outbuildings and facilities on the island. [Photo: CLLS]

lighthouse story. Thunder Bay Tug Services, for instance, helped with the moving of the 1873 Point Porphyry model, and Camp Bay local, Jim Dyson, was there to assist at every step of the way.

To keep things cool, the Thunder Bay Yacht Club's social committee coordinated with Lakehead Beer Company to create Porphyry beer in celebration of this momentous occasion. One young couple that had planned to visit the light earlier in the summer, were, until last week, delayed raising a glass of celebratory beer to toast 150 years of lighthouse living.

CLLS is grateful for the support of the local print media for providing an opportunity to share the story more widely. To the U.S. market, we had *Northern Wilds*; locally, *Bayview* and *Walleye* magazines shared some of our articles and events, also with the help of 99.9 The Bay radio.

Many times this summer, I met visitors who expressed interest in the weekly *Chronicle-Journal* column, "Lighthouse Dispatches". A big thank you goes to the readers of this column for their feedback and support. And to the *Chronicle-Journal* that posted images, articles and edited 11,000 words in 18 articles —thank you!

Next season is going to be very dynamic as many changes are being planned at the three lighthouses. In the city, we are hoping that residents will see CLLS's small installation at the Thunder Bay Museum next month, plus attend a few lectures; one that will focus on the Trowbridge Island Lighthouse and its 100th Anniversary.

Thunder Bay and area is fortunate to have access to these CLLS lighthouses under a 10-year lease agreement with the Department of Fisheries and Oceans Canada. Donations help too, and we are thankful to all of our supporters.

Looking forward to, next year, having the privilege to enjoy, to share and to educate people on the might and beauty of Lake Superior lighthouses.

LIGHTHOUSE DISPATCHES

2024

Now, a Veteran Lightkeeper

LIGHTHOUSE DISPATCHES

May 21, 2024

Island lighthouse being prepared for season

With the migration of birds, and spring in the air, the lighthouse is reopening for another season of connecting the community and visitors to our historic lighthouses on Lake Superior.

Our industrial trans-shipment city of Thunder Bay is abuzz with shipping traffic on Superior, and we are already seeing many shipments of potash leaving the port for far away destinations around the world.

Canadian Lighthouses of Lake Superior (CLLS) helps share the story of shipping and transportation by fulfilling its mandate to educate the public on the purpose and values of our nautical history and lighthouses. This work cannot be done alone, and requires the spirit of many to uphold an attraction that builds economic development and creates a strong tourism destination in the region.

Over the weekend, the docks were moved from their storage bay to Porphyry Harbour with the kind donation of time and expertise by Archie's Fishing Charters and Lighthouse Tours. This year, the water level is 0.45 metres, or 18 inches lower than usual, which will create more obstacles and obstructions for boaters to avoid.

The Porphyry Island lighthouse, located 43 kilometres east of Thunder Bay on Black Bay, is being readied for the season, with 24 host-keepers and eight accompanying artists-in-residence booked for their one-week terms.

We still have an opening for a host-keeper or couple from June 23-30 to help with lighthouse setup. Go online at CLLS.ca to apply, and to find further information.

The trees are starting to bud on the island, which is three weeks earlier than usual, and it's rather dry for this time of year. We've already noticed bear scat on the beach, as the bear could be giving birth away from the mainland. Moose tracks up and down the trail can also be seen.

Our first visitors arrived on the island, not only to offer a helping hand but also to celebrate Joe Marcella as a former board director, volunteer and founding member of CLLS. Marcella is well known on the North Shore, along with his former vessel, *Tug o' the North*. Visitors now enjoy the Paterson Sauna, named after the former Paterson Steamship company. Marcella was credited with the design and construction of this popular amenity at the lighthouse.

He also spent time with summer students, teaching them the craft of woodworking, as they erected another small building on-site. His volunteer spirit will live on in the form of a plaque acknowledging his dedication and appreciation by the board of directors for his can-do attitude.

Another director on our board, Kevin Graham, fashioned the stainless steel plaque with etched text stating, "In recognition and appreciation of Joe Marcella, *Tug o' the North* captain and CLLS founding member", and was presented by Archie Hoogsteen. The family enjoyed a picnic and the fresh spring air.

The lighthouse group operates three lighthouses on Lake Superior, and last year one of them was declared surplus by the government and transferred to the group. The Shaganash Lighthouse, also known locally as No.10 Lighthouse, is now owned and operated by CLLS, with more amenities being added as the season progresses.

At the end of last month, members, supporters, boaters and lighthouse enthusiasts came together to celebrate 100 years of the Trowbridge Island Lighthouse, established in 1924. The fundraising dinner was a success with 150 people in attendance, raising $8,500 for the cause.

The next celebration will be taking place at the Lakehead Beer Company on Park Avenue to launch another beer, "Trowbridge". It is with thanks to the social committee of the Thunder Bay Yacht Club for organizing the May 28 event at 7 p.m. Try the new rice beer, and win a door prize.

If you are looking to book a tour this summer, find out more information at the event as Canadian Lighthouses of Lake Superior volunteers will be available. Sunday tours begin on June 23 and leave from Silver Islet at 9 and 11 a.m.; also on Thursdays.

Now, I must get back to my 32-foot wooden vessel *Hidora*, as I prepare for her voyage back onto the lake. It's going to be another busy season connecting visitors to where we live.

Celebrating years of volunteer spirit, Joe Marcella stands with gathered family beside the Porphyry Island boathouse pointing out a plaque acknowledging his service by the CLLS board of directors. Jill Marcella, Jay Caldwell, Jeanne Marcella, Joe Marcella, Tanice Marcella, Dustin Holtz, Amanda Caldwell, Erin Marcella-Fui, and Jr Fui were also in attendance.
[Photo: CLLS]

LIGHTHOUSE DISPATCHES

May 28, 2024

Island coming alive as volunteers spring into action

From the heavens above to the waters below, lighthouse living captures a wide scope of experience that's the essence of lightkeeping on Lake Superior.

As I stood at the Porphyry Island boathouse, 43 kilometres east of Thunder Bay, the morning winds brought with them a strange and unidentifiable sound. Jumping into the golf cart and traveling to the point a kilometre away, a clatter could be heard as the Canadian Coast Guard arrived at the heliport. The big red and white chopper, adorned with every toy a boy could want, gently landed against a backdrop of the calm waters of Superior.

Wearing bright-coloured immersion suits, two technicians and a pilot were here to provide service to the light. They'd already been to Angus, Welcome, Trowbridge islands, and now it was Porphyry's turn.

An exchange of information took place regarding the construction dates of the light station's buildings. There had always been a bit of a mystery surrounding the boathouse's construction date, but last year at Library & Archives Canada a photo from 1916 showed a newly constructed boathouse, with a large fishing net beside as keepers would also fish to support their income.

The island trees are budding, and the grass is starting to grow. Last year we found the island to be very grey and slower to wake up.

This coming weekend, 33 volunteers will land at Porphyry from Silver Islet to participate in the annual cleanup. The rakes and shovels are ready, and a chain saw is standing by for the trail and homestead grounds cleanup. The Thunder Bay Hiking Association has many of its members coming, which is wonderful as they already know the island, and can again enjoy a BBQ prior to returning to the mainland.

If anyone is interested in volunteering further, Canadian Lighthouses of Lake Superior (clls.ca) has one opening for a host-keeper term from June 23 until the 30th. Host-keepers spend a week, do chores, some project work, and keep the site looking trim and neat.

This weekend also saw some hardworking volunteers from the Silver Islet Yacht Club, Silver Islet Campers Association and CLLS, a joint partnership of the Silver Islet Harbour Association, putting in docks using a big crane. The team gently floated the docks and locked them into place. In some cases, and due to the low water level, some adaptations had to be made.

Many years ago, "Friends of Porphyry Island", made up of Silver Islet volunteers, managed the lease for the light station. When the Silver Islet docks went into disrepair, it was through the actions of many volunteers that the funding of the breakwall and pier reconstruction began. This work helped our lighthouse group facilitate the transport of more tourists to the island safely. Nearly three million dollars was invested by all levels of government, and now four times the number of visitors enjoy the use of the harbour facilities. Let's remember, had it not been for volunteers in the first place these facilities would not have been able to serve the cruise ships.

Hovering over the Point Porphyry light station, a Canadian Coast Guard helicopter brings technicians and surveyors to assess the site. Leased by Canadian Lighthouses of Lake Superior, these sites are inspected every five years, while the light is checked every two years. [Photo: CLLS]

LIGHTHOUSE DISPATCHES

My wooden vessel, *Hidora,* my home away from home while at the light station, has been held in slings in the water overnight to soak the bottom boards. Last night, and whilst asleep, the boat rocked suddenly. I got up quickly, opened the door and said "get off my boat" only to find it was partly a dream. The end of the sleeping bag got soaked because as I got up it went into the bilge. So much for sweet dreams!

See you at the Lakehead Beer Company today at 7pm at the corner Park and Cumberland for the launch of a new beer commemorating "100 Years of Trowbridge" light station. Cheers!

With the newly painted Silver Islet General Store in the background, the place had become a busy hub over the weekend setting up docks to accept visitors. Locals gain much benefit from the wonderful facilities. Here, volunteers are working hard to meet the cruise ship and local boat traffic needs.

[Photo: CLLS]

June 4, 2024

Cleanup covers gamut on island

Inside the Porphyry Island boathouse, waiting for the annual cleanup volunteers to arrive, the spring weather was all around us. Using Starlink technology, we watched as a trough of weather starting in Duluth came up the North Shore passing Thunder Bay and heading straight for us. Unbroken, wet, inclement weather on the radar was all we could see for the next three hours, but attitude determines altitude; we were ready to go no matter what!

The first of three groups arrived, mostly from the Thunder Bay Hiking Association, ready for a day of chores and activities to make the lighthouse ready and safe for summer visitors who, last year, numbered 1,000. A campfire was set as a welcoming sign, and fresh, dry work gloves with shovels, rakes, crimpers and spades were at the ready.

Laughter filled the boathouse as chores were divvied up and further explained as to what the outcome of the work was. One team of four guys set off to the homesteads at the lighthouse point, one kilometre away, to make beds and clean windows, which received a bit of a chuckle!

Another team went to mulch up the garden to make it ready for some beans, peas and beets to be planted later, with the rhubarb already well on its way. The lighthouse garden helps visitors comprehend the challenges of living on a cold island isolated far from the mainland.

Back at the boathouse as another group was arriving to take on some of the trail network, a 5-meter wide bell tent was erected, in the drizzling rain! If you are looking for what makes a volunteer thrive and survive, it's pure determination to get a job done.

Later, after Archie Hoogsteen of Archie's Charters delivered the last boatload of volunteers, he offered his boat's power to pull the dock off the beach in anticipation of the local and transient boaters looking for a place to tie up in the coming season.

On the island in the summer months, many people love to walk the trails. Most of the island is part of Porphyry Island Provincial Park Nature Reserve, while the lighthouse footprint, road and harbour area are under Department of Fisheries and Oceans Canada jurisdiction, which are in turn leased by Canadian Lighthouses of Lake Superior. For more than 120 years while lightkeepers lived on Porphyry, there had always been a shoreline trail all the way around the island. There were practical reasons for this. The shoreline trail was used to reach the many beaches where, in the event of a shipwreck, survivors might be found. The trail was also used to search for driftwood and other things that would blow ashore. Former lighthouse children who now come as visitors always relate to their journey on these trails of discovery in the rich and dense boreal forest with occasional arctic-alpine disjunct plants.

Discovery was afoot for the many volunteers, too, as they walked the trails to re-flag them. Most hikers took to the beach, cleaning up plastics and debris swept in over the winter months. The main road through the centre of the island towards the light was given a good going- over, with leaves raked up and deadfall cut from winter blow downs.

As the smoke from the campfire encircled the boathouse, volunteers were found around the barbeque fixing up hotdogs and hamburgers. There were lots of tasty treats as many had baked cookies and some presented chocolate. A fitting reward to a great group of volunteers who, beyond self, are making a difference to help safely connect people to our beautiful North Shore environment. Porphyry Island is also part of the TransCanada Trail system (also known as the Lake Superior Water Trail) which supported the clean-up with a small grant.

Next Wednesday, June 12, at the Prince Arthur Hotel at 7pm, join us for the CLLS Annual General Meeting and hear from Allan McNeice, former lighthouse technician, as he shares some outstanding facts of "100 years of Trowbridge" including the amazing light apparatus.

Now, I'd better go find some dry clothes and get myself a hot cup of tea. It's been a busy start to the season thanks to our volunteers!

After a few hours of work on the Island, colourful volunteers gather to swap stories and enjoy a tasty barbeque by the Porphyry boathouse as the rain abated. [Photo: CLLS]

Lake Superior Water Trail

Celebrating Canada's 150th anniversary included the opening of a new route called the Lake Superior Water Trail (LSWT) in 2017. Established after many years of research and consultation, the water trail runs from Thunder Bay in the east and south following the north shore of Lake Superior to Sault Ste. Marie. This is part of the TransCanada Trail system which is the longest network of multi-use trails in the world. Two stops are featured on the LSWT — the Porphyry and No.10 lighthouses — and these include comprehensive visitor information sign boards that focus on the history of the area, maps of the region and safety information for paddlers.

Canadian Lighthouses of Lake Superior's journey in the early days to establish two of the sixteen stops along the trail can be credited to the work of Joanie and Gary McGuffin. Working from their own experiences canoeing around the lake and being part of the Lake Superior Watershed Conservancy (a bi-national organization protecting the health of the aquatic environment), they engaged communities, organizations and parks along the Canadian shoreline of Superior.

Educating the public on the opportunities to explore the vast expanse of the lake along with making it accessible were among the main reasons for establishing the LSWT. Connecting with First Nations, Ontario Provincial Parks, and other organizations, the water trail also helped to create economic opportunities in the region.

The TransCanada Trail system has provided many years of annual funding to help with the maintenance of the trail structure on Porphyry Island. Help has also come from many volunteers including the Thunder Bay Hiking Association which brings dozens of volunteers every year to help maintain the trails. Young and old can now access these trails. For kayakers and canoeists, the Porphyry site offers tenting areas and a sauna in which to unwind after a day on the lake.

The safety signage has played a big role in educating people who venture onto the lake as it provides information that many are not aware of. As an example, in 2016, a visitor to the island was swept out into the lake by a rip current. Although the lightkeepers back in the day were aware of these currents, visitors today are not. Now, the signs help to keep everyone safe.

LIGHTHOUSE DISPATCHES

June 11, 2024

Preparation for season ongoing on island

As the trees start to unfurl their leaves and the rhubarb patch is out of control, spring is moving along quickly. The monarch butterflies have returned to the site in bigger-than-usual numbers, finding many tantalizing dandelions along the way. Dancing in the wind, these well-travelled insects, with brightly coloured wings, seem not to be affected by the wind that's been coming from the north over the weekend.

Thunder claps and clouds keep us watching as the weather can change rapidly on the lake. Fortunately, Porphyry Island light station has a huge panoramic view of the lake, and in some directions we can see 40 kilometres.

This weekend saw some Canadian Coast Guard search and rescue action past Passage Island and Isle Royale as the 689-foot *Michipicoten*, carrying low-grade ore, hit something on its outward journey from Two Harbors, Minnesota. The radio chat was impressive, with calls from an overhead Canadian Forces Hercules, ready with a parachute jumper if the case warranted. It was only the day before that over Black Bay another search and rescue exercise was underway, but this was for training purposes.

With more passenger traffic on the lake, it's becoming a yearly ritual for everyone to work together and to co-ordinate and practice for any eventuality. By offering fixed aids to navigation, the lighthouses are one part of the boating picture in regards to safety.

Captains need to have up-to-date charts, a good compass and radio, and let someone know about their trip plans. Lake Superior and the work done by the light stations help keep boaters navigating a safer passage, because who knows what you will do if you drop your phone in the water!

At the station, we had a work team of two Andrews and two Pauls, which created some fun moments as docks were slid into place. Docks used for the commercial boats were refloated, fitted and anchored with an adjoining short boardwalk, to help reduce the amount of caustic sand arriving on the vessels.

The many newly built picnic tables from last year are in place, allowing many visitors over the summer to enjoy a peaceful view, or lunch with friends. We often see Black Bay fishermen use the facilities for a break, or cook up a shore lunch over the fire. You can book your own tour online at clls.ca that departs on Thursdays and Sundays from Silver Islet to Porphyry Island, or check out Sail Superior for the Lighthouse Trail Discovery Tour on five set dates during the summer, departing from Thunder Bay.

Cold, fresh water was pumped from the lake and into the basement cistern of the keeper's dwellings for our water supply.

The cisterns need to be filled again later in the summer as water is used for the garden, dishes, and sometimes laundry.

This weekend saw the keeper's dwelling filled with two 30th birthday celebrations from a visiting group of friends. As usual, the retort upon return to the mainland was, "we needed more time to visit the island."

When we think of attractions in the area, Lake Superior is the elephant in the room. It's so pristine, clean and wild that it's always refreshing for visitors to explore. Sometimes I wonder how living behind a ribbon of rail, trans-shipment facilities and other barriers in the city of Thunder Bay holds us back from exploring our own backyard.

With the lower water level, the island has more real estate than in previous years; many are able to hike along the shoreline, which is a nice addition.

Coming up on Wednesday of this week at the Prince Arthur Hotel, Canadian Lighthouses of Lake Superior will be conducting its Annual General Meeting. This year we celebrate 100 years of Trowbridge, and Allan McNeice, former Canadian Coast Guard technician, will be sharing with us one of the most historic and beautiful lights on the Canadian side of Lake Superior. He will be talking about Trowbridge's Fresnel lens from around the 1890s, made of brass and cut glass. Also some updates will be shared regarding the Trowbridge Island infrastructure upgrades that have recently taken place.

It's time to be going as there is more to do to prepare for the season, and until then, enjoy the day.

White fluffy clouds pass by as the docks fill up with boaters who come to enjoy the serenity and silence at the Porphyry Harbour. [Photo: CLLS]

June 18, 2024

Adventure on Trowbridge Island

Inclement weather, fog, swell, chop and more was coming our way as our charter boat's windows steamed up with excitement. Preparing for the adventure to Trowbridge Island has been going on since February with most volunteers from the Thunder Bay Hiking Association booking a seat. As the first of two crews left for Trowbridge Island Lighthouse located near to the feet of the Sleeping Giant, the fog closed in. Mixed with the emotion of being on a charter, and the question about how our landing might be, our captain brought us safely to shore.

Trowbridge Island is a small craggy island with a dash of boreal forest atop, arctic-alpine disjunct flora around the shore; with little mammal life but lots of birds catching insects in the air.

The first duty was a safety orientation to the island — not to scare volunteers, but to give them the heads-up on hazards on the work sites. Years before, the lightkeepers had to work in many difficult weather conditions including high seas, and sometimes freezing rain.

The weather picked up as the first crew ventured to the summit for a spectacle to behold... an 1890's Fresnel lens that's a whopping five feet high, of cut glass and brass. This light operated until 2003 and was part of last week's presentation by Allan McNeice. The poured concrete tower is a taller version of the famed Peggy's Point lighthouse at Peggy's Cove near Halifax, Nova Scotia.

Once the crews had their curiosities quelled, it was onto the work portion to clear trails, open the keeper's yards and scour off moss from the raised-concrete path to the machine shed and other outbuildings. Not only has Canadian Lighthouses of Lake Superior been busy preparing for the "100 Years of Trowbridge" celebrations, so has the Department of Fisheries and Oceans Canada which replaced the 100 steps from the lake level to the tower — a monumental feat. Two weeks earlier, two work crews and a big helicopter slinging wood had arrived to take on this big task. Thanks from the volunteers for the pressure-treated lumber with their perfect angle-cuts; a testament of a job well done! Visitor experience signs had been installed in 2022 to give boaters and tourists an opportunity to understand the significance of these structures to mariners.

Kevin Graham, son of Eve Graham and Gordon Graham (deceased), former lightkeepers at Trowbridge, is spending a week as a host-keeper. This work is challenging as there is not a set routine, nor full support, as it's still early days. Graham is excited to be back on the island — he was three years old when last lived there. Memories for a lifetime are made from these experiences.

After some tinkering with fuel, power and pumps, my boat, *Hidora*, sails on Lake Superior once again after a winter break. *Hidora*, made of wood and powered by a 6-cylinder, flat-top Gray Marine gasoline engine, also includes a wood stove. She is 32 feet in length and glides

Standing proudly on newly constructed pressure-treated steps, volunteers enjoy a day's outing to the Trowbridge Island Lighthouse.
[Photo: CLLS]

over the water with ease, "like a duck", as her former owner once said. She was built at Port Arthur's Perry Marine in 1963, and has already made a trip this season to Porphyry Island and Silver Islet. She will be used as my accommodations at Porphyry this summer.

If you are in the city of Thunder Bay this summer, you can take advantage of Sail Superior's (charter) Lighthouse Trail Discovery Tour leaving in the morning on Saturday June 29th, to see a few local lighthouses, with a stop at Silver Islet. Archie's Fishing Charters and Lighthouse Tours leave Silver Islet on Thursdays and the Sundays for excursions to the Porphyry Island Lighthouse.

Well, as I bob up and down in *Hidora* at Porphyry Harbour and watch the mergansers on the beach, the tea pot whistles, signaling it's time for me to take a break.

Two volunteer crews assemble under the Trowbridge Island lightkeeper's veranda and watch the swallows swoop as ships pass on their way to Thunder Bay. Three CLLS lighthouses are maintained through the generous help of a large pool of volunteers. [Photo: CLLS]

June 25, 2024

1st tour of season, people-mover on-site

As the Canadian flag was hoisted up the pole, the Point Porphyry site was ready to accept the first scheduled tour of the season. With much anticipation and with the help of many, we are now ready for the season... two hundred volunteer hours; by community for community!

Andrew Ehn, a volunteer, is accompanying me as an assistant at the start of the season to help with the host-keeper and artist-in-residence programs. Thirty people will be staying on Porphyry Island, each for the various one-week programs which help sustain the lighthouse and visitor programing.

This week, we will be working to accommodate our future visitors by preparing our gift shop, cutting the grass and installing the final set of visitor information signs.

Our solar powered "people-mover" that came via a grant from Parks Canada's Lake Superior National Marine Conservation Area is now onsite. This vehicle will help our visitors beat the mosquitos on the 1.3 kilometre Porphyry Island lighthouse road by transporting them quickly from the harbour to the point. It will also help us with accommodating potential larger groups from cruise ships, and make it easier to keep people together during the tour.

Visitors are often amazed at the environment that we live in surrounded by this Great Lake. Porphyry Island is home to a Provincial Park Nature Reserve that helps us showcase a typical boreal forest and "Old Man's Beard" (*Usnea florida*), a lichen that hangs from the trees and is a blight for the forest, killing the lower branches as it works its way up the tree. When the Lake Superior fog meets the lichen hanging in the trees, water droplets condense onto the fungi hydrating it and allowing it to live. It looks pretty and whimsical, but it's slowly killing the trees and changing the make-up of the forest.

The island is also surrounded by the Lake Superior National Marine Conservation Area which supports our goals to connect people to the history and natural environment. Many visitors are surprised to find, underfoot, black volcanic sands cast by hot volcanic action, some 1.1 billion years ago. We are left today with an archipelago of islands stretching from Porphyry to Rossport.

With Canada Day just around the corner, we are expecting local boaters to venture out from the city of Thunder Bay to visit us displaying the flag. The water here will provide a shock to anyone jumping in as it has been registering 47°F recently — too cool for me to go for a swim, but that hasn't stopped sauna users who take advantage of the facilities.

Our large bell tent has already had a few kayakers test it out and is available for booking along with the host-keeper's dwelling.

My boat, *Hidora*, now docked at Porphyry, is my home away from home. It's been a busy time as I had some engine trouble which required changing of some filters and tightening up the fan belt. Now, while in Porphyry Harbour, I can enjoy the sunsets and talk to visitors about their future adventures on the lake.

If you're interested in a historic lighthouse discovery tour, start by booking with Sail Superior's *Rocket* at the Thunder Bay Marina. The charter takes you past Welcome Island, Trowbridge Island, and the Point Porphyry lighthouse, where you can take a tour. This is then followed up with a visit to Silver Islet for a walk down the avenue.

Hidora's tea kettle is whistling and bellowing steam, summoning me to take a break.

Next week we will share the happenings of our first of the season artist-in-residence.

Doing a test run with the new solar powered people-mover with a family who enjoyed a day's outing and tour to the light at Porphyry Island. The light station is located 15 kilometres east of Silver Islet, on the other side of Black Bay. The keeper's dwelling and tower can be seen in the background. [Photo: CLLS]

July 2, 2024

Visitors commune with nature at island

Reaching for another log to put on the fire has been the routine the last few days as the summer holidays begin. The weather has been very good for ducks, but for us humans helping engage visitors to a Superior experience, it's been challenging.

The lighthouse road to the point has gotten muddier as the last few days have worn on, and the solar powered people-mover is starting to lose its charge with little sunlight; but the show must go on.

Boatloads of families and friends arrive to take in a wet start to the weekend. The sauna is packed up with wood; fire is ablaze as the door swings open and visitors dip in the lake. BRRR, it's cold at 8° Celsius. The children are playing on the beach with no rock left unturned. The forest is active as visitors walk the trails and commune with nature.

Our visitor tours to the lighthouse have been filled up with a tour on Saturday from Thunder Bay and one on Sunday from Silver Islet. One young lad who came from London, England, to visit family and friends said, "It was the highlight of our visit to Canada." Coming from Britain, incessant rain is something I grew up with!

The wooden vessel, *Hidora*, measuring ten meters in length, has a small wood stove, called a Sardine. It's a small, square cast iron stove with a removable top insert, and a chimney that helps create a good draw. Under wet skies and after chopping wood, birch logs are preferred because, when they burn, they emit good heat.

Meanwhile, at the keeper's dwelling, our artist-in-residence, Lee Angold, is using watercolors to showcase a tree branch with unique bark, lichens and fungi. It's not only taking in the panoramic views that are popular at the light station, but also focusing on the minutiae. Small plant life, especially the arctic-alpine disjunct plants, appear in quantity throughout the island — all you have to do is look.

Angold is a visual artist who enjoys illustrating the botanical and natural science worlds. She is hoping to use her watercolours to exhibit several pieces that could, in future, be shown in Thunder Bay or here, on-site, at the Gordon Graham Gallery.

The Porphyry Island lighthouse also accommodates host-keepers and, next week, we will be hosting our first of several who will be responsible for site upkeep. No.10 Lighthouse will also see some activity next week as we build more amenities for boaters and kayakers.

Today, Canadian Lighthouses of Lake Superior directors, Darcy and Thomas Trist, are busy preparing for future visitors by supplying the wood piles for the sauna and fire-pit. It's through the kindness of volunteer time that a welcoming spirit is created.

One visitor remarked on the site organization and information signs — how helpful they were to understanding the lighthouse experience.

In the evening, the sun was setting, and still a cool breeze continued to blow from the north. On the lake, you always need to layer up your clothing. This is because the weather is always changing and you never know what Superior is going to throw at you next!

In the forest, we can still hear the birds sing, even when travelling on the solar powered people-mover as it is so quiet. One person's bag was picked up by stragglers as our baggage-handling procedure is still in its infancy with the new vehicle.

This weekend, it has been a joy to watch a family take over the keeper's dwelling and go and explore. Memories are made from these moments, later to be brought back and shared around the dinner table. With the exotic flora and fauna, stellar panoramic views, interesting history, all atop a volcanic isle surrounded by crystal clean water, how could you go wrong?

Steam fills the cabin as the copper kettle whistles away. Time to prepare for the next visitors.

Next week, we will hear about our next artist-in-residence and what stories he brings to the lighthouse.

In the keeper's dwelling, artist-in-residence, Lee Angold, prepares a canvas for her watercolour art. She has met many people who have come to share the lighthouse experience. [Photo: CLLS, Andrew Ehn]

July 9, 2024

Porphyry making memories, draws boatloads of people

The summer is now upon us at the lighthouse with calm seas and sunny skies after a string of rather wet (nasty) weather. Our wood supply dwindled as the fireplaces were fed to keep the atmosphere inside dry and warm.

A family ventured to Porphyry aboard the sailing vessel *Frodo* to enjoy some of the amenities at the Point Porphyry Lighthouse, including a hot sauna and a cold dip in the lake. Taking a tour and enjoying the view for the family was a "memory-maker" as the lake swelled and rolled around the reef at the point creating just the right atmosphere. This was followed by the family enjoying a barbeque at the harbour.

On Sunday, the lighthouse had two full tours plus three full boat-loads who enjoyed the forest green, especially when taking the solar powered people-mover with the mosquitos falling far behind.

The garden has been tilled and planted, although a late start, with the lilac bush now in full bloom. What a beautiful sight!

Lee Angold with her accompanying dog, Ember, finished her artist term collecting specimens of fungi on tree limbs for watercolour paintings. Just to look at her pallet of colours was inspiring for how carefully colours were blended.

Meanwhile, our other resident artist, photographer Jon Babulic, who was the former CAO of the City of Barrie, collected photographic images of the site. His goal is to create a coffee-table book of life on the island. From the very small to the very large, he captured images to showcase the diversity of this Lake Superior island and its people.

Porphyry Island is operated by Canadian Lighthouses of Lake Superior and is situated 15 kilometres east of Silver Islet. The not-for-profit organization relies on donations and fees collected at the site to carry on. Parks Canada has offered some funds for capital improvement projects, but operating funds come from the support, mostly in the summer, from visitors. Under the Lake Superior National Marine Conservation Area's mandate, our lighthouse group can continue to build and expand on the services and connections to lighthouse history that visitors enjoy.

Two studies are currently underway at Trowbridge Island Lighthouse (near the feet of the Sleeping Giant) with the old slip and boathouse being investigated from past records and plans re-drawn for future consideration; with another project looking at the feasibility to replace the floor of the keeper's dwelling.

This weekend will see a small celebration of the "100 Years of Trowbridge" wrapping up a schedule of many events including a lecture on the lighthouse at the Thunder Bay Museum, a community fundraising dinner with guest speaker Allan McNeice, and the launch of a tasty new beer, "Trowbridge". The brew, made from rice, has been selling so well it's flown off the shelves at Lakehead Beer Company with a new batch to be ready next week.

This week, the boathouse squirrel has decided to target my boat, *Hidora*, and other boats, looking for snacks which, unfortunately, included my chocolate covered almonds. Now, I look to the grace of other boaters to provide me with some sweets to keep me going.

The fog is rolling around this morning as I complete my dispatch, and it's parted by the blast of my steam whistle atop the kettle — coffee time!

Next week, we will hear about our new host-keeper and new artist-in-residence.

Paul Morralee and a visitor enjoy the view to the east from the lantern of the Point Porphyry Lighthouse with the rich, boreal forest below.

[Photo: CLLS, Andrew Ehn]

July 16, 2024

Visitors bring party mood

The wind and waves battled the southwest edge of Trowbridge Island as an excited crew of party-goers anticipated the landing. Celebrations for the lighthouse's 100th birthday event were in good hands after months of preparations.

An alternate landing route was hastily established as eager visitors excitedly jammed the passageways to be the first to disembark.

Trowbridge Island, named after Charles Trowbridge, former Silver Islet Mine shareholder, harkened back to the challenges of days gone by as visitors climbed to reach the tower way above. Splendid in the sunlight and surrounded by the Superior's turquoise waters and watched by the Sleeping Giant, the 1924 reinforced concrete tower was ready to be opened.

Visitors to the island are very infrequent, except for some kayakers and local boaters from Silver Islet. Swallows were in the air, gliding along and catching insects as visitors watched from the tower after looking at the large Fresnel lens. Near to the island, the Canadian Coast Guard in their red ship with a white stripe was seen actively doing soundings of the bottom of Superior in the area for future charts.

Descending 100 steps of newly constructed stairs, visitors assembled in front of the keeper's dwelling for some lunch, cake and refreshments. Paul Capon, representing the board of directors of Canadian Lighthouses of Lake Superior, provided words of recognition after visitors had explored the interpretive signs and outbuildings on-site.

The light station is located a few kilometres from the feet of the Sleeping Giant, having been established there after the wreck of the ship *Theano* in 1906 on Trowbridge's shoals.

Meanwhile, the Porphyry Island Lighthouse was filling up for the weekend with a fleet of power boaters from Thunder Bay. Margaret Mol, resident artist for the week, shared her art and provided opportunities for boaters and visitors to make their own Christmas ornaments and toy sailboats. On a glorious, sunny afternoon, perched on the point, Margaret created a wonderful oil painting of the large rock off the point with its yellow lichens and dark colours. What talent!

Karen St. John and Fiona Johnstone were in for a one-week host-keeper stay helping to make everyone's time on the island more comfortable and safer. Each week, our lighthouse group holds a safety meeting to discuss on-site hazards and emergency protocols. Fiona and Karen took stock and consolidated our first-aid boxes and stations. We received some training tips on our new AED device to treat heart attacks.

Boaters this week have enjoyed calm seas and good weather. As the warming climate hits the mainland, we are seeing the effects as fog shrouds the shore. The cool waters of Superior are especially inviting as many visitors are taking advantage of a cool dip. The black sand beaches are heating up and visitors are enjoying lying on the sand and just taking in the lapping of the water on the shore. If you'd like, there are tours on Thursdays and Sundays from Silver Islet for the day.

As it is still morning as I write, I'm going to make another coffee over the propane stove aboard my wooden boat and listen to the birds before it gets busy again.

There was a sense of discovery on Trowbridge Island as it is very isolated and difficult to reach. Many pictures were taken, and many memories were made. [Photo: CLLS, Andrew Ehn]

Canadian Lighthouses of Lake Superior welcomed many people from the area to celebrate "100 Years of Trowbridge". Visitors view the island from the lighthouse lantern as they admire the original Fresnel lens.

[Photo: CLLS, Andrew Ehn]

LIGHTHOUSE DISPATCHES

July 23, 2024

Summer sunsets a treat for Porphyry visitors

The sun is now setting further north, near to the head of the Sleeping Giant, as boaters and host-keepers get ready to dream the night away. Rocked by the waves and gentle breezes, boaters wake well rested, ready to take on the challenges of island life.

For me, the day usually starts with the squirrel looking for treats by scratching at the door early in the morning. Living on a boat in the summer at the light station provides some comfort away from all the activities on-site. The station is in full swing as many operational projects are underway, and volunteers are making a dent in the "to-do" list.

Many visitors are still amazed to see the Sleeping Giant from the east side as the head appears on the other side relative to the view from the city of Thunder Bay. The Point Porphyry Lighthouse, located 43 kilometres east of the city, along with two other lighthouses, is operated by Canadian Lighthouses of Lake Superior, a non-profit charitable organization.

The Lavender family, made up of grandparents, grandchildren and parents, rented the house and freely volunteered their time. With gusto, they took on the repainting of the helipad by carefully scraping the paint chips and then applying the standard red and white colours that looks like a target when finished.

As they covered the landing pad with white paint, surrounded by a huge panoramic view, they found time to take in the sight. Due to some inclement weather, the library in the keeper's dwelling served up a good way to take a break. Meanwhile, the grandchildren were given the jobs of sweeping out the bell tent, cleaning up the fire pit and setting it up for the next fire. Every effort helps keep things running. The memories of their visit will be indelible and will be rekindled around the campfire later while taking in the constellation of stars.

Artist-in-residence, Heidi Burkhardt and her niece Rike, enjoyed a week at the light station. Heidi organized an art lesson for the children and the rest of the family. What a great time to spend together as a family!

Not only were the host-keepers blessed with an art lesson from Burkhardt, but so were the rest of the visitors who found her painting many landscapes around the point. Filling seven canvases with island vistas, she shared many landscapes with visitors who had come for the day aboard charter boats.

There are still some openings on the tours on Thursday or Sundays to Porphyry Island from Silver Islet.

Most visitors are amazed at seeing several extinct volcanoes and hearing about how the island was formed a billion years ago, along with the lighthouse story. I enjoy hearing people's observations of the area. Most are just surprised at the clean water, ecology and interesting lighthouse anecdotes.

Save the date of August 17th for the annual carnival on Porphyry Island which, this year, consists of an eco and history tour, a lighthouse film from the 1980s, a fish & chip dinner, and entertainment provided by Scott van Teeffelen. Parks Canada will also be hosting a ""Painting Superior"" activity so visitors can capture their experience through art on the day when boaters also serve visitors a tasty meal. Bring your deck chair and enjoy the entertainment.

Time to get going as the tea kettle is about to whistle its tune.

Next week we will learn about our two new host-keeper teams and the work being undertaken at the No.10 Lighthouse.

Surrounded by Lake Superior, host-keepers scrape and clean the helipad. Still active today, the heliport is used by the Canadian Coast Guard to service the light. Porphyry Island is on the other side of the Sleeping Giant, east of Thunder Bay.

[Photo: CLLS, Andrew Ehn]

LIGHTHOUSE DISPATCHES

July 30, 2024

No.10 lighthouse host-keepers comfort visitors

Stepping out of the sauna and looking up to the heavens above, I am left bewildered by all the stars, and the quiet now that the storm has passed. Superior kicks up often and, over the last few days, the waves have been pounding the shores and keeping some boaters at bay.

Karin and Gordon Mackenzie left this morning on their vessel *Fair Haven*, heading north to Nipigon. They'd been waiting a day for calmer seas. They had been serving again as host-keepers, and this year they took on another challenge: No.10 Lighthouse! Also known as Shaganash Lighthouse, it is 54 kilometres directly east of Thunder Bay. The old wooden tower built on Number 10 Island in 1922, now has a temporary dock, a full service outhouse, picnic tables and groomed hiking trails. The Mackenzies' dedication to building economic development opportunities, tourism and recreation in the area through their volunteerism is well recognized. Many thanks to them!

The Gauley-Walker family consisting of Oliver, Jaclyn and Addison, secured the home front in the bunkhouse as staff and volunteers were working the day at the No.10 Lighthouse. As host-keepers, they provided comfort to visitors who have been continuing to pour in while also completing some chores. Addison enjoyed swimming at the beach, riding her bike, and visiting the sauna. Jaclyn is the daughter of Foster Gauley, a retired photographer for the *Chronicle-Journal* newspaper.

The Sunday and Thursday tours have really ramped up. Now with warmer, dry weather, operations are in full swing. The water temperature has changed again as the lake rolls over and cooler water comes to the surface. Swimmers in the bay have enjoyed a cool and refreshing dip at 17°C.

Ten kayakers from Such A Nice Day Adventures, starting from Silver Islet, took advantage of all the amenities and enjoyed a tour at Porphyry Island. This included the new solar powered peoplemover. Gliding effortlessly through the boreal forest and hearing the birds singing was a real treat for the senses.

Our guests arriving by charter boat often ask about travelling on Lake Superior with some windy weather and storms present in the forecast. On Saturday, when the *Superior Rocket* came out from Thunder Bay, and when Archie's Charters came out from Silver Islet, winds reached speeds of 25 kilometres per hour. Seasoned charter captains last year did more than fifty charters trips to Porphyry with only two cancellations due to weather.

On Sunday, the guests arrived in comfort and enjoyed a comprehensive tour of the site, with some bigger-than-usual waves. Point Porphyry offered beautiful views of the surroundings including a freighter upbound to Thunder Bay.

Experiencing Lake Superior is a real memory-maker for visitors; not just because of its bigness, but also because of the diversity of things to experience.

"Painting Superior", a program offered by Parks Canada, is an example of collecting the experiences around you. On August 17, the annual all-day Lighthouse Carnival fundraiser is taking place at Porphyry, and what a great time to learn about the area in which we live!

Gathered around the lightkeeper's breakfast table in the bunkhouse at Porphyry Island, host-keepers along with lightkeeper Paul Morralee (Managing Director) gather to enjoy a meal and discuss the day's chores.　　　　　　　　　　　　　　　　　　　　　　　[Photo: CLLS, Andrew Ehn]

The event will include tours, a fish dinner and local entertainment. Tickets are available online at clls.ca for this unique outdoor experience. Bring a friend.

Each day working at the light stations brings me a unique view of just how much trans-shipment means to the area and how these lighthouses protect that commerce.

Now as I hear the lapping of the waves, and the boiling of my hot water, it's time for a cup of tea and to enjoy the sights.

Seen from a drone above Porphyry Island, ten kayak venturers arrive on shore. They are enjoying a trip on Lake Superior with Such A Nice Day (SAND) Kayak Adventures and in nine days' time will be in Rossport.
[Photo: CLLS]

August 6, 2024

Forest bathing, friendships in order on island

The warm weather continues to attract kayakers and other boaters to these volcanic island shores. Visitors are often surprised to find how different the island is in comparison to the mainland. With the long weekend, we saw lots of sailboats from SUNORA, and boaters coming to enjoy a swim.

The ice-cold waters of Superior have warmed up enough for swimmers to take the leap. Many at Porphyry enjoy a dip at the harbour, which is sometimes accompanied by a yell as a way of acknowledging that the water is colder than expected.

Now in the mid part of the summer many boaters are out and about on the water exploring the coves and bays. Here we find that the hike on the trails is of great satisfaction, with some calling it 'forest bathing'. There is always a new plant species to discover or to just enjoy the silence.

The host-keeping family of Rebecca, Drew, Mathew and David enjoyed the week immensely as they worked at chores and projects. They had travelled from Saskatoon to give their children an experience to remember including a bit of a sunburn. With each day, tasks were laid out and the family took on the work with spirit and vigor.

Marjorie Neill from Cornwall in southern Ontario, enjoyed the experience of host-keeping and kept up with emptying the sauna fireplace, cleaning up the yard, and sharing the odd yarn with visitors.

The Voyageur Outward Bound Ely, Minnesota, group of kayakers travelled across the archipelago of Superior islands in search of an opportunity to give back. Landing at Porphyry, the group took to repairing the road and clearing up the storage area behind the boathouse. It's through this experience, when no one is watching, that volunteers build networks of friends and learn new skills.

As the home front is being well managed by the volunteers, the assistant lighthouse keeper, Andrew Ehn, and myself as the managing director took some time to work at the Trowbridge Island Lighthouse.

Starting early in the day, we took timbers to the island for some further restoration work. The view from the rocky island with a small forest is amazing as we took a moment to watch the holiday boating traffic far away on the north shore.

Midway through the early afternoon, I decided to take a swim, and a few moments later Andrew joined in. The water was so refreshing, and just what was needed to break the humidity. It was very peaceful, and I suggested to Andrew that we sit on a ledge to warm up as we watched swallows swoop over the water catching bugs. Suddenly and without notice, Archie's Charters ferrying passengers, rounded the corner! There was immediately a concern as us swimmers were not dressed for the occasion. Like a walrus, and a baby seal we unceremoniously got back into the water to the chuckles and laughter of the charter passengers. Andrew's toe got bruised in the process. He was quickly attended to by a retired nurse and we wrote up an accident report.

Our Lighthouse Carnival event is taking place a week this Saturday, on August 17, and it includes food, entertainment, tour, films and "Painting Superior" by Parks Canada. Departing from Silver Islet, it's a great way to connect with Lake Superior and meet new and old friends at the lighthouse. Reservations are available at clls.ca.

Visiting from the United States and doing community service, a crew from Voyageur Outward Bound, Ely, repairs the road at the light station.
[Photo: CLLS, Andrew Ehn]

August 13, 2024

Capturing scenes, admiring Northern Lights

Summer-like weather has returned after a cold blast from the north that was accompanied by high winds. I presume this is a notice sent to wildlife that colder weather will return with the ice and snow; but not too early please!

Our host-keepers, Chancy Atwood and son Aaron, were enthusiastic to take on the tasks of helping to operate the light station during their term. There were many visitors to help guide them and with whom they could share the experience and observations while the day-to-day chores were completed. To finish, a swim at the beach was in order.

Artist-in-residence Mary Espinosa continues to paint and create during her term with Canadian Lighthouses of Lake Superior. Constantly amazed by nature, Espinosa has enjoyed capturing the North Shore on canvas. On Saturday and while staff are continuing to work at the Trowbridge Island site located near to the Sleeping Giant, Espinosa painted the scenery around the keeper's dwelling and light tower. We are all excited to see the results.

The birds are filling the trees and chirping away as usual, but the other day, while cycling the forest path, I heard a strange call from a bird high in the branches. This was a signal as there was a big mammal about, and it wasn't riding a bike. It was a black bear, possibly two years old, out for a morning sojourn through the woods. Darting across my path, the bear crashed its way through the woods, knocking over saplings as it went. As I peddled faster and looked over my shoulder, the bear disappeared, but the bird kept up the alarm.

Reaching the point, and watching the flag, high winds continued to push waves hard against the rocks. I found myself mesmerized by the constant motion, the soundscape and vista. The black volcanic rocks topped with orange coloured lichen surrounded by turquoise waters made me think as to how vibrant these naturally occurring colours are. The experience of being on the island continues to awe me with how quickly things can change.

Last night we were able, as a group, to connect with the Northern Lights from the point at Porphyry Island. Starting from the north and moving eastward, as we looked up towards the heavens the sky was filled with dancing colours of green and some reds. Some of our newly arrived host-keepers hadn't seen the lights for years! These are special moments to remember — the experience of being at the light station surrounded by nature.

LIGHTHOUSE DISPATCHES

This past week, we heard the sad news that former volunteer and CLLS board member, Joe Marcella, passed away. He was an ardent supporter of the lighthouse group and readily offered up his experience of the North Shore. Marcella will be remembered for his happy spirit and his can-do attitude while building and designing the Paterson Sauna on site. He will be missed.

This coming weekend, tickets are still available (clls.ca) for the Lighthouse Carnival event featuring Scott van Teeffelen, a fish & chip dinner, historic tours, films and "Painting Superior" with Parks Canada. If you are looking to have an experience on a Lake Superior island, come for the day, meet some local boaters, tour the island and make some new friends.

Time to take a dip in the cool water, wash up and enjoy the day.

At Porphyry Island Lighthouse, Mary Espinosa, artist-in-residence, paints a landscape of the point. She will be showing and selling her work at the annual Lighthouse Carnival this weekend. [Photo: CLLS, Andrew Ehn]

August 20, 2024

Carnival rolls through, artist finishes term

The wind from the east today creates a soundscape that travels across the island to our ears in the harbour. With boats safely nestled away and the weather travelling around us, the sunshine today is very bright. This makes everyone happy because the solar systems are charging the batteries as the days get shorter. Some boaters even started their day with some yoga.

Our four host-keepers, Nicole, Bethany, Donna and Bonnie, enjoyed some time to relax after a busy week of preparations for the annual carnival. Boaters from the Thunder Bay Marina and the Thunder Bay Yacht Club arrived early to prepare the site for our fifth Lighthouse Carnival event. Entertainment, tours, "Painting Superior" with Parks Canada, and the Scott van Teeffelen Band "unplugged" provide everyone with lots to do. Fueled by volunteer spirit, the boaters cooked up a delicious fish & chip dinner. What a wonderful way for our on-site volunteers, visiting guests and family to enjoy this island.

Staff member Andrew Ehn and Canadian Lighthouses of Lake Superior managing director Paul Morralee, both had visiting family to share some time with. With the fire burning bright, the tunes wafting over the water, and the sauna in full use, everyone enjoyed a Superior experience.

For the more adventurous, Parks Canada staff offered up painting with acrylics on the point surrounded by nature. With blankets spread across the lawn, visitors were instructed for one half-hour on how to prepare their canvas and select something to sketch. This provided a break between the historic site tour and screening of a documentary film captured in 1980. Back then, there was a discussion that was ramping up around the future automation of the site. Gordon and Eve Graham were featured along with their sons on what it was like then to live at a light station.

Situated on the eastern side of Black Bay, Porphyry Island is only 15 kilometres away from the hamlet of Silver Islet at the end of the Sibley Peninsula. For visitors from Thunder Bay, they are most amazed at the panoramic views, the magical reversal of the Sleeping Giant, and the pristine nature.

This week, we've seen two pine martens on the road leading to the light station, along with a hawk waiting in the tree branches for a meal. Lots of voles and mice running about as summer starts to fade into cooler evenings with moonlit shores.

Capturing some wonderful scenery, our artist-in-residence has finished up her term with many paintings in tow. This year, Mary Espinosa was provided an opportunity to celebrate "100 Years of Trowbridge" by accompanying a work party. She painted a beautiful picture of the Trowbridge keeper's dwelling and tower.

As my Mum picks gooseberries, we are all excited to do some pie-tasting later.

Boaters attending to and volunteering at the Lighthouse Carnival took to the black sand beaches of Porphyry Island to do some yoga. This is part of the mid-continental rift that left its mark 1.1 billion years ago, by creating this volcanic island.
[Photo: CLLS, Andrew Ehn]

With a host-keeper assisting and with some spare hands, the berries are plucked end and tail for processing. Bubbling up on browning pastry in the propane oven, our lunch guests are anxious to have a taste of what it was like to be a lightkeeper at the station. It took six hours to pick, clean the berries and cook up the pie.

Smiles all around as the pie is devoured in seconds followed by hot coffee and steeped tea. I raise my teacup in a toast to all the volunteers who help to make this place run. Thank You.

As a reminder, charters are still running for another three weeks before the season ends at the lighthouse.

Seen from above from the light tower, "Painting Superior" took place on the front lawn of the keeper's dwelling. Parks Canada provides this activity so that people can engage in another form of connection with where we live.
[Photo: CLLS]

August 27, 2024

Something always delights at Point Porphyry

Mist and fog surrounded Point Porphyry as the temperature and humidity climbed. Recently arrived artist-in-residence, Beth Dugan, from Minneapolis, waits patiently to see the much-anticipated Sleeping Giant.

As the lighthouse crew cooked their wieners over the open pit fire, the fog rolled back slowly to reveal Hardscrabble Island, a natural dike formed 1.1 billion years ago as part of the mid-continental rift. With excitement mounting, the Sleeping Giant was next to be revealed to the joy of Dugan. Something is always new to delight visitors each day at the light station.

Life continues with day-to-day chores. A bucket is filled with fresh water, biodegradable soap and dirty laundry which is turned and beaten with a stick. The rinse cycle is next completed by pouring the contents onto the dock, filling the bucket with cold water, then rinse and repeat. Creating that wind-blown fresh-air scent to sleep upon, what could be better?

Today, there was a clatter from the air, and everyone at the station dashed to the helipad. It was like a scene from a M.A.S.H. television episode from the past. Arriving from the sky was an *Ornge* Air Ambulance ready to do a test run and to survey the site. Aboard were two paramedics, two pilots and a technician coming to take measurements.

Health & Safety is part of the culture at the light station. After making a request to *Ornge* to have the site available in case of emergency, the exercise was necessary. Speaking with *Ornge* representatives helps the onboard crew and staff to learn about the delivery of services to this isolated island. We are grateful for their time and attention as just under 1,000 people visit here every year and, possibly in the future, we will be visited by a cruise ship?

Our solar-powered golf-cart, now christened the "Mosquito Express", is moving people from the harbour to the point in silence, surrounded by trees, birds and a beautiful blanket of moss that covers the forest floor.

Taking a break, our staff practiced "forest-bathing" this week. We entered the forest and selected a place to lie down and look up at the trees while using all five senses. The mosquitoes have left, so the experience was very rewarding without being a blood donor. I was amazed by the sounds of silence, and how still everything was. We could hear in the background families passing by on their way to the lighthouse, but being immersed in nature was a real treat to experience. As we now work to consolidate our reports, build our shutdown lists, and consider next steps, it's wonderful to own a moment of time and just "be".

Our host-keepers, Raija Zatti and Bill Boyce, enjoyed their time replacing steps to the bunkhouse and keeping the fires burning bright for the many visitors this week. During their off time, they kayaked and fished their way around the point and explored the trails on the island. Well done!

Katerina Lanfranco, last week's visiting artist-in-residence, left with all smiles as she was able to connect with visitors who enjoyed and purchased her artwork. Making two dozen fridge magnets, she created a mosaic mounted in a disused window frame! Part of the sale included a donation, which in turn helps keep the "wheels turning".

Next week we are looking to share more experiences from this island, surrounded by Lake Superior and the adventures that come with it. Time to dash to the dwelling for lunch.

Dropping in to survey and inspect the Porphyry Island helipad, technician Jeff Dennison and paramedics David Boer and Philip Marks are joined by pilots Federico Riva and Kief Khanlauian. *Ornge* serves the region with its air ambulance helicopter and fixed-wing aircraft. [Photo: CLLS]

LIGHTHOUSE DISPATCHES

September 3, 2024

Island reflects, looks ahead

The island has been surrounded by windy times this the last week as the summer slowly ebbs away. Life goes on, and the waves rock us to sleep at night, ready to meet the next day and whatever adventures come our way.

Boaters at the dock enjoy the brisk, fresh winds as another gin and tonic goes "down the hatch". With the richness of island life recognized by our visitors they are often overtaken by option fatigue. They ask "What should we do?" Forest bathe, walk in the woods, sit on the black sand beach, or go for a swim?

For our staff, this morning is different. We're in the keeper's dwelling with coffee and breakfast as we prepare ourselves for 32 visitors in the next hour! The visitors climb the tower — the winds are calmer now — and the view is incredible with the turquoise waters churning over the reef. Labour Day is a time for rest and reflection prior to back-to-school and back-to-work after the summer holidays! There are four more tours available online to book in September if you're interested in coming for a visit (clls.ca).

Our final week of regular operations finishes with artist-in-residence Beth Dugan who captured a variety of scenes with her different art forms. One technique she used was to look at her subject and sketch without looking at her hand. The line drawings she created were of familiar horizons including the Sleeping Giant. Another art form was to use photographic paper, laid down with an item on top, such as a twig, and then, by exposed sunlight, it leaves a shadow on the paper. The most prolific of her works were the miniature watercolours. In the end, she filled the artist studio wall with her art. What a delight!

The leaves are starting to turn a little with the mountain berries showing up in bright red. Monarch butterflies have returned this year, but not as many as in years previously. Still, a beauty to behold. In full bloom of bright orange, the tiger lilies huddle at the corner of the keeper's dwelling. This reminds us of previous keepers who lived here, such as Fran and Clifford McKay who were amazing gardeners.

As the season starts to wane, boaters are finding the right time to make the journey and, as was the case with the winds of the last few days, many were held up in Thunder Bay. We watched on radar to see big storms heading our way! One monster of a storm arrives with flashes of light, roars of thunder and huge waves, but we are safe. It's during these nights, as the wind howls around the dwelling and the windows rattle from the thunder that it's good to be inside.

It's also exciting as things start to slow down so that we can take a moment to reflect on the season and start to plan for next year. Our focus will be towards future sustainability of the three light stations operated by Canadian Lighthouses of Lake Superior and how we share these historic gems with others.

As the tea kettle whistles in the kitchen, I must make a dash, for it's teatime; time to look out the window and wait for the next ship to pass.

With amazing skill and perseverance, artist-in-residence, Beth Dugan, shares some of her work on the wall. Porphyry Island enjoys the opportunity each season to host artists-in-residence and host-keepers for one-week terms.

[Photo: CLLS, Andrew Ehn]

September 10, 2024

Calm moments set in as site winterization begins

Now, things are starting to settle down; the island has been bombarded by wind for the past ten days. I presume, with global warming, the weather systems are getting bigger and staying longer. Whatever the weather, we persevere to complete our chores, knocking off items on our wind-down list while still greeting visitors.

It is a nice time of year when the boater traffic starts to tail off and lightkeepers get to enjoy the island. The other day sitting on the harbour's black sand beach, we could see Turtle Head (part of Pie Island), the Sleeping Giant, and between both, on the distant horizon, another, smaller version of the Giant. It's magical to think what the First Nations peoples would have thought about seeing these landforms on the horizon along with the mysteries of thunder and lightning.

Clear skies at night are starting to bring out the constellations with the Milky Way ever-present. Upon the windowsill and across the foot of the bed each night, the tower's light blinks. It's calming to know that, in rough seas, this light is a beacon for sailors and boaters.

The Canadian Coast Guard search-and-rescue lifeboat, *Cape Chaillon*, came for its annual visit. Sailors Dave and Kate DeJong were here for a few days with their three children and were welcomed aboard for a tour of the vessel.

Mr. DeJong helped later with lifting some docks and started by saying, "I can't watch other people work without helping out". It's nice to have people who come and assist in winterizing the site, as many hands lighten the load.

Now, it is all quiet again as the weekend traffic has left to go home, and the waters are calm and temperatures warm. On the horizon, I can see that there is a cruise ship at Silver Islet with its many guests visiting the shore.

Today is laundry day with the usual bucket of warm water from the sauna to complete the task. This past week also included doing some stitching of a favourite pair of shorts. I used a zigzag stitch (thanks Dad) that I am hoping can last to the end of the season.

Planning continues for the next season with our new intern, Andrew Ehn, looking into cataloging and listing items to attend to in 2025. It's wonderful to have the support of the Northern Ontario Heritage Fund to help build up the organization's economic diversity and tourism potential on the north shore of Lake Superior.

Time to tackle the to-do list and take a moment to enjoy the beauty of this island in Lake Superior.

LIGHTHOUSE DISPATCHES

A family visits aboard the Canadian Coast Guard search-and-rescue lifeboat *Cape Chaillon* at Porphyry Harbour. Beatrix, Finn, Oak and Dave enjoy their visit to the Island to explore nature and learn about the movement of ships on Lake Superior. The role of the Canadian Coast Guard search-and-rescue crew was also part of the day's lesson. [Photo: CLLS]

Aboard the wooden vessel *Hidora* at Porphyry Harbour, Paul Morralee, managing director of Canadian Lighthouses of Lake Superior, attends to mending his favourite shorts.
[Photo: CLLS, Andrew Ehn]

LIGHTHOUSE DISPATCHES

September 17, 2024

More winter prep, reflecting on happy memories

Warm weather and calm seas greet us each day as we take time to enjoy the sunshine. The season here is nearing the end, and what a season it has been!

Our visitor numbers to the site this year are equal to that of last year, totalling over 1,000 people. It's nice to know that this destination on Lake Superior continues to educate, entertain and be a space to enjoy the environment. Last week, we managed to see the cruise ship, *Le Champlain*, in the shipping channel near Isle Royale as it passed by heading for Terrace Bay and other North Shore communities.

It's wonderful to share the lake with out-of-town visitors because it helps remind us of what we have. On the night the ship passed, with moonlight glowing off the water, we lit up the lightkeeper's dwelling to send a message, "We live here."

Our work this week has included cleaning up the brush around the keeper's dwelling so that the building might be presentable next summer. This work was completed with a very satisfying bonfire that cast shadows up the light tower.

The steps and sidewalks were also painted standard coast guard battleship grey. Also this week, we drew up the Trowbridge dock and transported it back to Porphyry Island for safekeeping over the winter months. Trowbridge Island is rugged and has little space to store anything because of its rocky cliffs.

Next, keeper's assistant Andrew Ehn, helped haul No.10 lighthouse's dock up the beach for winter storage. After a swim and a lunch at the site, we had a moment to look at the Black Bay Peninsula from a different perspective of the extinct volcanoes. A sailboat passed us by, and we exchanged a wave to send them on their way.

On Thursday, we had our final charter tour of the season with lunch at the keeper's dinner table along with a film screening. And the next day, we had a corporate group of 13 turn up for an exclusive tour of the island, including a walk to the point along Porphyry's south shore.

We had a flock of blue jays pass through, and a few pileated woodpeckers were tapping out their morse code in the woods — tap – tap – tap. Some of the bird life and other wildlife are starting to pack up to move out.

The loons in the bay are also starting to congregate, and the Canada geese have come to leave their calling card on the keeper's lawn. Negotiating the poop is a tricky affair!

We dismantled the Point Porphyry lighthouse model, constructed by the Hammerskjold High School woodworking class. The model is helpful to showcase what it might have been like back in 1873. Imagine, former light keeper Andrew Dick with his wife Caroline having nine children in that place!

With the season nearing the end, it's nice to reflect on the many happy memories of the Lighthouse Carnival, "Painting Superior" activity, the artists-in-residence sharing their work, and the ambitious host-keepers helping to create some order to the site.

The visitors that came this year, while exploring Ontario Superior Country's Lake Superior Circle Tour, certainly helped fill charter seats.

Archie's Fishing Charter helped this year by providing service to bring our many visitors, participants, volunteers and guests to the island. It is by all working together that we can continue to connect visitors to our beautiful area.

Time to drink a cup of tea before settling back into the to-do list.

Casting shadows upon the Porphyry lighthouse tower as the bonfire burns bright, work is nearly completed as the Canadian Lighthouses of Lake Superior closes its three light stations on Lake Superior. [Photo: CLLS]

LIGHTHOUSE DISPATCHES

September 24, 2024

Another season wraps connecting people to island

Seasons come and go and, with autumn in the air, it's time to put the docks up for the impending winter months. This season has been filled with much joy and excitement as we have now completed our tenth season; serving a mandate to connect visitors to our history and natural beauty.

Many of our visitors who departed from the newly created Silver Islet Harbour are excited that, due to volunteer efforts the harbour now attends to the needs of the public, international cruise lines and charters. Archie's Charters and Sail Superior use these facilities to get hundreds of people out onto the water to explore where we live.

Parks Canada, for this season, helped us bring more art to the island through the "Painting Superior" program during the annual Lighthouse Carnival. Participants enjoyed the exposure to art lessons on how to stage a painting and ways to put brush to canvas.

Volunteer groups such as the Thunder Bay Trails Association helped to make sure that the Porphyry station was ready for visitors. The Thunder Bay Yacht Club's SUNORA regatta utilized the site for its annual awards and celebrations after visiting the north shore of Superior. Voyageur Outward Bound, Ely, USA, played a big role in brush work with their kayaker crew who were travelling through the region and enjoying their 45th day in the outdoors. Watching the beach yoga on the black sand beach this summer showed how different groups are taking advantage of this beautiful place to be.

The Trowbridge Island Lighthouse, located near to the Sleeping Giant, also operated by Canadian Lighthouses of Lake Superior, celebrated its 100th year of operation as an aid to navigation. Thanks to many volunteers, the annual spring clean-up was a success and the Department of Fisheries and Oceans Canada also stepped up to fix the wooden stairs to the lighthouse. The site was also home to the first host-keeper term in many years that focused on keeping a safe place for visitors.

Shaganash (No.10) Lighthouse, east of Porphyry Island, also saw lots of activity this season with the installation of a working dock and a new outhouse. This site continues to attract a lot of kayakers, with over forty taking the route to Rossport across the North Shore.

Back at Porphyry, *Ornge* Air Ambulance practiced a trial run after the helipad was freshly painted days earlier by volunteers. The operation and experience were good for all, as we were able to exchange and update information on our health and safety practices.

Back in town this season, we saw the Thunder Bay Yacht Club's "Trowbridge" beer launched by Lakehead Beer Company sell-out, twice! The unique rice beer, cold and with a crisp taste, was a real winner. CLLS is thankful as money from each beer sold is donated to a fund to help keep the lighthouse sustainable into the future. Also, we thank the Thunder Bay Museum for supporting our speakers' series in the spring.

Thanks to the CLLS board of directors, volunteers, sponsors and supporters for helping to make the season a success. Many hands lighten the load. A special thanks goes to Andrew Ehn, our intern, for his hard work, his passion and dedication, and to you the readers for staying with us during this adventure on Lake Superior.

Watch out near Christmas time with the launch of my book titled *Lighthouse Dispatches: Ramblings of a Modern-day Lightkeeper*, which will be sold locally and featuring the last ten years in print accompanied by pictures.

Until then, have a great winter and see you next year!

Projecting images of the island on the Porphyry keeper's dwelling gets your imagination going seeing all of the options for things to do. Next season, the lighthouse will be ready to take on visitors for a day, a night or as a host-keeper or artist-in-residence for a week. [Photo: CLLS]

2025 and Beyond

LIGHTHOUSE DISPATCHES

These "Lighthouse Dispatches" have showcased a variety of milestones accomplished at the Point Porphyry, Shaganash, and Trowbridge Island lighthouses. They also pay tribute to the commitment of volunteers who have tirelessly worked to maintain these light stations and to share their histories with the public.

Canadian Lighthouses of Lake Superior acknowledges the tremendous efforts made by numerous individuals and our lighthouse group is dedicated to preserving all of their contributions by ensuring sustainable operations for the future. To achieve this, diversified revenue streams and increased opportunities for a broader audience to engage with lighthouses are essential. Notably, while significant advancements have occurred at Porphyry Island, both the Shaganash (No.10) Lighthouse and Trowbridge Island Lighthouse are experiencing a rise in visitation and programming, alongside crucial infrastructure improvements such as docks and pathways.

As soon as visitor access to Trowbridge Island is secured and a comprehensive safety plan is established, the site will be equipped to welcome more guests and offer expanded programming. The stunning Fresnel lens and the view from inside the lighthouse lantern atop the concrete tower, alongside its closeness to Silver Islet, will provide tourists with a unique experience that cannot be found elsewhere on the Canadian side of Lake Superior. The island's seclusion will serve as a breathtaking backdrop for appreciating the majestic beauty of Lake Superior, while also allowing reflection on the solitude experienced by past lightkeepers.

Under CLLS stewardship and ownership, the Shaganash (No.10) lighthouse has seen a increase in amenities over the last two years. These improvements will create more opportunities for host-keepers and artists-in-residence to engage in additional residencies going forward. The lighthouse group is also considering the possibility of reconstructing the original 20ft x 20ft lighthouse near the original foundations. This could function as a fully serviced, year-round, off-grid research facility, or used for lighthouse programming during the summer months. The site will continue to act as a hub for kayakers navigating the North Shore.

The potential addition of other lighthouses is currently under review. With recent public use of the Thunder Bay Main Lighthouse (on the breakwater in Thunder Bay harbour) for fundraising activities, there is hope that CLLS could gain regular access to this lighthouse and invite people to enjoy an unobstructed view of the magnificent Sleeping Giant. Providing the public with a platform to connect with nature while learning about the lighthouse's story opens new possibilities, acting as a gateway to other lighthouses and other opportunities.

The sustainability of CLLS operations relies on the dedication of members and volunteers who contribute thousands of hours of support each year. The lighthouse group will have to aim to broaden its mainland activities through additional fundraising events, speaker series, and educational programs in schools. By leveraging additional resources from these initiatives, CLLS hopes to enhance human resources, whether part-time or full-time jobs, to ensure that tourism and economic development continue to flourish in the region.

The lighthouse group will continue to apply for capital funding from federal, provincial, and municipal sources, as well as from other non-profit organizations to build its infrastructure. Maintaining these relationships will only strengthen the social capital already established on these isolated lighthouse islands. While the future appears bright, it requires constant attention to detail and a steadfast commitment to protect, promote, and preserve Canadian Lighthouses of Lake Superior.

Standing on these ancient volcanic islands, with a history that stretches back thousands of years, we pay tribute to those who paved the way for us. We honor the First Nations and Métis peoples who shared their knowledge with settlers to help them thrive in this demanding landscape. We express our appreciation to the lightkeepers and their families, who ensured safe passage on *Gitchee Gumee*, allowing our society to grow and flourish. We recognize the founding board of directors of the Canadian Lighthouses of Lake Superior for their vision and dedication, which cultivated social capital and economic progress along the North Shore.

Our gratitude extends to the federal, provincial, municipal, and non-profit organizations that provided the financial support and guidance needed to develop a welcoming infrastructure and visitor resources. We are thankful for those who contributed their time and expertise during the early days when our path was uncertain. Today, we celebrate the invaluable contributions of our host-keepers and artists-in-residence who bring the lighthouse sites to life. We also honor the community of sailors, power boaters, and paddlers who bravely navigate the elements, embodying the spirit of this magnificent inland sea.

To future travelers, may your journey reflect my own—a beautiful, lasting love affair with the water, land, stunning vistas, and the rich lighthouse history that has shaped our shared legacy!

LIGHTHOUSE DISPATCHES

Index

(*p* = photo caption   *c* = photo credit)

– A –

Adams, Dan   136, 137*p*

Adams family   58*p*

Adderley, Barb   90*p*

Adirondack chairs   226, 279

AED device   310

Ailey, Char   226*p*

Air Ambulance – see *Ornge* Air Ambulance

Aitken, Ashley   237*p*

Alexander Henry – CCG ship   50, 86, 99, 119, 197, 207, 217, 218, 246, 248, 249, 276, 287

Alexander, Mirabai   205*p*

Allain, Suzanne   243*p*

Allin, Melissa   90*p*

Amateur Radio Lighthouse Society   184, 185

Amethyst Harbour   136

Anderson, Allison   237*p*

Anderson, Kraig   23, 28, 235

Angold, Lee   259, 305, 306*p*, 307

Angus Island   292

Angus Island Lighthouse   44, 59, 135

Annual General Meeting (AGM), Canadian Lighthouses of Lake Superior (CLLS)   159, 203, 206, 207, 208, 245, 246, 248, 296, 299

Appleton Judith   104, 105*p*, 106

Archie's Fishing Charters and Lighthouse Tours – see also Hoogsteen, Archie   20*p*, 44, 53, 124*p*, 131, 148, 154, 155, 156, 192, 246, 254, 286, 290, 295, 302, 314, 318, 331, 332

Arctic-alpine disjunct plants   29, 39, 50, 179, 180, 210, 223, 265, 296, 300, 305

Ariss, Iloe   53, 60, 61, 61*p*, 62, 63, 68

Arlo the dog   281*p*

Ashland, Wisconsin   121, 122*p*

Atwood, Chancy   247*p*, 319

– B –

Babulic, Jon   307

Bagdon, Elaine   274*p*

Bailey, Jim   182
         Max   101

bald eagle   185, 270

Balec, Ray   237*p*

balsam fir   179, 252, 265

Bamboulis, Jim   229

Barnhatt, Randy   107*p*

Barrie Canoe and Kayak Club   57

Battle Island Lighthouse   14, 17, 23, 36, 42, 252

Bayview magazine   288

Beatty, Abigail   204, 205*p*, 213*p*, 225, 226*p*, 238

Bedard, Otto   107p

Belanger-Boeckermann   124p

Bell helicopter   218

bell tents   204, 229, 263, 279, 295, 304, 312

Bell's map, 1869   144, 152

Belliveau, Claire   107, 136, 157

Bellman, Ann   107p

Berube, Diane   235

Besignano, Carol   281p

BINGO   121

Bishop-Legowski, Sallie   234p

Black Bay   14, 26, 36, 48, 50, 53, 64, 65p, 76, 85, 106, 107, 110, 117, 121, 125, 137, 138, 140, 148, 157, 161, 162, 167, 174, 184, 186, 194, 195p, 203p, 219, 221, 227, 248, 249, 256, 257, 260p, 279, 283, 298

Black Bay Peninsula   28, 74, 144, 146, 152, 252, 273, 285p, 330

black bear   40, 46, 161, 162, 163p, 197, 210, 231, 266, 273, 290, 319

black sand beach   31, 39, 44, 50, 87, 95, 101p, 150, 166, 177, 178p, 204, 207p, 211p, 226p, 229, 231, 252, 253, 257, 258, 270, 274p, 276, 310, 322p, 332

blue jays   169, 237, 243, 283, 330

Blueberry Festival, Nipigon   282

Blyth Academy   50

Bockus, Diana   124p

Boer, David   325p

boreal forest   10, 179, 252, 265, 296, 303, 308p

Bosquet, Joseph – lightkeeper   21, 23, 58

BOSS program   203, 210, 212, 213p, 238

Bossio, Tony   189

Bottle Point   256

Boudreault, Simon   144, 147p, 153, 154p, 158p, 161

Boutillier, Stella   245p

Boyce, Bill   243p, 325

Bradley, Dave   100

British Columbia   252, 265

Brooks, Adrian   91, 92p, 93
Jane   91

Bruyere, Arden   156p

Buckley, Abbi   205p
Paul   243p

Budd, Sandra   154

Builders On Superior Shores – see BOSS

Burkhardt, Heidi   312

Burlington – ship   248

Buske, Anna   227, 228c

butterflies   15, 46, 123, 125, 126p, 128, 149, 155, 157, 169, 172p, 179, 188, 192, 229, 243, 244, 246, 257, 263, 276, 280, 298, 326

Buzzi, Gayle   26, 30, 31, 32p, 34, 50

– C –

Cain, Pamela   219, 220p, 256, 258, 258p

Caldwell, Amanda   291p
Jay   291p

Canada Day   139, 210, 213, 242, 250, 253, 303

Canada Summer Jobs program   10, 27, 29, 68, 97, 125, 180, 206, 238, 261

Canadian Coast Guard   7, 8, 33, 50, 59, 186, 196, 217, 218, 235, 238, 292, 293p, 298, 299, 309, 313p

Canadian Coast Guard (CCG) ships   60, 99, 119, 207, 218, 328, 329p

Canadian Hydrographic Service chart   3, 4

Canadian Lighthouses of Lake Superior AGM – see Annual General Meeting

Canadian Wildlife Federation   175, 182

Cape Chaillon – CCG ship   328, 329p

Capon, Paul   18, 66, 86p, 189, 247p, 309

Carlson, Joyce   243p
Sage   285p

INDEX

Carnival – see Lighthouse Carnival

Carpenter, Larry 112

Carpick, Betty 83, 85, 104, 105p, 107

Catherine Street Book Society 66

CBC (Canadian Broadcasting Corporation) 59p, 66, 79, 116, 155, 192, 196, 225

Cetz-Huchim, Zack (Zaqueo) 259, 260p, 262p, 267

Chekki, Chen 2

Chimenti, Victor 38, 39p

Chronicle-Journal newspaper 2, 3, 7, 239, 288, 314

CLLS Annual General Meeting – see Annual General Meeting

Coffey, Marlene 223, 224p

Cohen, Simon, 74

Collingwood, Ontario 119, 245

Colourful Communities Project, Dulux Paint 76

Conrad, Alden 141p
       Heather 124p, 139p, 141p, 243p

Cooke, Jack 254p

Cop-Rasmussen, Jacalyn 145p

Coral Wave – sailboat 275p

Country 105 – radio station 19, 20p, 44

Country Neighbours Book Club 123, 124p

COVID-19 128, 171, 199, 236

Cowley, Marie 243p

Coyne, Jen 90p

Cressman, Stephanie 29, 30p

Cristobal – storm 131

Cristofaro, Kain 58p
       Keaton 58p
       Keli 58p
       Sal 58p

Crouse Hinds – electric light 99

Crowell, Colin 205p

Current River Bakery 162

Cuthbertson, Manon 205p

– D –

Dacey, Jim 95

Dahl, Libby 118, 121, 136

Daley, Mark 89
       Steve 89

Dalicandro, Lauren 267, 269p

Dawson, Garry 254p

de Bakker family 223

DeFranceschi, Claudio 243p
       Helen 243p

DeJong family 328, 329p

Delgati, Molly 182

Delta Hotel 203, 207

Dennison, Jeff 325p

Department of Fisheries and Oceans (DFO) 7, 28, 42, 72, 76, 78, 106, 163, 165, 166, 168, 177, 179, 194, 196, 199, 238, 245, 280, 288, 295, 300, 332

Department of Marine 23

de Pencier, Adam 40, 41p
       Hannibal 40

DeProphetis, Kaia 213p
       Paige 213p

Desorcy, Kristen 158p

Devil's Club – plant 92, 179, 197, 252, 265

DeWitt, Josh 158

DFO – see Department of Fisheries and Oceans

Dick, Andrew – lightkeeper 21, 23, 38, 47, 48, 48p, 58, 83, 131, 133, 140, 146, 173, 175, 331

Dick, Caroline 48, 173, 331
       Thomas 244

Dishaw, Daniel 79c

Dittman, Renate 214, 215p, 216

Dool, Berit 237p

Dorian, Ontario 263

Dowds, Liam 85

341

Dowhos, Rosalyn 124p

Dryden, Ontario 35

Dugan, Beth 324, 326, 327p

Duke, Ted 197

Dulux Paint 76

Dumont, Michel 66, 67p, 247p

Dupuis, Nicole 158p

Duquette, Dani 222p

Dykstra, Susan 227

Dyson, Jim 123, 146, 248, 249, 253, 254p, 288

– E –

Eby, Chris 255, 256p

Eckert, Nicole 205p

EcoSuperior 144, 146, 148, 153, 154p, 156, 157, 160, 175, 179, 182, 188, 192

Edinburgh, Scotland 48

Edmund Fitzgerald – ship 137, 270

Edward Island 13p, 45p, 74, 95, 174, 182, 216, 252, 273

Edwards, Wanda

Ehn, Andrew 2, 303, 306c, 308c, 310c, 311c, 313c, 315c, 317, 318c, 320c, 321, 322c, 327c, 328, 329c, 330, 333

Ella the dog 281p

Ellchook, Michael 44

Emerson – ship 247

Emmons, Clair 121, 122p

Espinosa, Mary 266, 268p, 319, 320p, 322

Etreni, Kasey 281p

Exquisite Gold and Gems Inc. 121

– F –

Fabius, Mike 13

Facebook 180

Fair Haven - boat 314

Fathom Five Marine Conservation Area 236

Fecteau, Cyndi 87

Fedorus, Sarafin 222p

First Nations people 48, 116, 144, 151, 152, 177, 179, 194, 197, 200, 221, 229, 252, 265, 274, 279, 297, 328

Fisher, Bob 75

Fisherman's Park – see Lorne Allard Fisherman's Park

fog alarm building 12, 23, 23p, 33, 42, 48, 48p, 50, 59, 117, 135, 145, 196, 197, 235, 235p, 284

Folk Festival, "Live From The Rock" 225

forest bathing 286, 317

Fort William 14, 97, 98p, 135, 233, 244, 276

Franco, Carlo 173, 180, 192

Fresnel lens 23, 28, 59, 233, 235, 246, 247p, 299, 300, 309, 311,336

Frève, Carole 60, 61p

Friends of Battle Island Lighthouse 42

Friends of Porphyry Island 65, 293

Frodo – sailboat 44, 244, 307

Fui, Jr 291p
    Marcella 291p

– G –

Garcia-Lebuis, Lara 226p

Gardner, Tracy 124p

Gauley, Foster 194, 314

Gauley-Walker family 314

George's Market 174, 192, 238

INDEX

Georgian Bay 48

Gerow, Frank 14

Giant – see Sleeping Giant

Giffin, Liam 205p

Giroux, Glenda, Luke and Norm 243p

Glennie twins 100

Gordon Graham Gallery and Theatre 33, 34p, 50, 62, 66, 73, 89, 140, 171, 305

Gould, Doug 106

Graham Family Collection 59

Graham, Gordon – lightkeeper 17, 21, 23, 31, 33, 35, 56, 57, 59, 61, 89, 104, 116, 131, 153, 155, 235, 263, 300, 321

Graham, Eve 33, 59, 59p, 89, 104, 105p, 116, 118, 153, 177, 188, 189, 225, 300, 321

Graham, Kevin 57, 59, 177, 189, 290, 300, 301
    Sandy 124p

Gray Marine engine 130, 301

Great Getaway radio contest 19, 20p

Great Lakes Cruising Club 199, 287

Great Lakes Forest Products 130

Great Lakes Foundation 186

Great Lakes Guardian Community Fund 26, 45, 97

Great Trail network 51, 53, 64, 65, 66, 68

Grebe – shipwreck 52, 123

Gross, Brontë 121, 122p

Guerrero, Rebecca 251p

– H –

Hajdu, MP Patty 155, 206, 238

Halonen, Jorma 274p

Hamilton, Kennedy 175, 180, 184, 186

Hammarskjold High School 86, 210, 220, 242, 249, 251, 254, 255, 263, 272p

Hansen, Bruce 111, 113p
    Sandy 111
    Svenja 205p
    Teagan 285p

Hansmeyer, Rose 223

Hardscrabble Island 93, 252, 278p, 324

Harper, Prime Minister Stephen 279

Harries, Tom 236

Harris, Naomi 97, 98, 98p

"Heartland," CBC series 59, 66, 196, 225

helicopter 15, 16p, 44, 57, 85, 93, 119, 218, 292, 293p, 300, 325p

helipad (heloport) 15, 16p, 62, 63, 86p, 93, 114, 115p, 217p, 218, 263, 282p, 312, 313p, 324, 325p, 332

Hens & Chicks 265

Hercules aircraft 298

Herglotz, Kelsey 144, 147p, 158p, 161

Heriandez, Cesar 90p

Heritage Lighthouse Protection Act 7, 28, 166, 168, 245

Heron, Wendy 90p

Heroux, Greg 72, 81

Heywood-MacLeod, Ben 83, 84p, 86c, 186

Hidalgo, Ale 216, 219, 220c

Hidora, wooden boat 166, 173, 175, 212, 273, 286, 291, 294, 301, 302, 304, 305, 308, 329p

Hintikka family 150, 152p

Hoard, Alina 182

Holmes, Bruce 243p

Holtz, Dustin 291p

Hoogsteen, Archie – see also Archie's Fishing Charters and Lighthouse Tours 20p, 45p, 53, 124p, 131, 170, 181, 189, 195, 197, 243, 243p, 291, 295

Hoogsteen, Corrine 243p
    Kelsey 237p

Hopkins, Frances Anne 97, 98

343

Hrabok, Dallas 44, 45p
    Melissa 44, 45p
Hunt, Emily 83, 84p
Hyer, MP Bruce 279

– I, J –

iNaturalist 161, 182
Isle Royale, Michigan 44, 76, 190, 204, 246, 249, 252, 298, 330
Istiefson, Shelly 124p
Ives, Kristin 78, 79p

J.A. McKee – ship 14
James Whalen – ship 119, 197, 218, 276, 287
Jefford, Katelyn 105, 105p, 109p, 120, 120p, 259, 261
Jellema family 190, 191p, 193p
Jensen, Curtis 174p
Johnson, Brenda 251p, 254p
    Charlie 243p

– K –

Kaministiquia River 130, 155, 163
Kasper Transportation 190, 192
Kawagha-mish 138, 144, 150, 152
Keetch, John 270, 271p
Keg restaruant 162
Khanlauian, Kief 325p
Kilpatric, Kim 107p
Kim family 120, 233
Kim, Sean 115
King Edward VII (as Prince of Wales) 48
King George V 48

"King of Kensington" television series 192
King, Ti 243p
Knockaert, Ravin 185
Koeppen, Charleen 132, 133
Koivu, Deb 154, 189
Kornell, Denise 146, 148
    Mike, 146
Kruzins, Zack 89, 90p

– L –

Labour Day 121, 326
Lagre, Anna 90p
Lake Superior Circle Tour 331
Lake Superior islands (archipelago) 118, 252, 265
Lake Superior magazine 40
Lake Superior National Marine Conservation Area 26, 30, 57, 74, 205p, 236, 238, 258, 260p, 279, 287, 303, 307
Lake Superior Watershed Conservancy 297
Lake Superior Water Trail – see also TransCanada Trail 17, 53, 64, 66, 297
Lakehead Amateur Radio Society 184, 185
Lakehead Beer Company 243, 245, 247, 251, 254, 275p, 283, 288, 291, 294, 308, 332
Lakehead Motors 254
Lakehead Nurse Practitioner-Led Clinic 250
Lakehead Technical Diving 44
Lakehead Transportation Museum Society – see also Transportation Museum of Thunder Bay 217, 238, 246
Lakehead University 10, 29, 36, 204, 244
Lamb Island Lighthouse 78, 83
Lanfranco, Katerina 325
Langille, Timothy 229
Lavender family 312

INDEX

Lawson, Jennifer 237p

Le Champlain – cruise ship 330

LED light 196, 209

Leduc family 93

Lem, Robert 156p

Lester, Susan 180, 181p

Leverty, Robert 80

Lightfoot, Gordon 137

Lighthouse Carnival 149, 152, 153, 155, 156p, 187, 189p, 190, 191p, 192, 193p, 199, 209, 214, 215, 215p, 216, 243, 257, 259, 261, 262p, 263, 266p, 315, 318, 320, 320p, 321, 322p, 331, 332

Lighthouse Trail 66, 150

Lighthouse Trail Discovery Tour 298, 302

Lighthouse Trail film 130

Little Havana 54p

Logan, Rob 110

Loon Harbour 100, 121

loons, common 128, 180, 208, 237, 273, 330

Lorne Allard Fisherman's park 66

Luckai, Phil 267, 269p

Luhrsen, Michael 100

Lumina, Dawn 251

Luomala, Dawn and Paul 254p

Lynch, Elaine 95, 189

– M –

MacAskill, Lorna 243p
        Scott 243p

Macfarlane, Thomas 151

Mackenzie, Gordon and Karin 212, 213, 214, 257, 258p, 282, 314

MacLean family 223

Magic 99.9 – radio station 19, 20p, 44

Magnet Point 273

Makin, Darrell 57, 118

Malenfant Alec 121, 122p

Mallon family 93

Marathon, Ontario 130, 252

Marks, Philip 325p

Martin, Frank and Renee 243p

McBrien, Marlene 205p

McDonald, Craig 219

McGoldrick, Curnis 115p

McGonagle, Dennis 53, 54, 54p, 55

McGuffin, Gary and Joanie 54, 297

McIntosh, Pete 10, 11c, 12, 16c, 18, 18c, 20c

Mckay Drive 60, 61p, 253

McKay family 21, 36, 52, 58, 60, 131, 208, 214

McKay, Fran 326
        Gloria 123

Mckay Family Collection 14c, 36c, 99c, 119c, back cover photo (c)

McKay - lightkeepers
    Bill (William) 36, 148, 203
    Bob (Robert) 15, 35, 36, 52, 60, 119, 123
    Charles 36, 36p
    Clifford 23, 52, 60, 326
    Ed 13, 14, 23, 36

McKay's Harbour (Rossport) 36

McLean, Roy – lightkeeper 21, 23

McLeod family 93

McMillan, Doug and Harriet 243p

McNeice, Allan 296, 299, 300, 308

Meingast, Carolyn and Wolf 107p

Merritt, Brian 132, 134p, 135p
    Charleen 118, 132, 134p, 135p
    Charles – lightkeeper 20, 23, 118, 132, 134p, 135, 268, 269p
    Dorothy 132

Merritt family   20, 21, 58, 118, 131, 132, 133, 135, 147, 218

Merritt Family Collection   134c, 135c

Métis Nation   35, 337

Michipicoten – ship   298

mid-continental rift   245, 252, 285p, 322p, 324

Midland, Ontario   159

Milky Way   228p

Miller, Vic   42, 112

Ministry of Natural Resources and Forestry, Ontario   57, 68

Mitchell, Bill and Karen   20p

Mol, Margaret   106, 108, 109p, 192, 309

Mölkky – game   232

Montreal Mining Company   151

monarch butterfly – see butterflies

moose   93, 111p, 161, 177, 216, 283, 290

Morralee, David   230c, 271p, 272c

Morralee, John   2

Morralee, Paul   3, 8, 43p, 63, 79p, 86p, 113p, 130, 130c, 200p, 205p, 230p, 271p, 281p, 308p, 315p, 321, 329p

Morralee, Steven   271p

Mosquito Express   324

Mount McKay   36

– N –

Nadeau, Jayda   145p

Nardo, Viviana   243p

Naturally Superior Adventures   73, 74, 106, 174, 175, 184, 221, 286

Nault, Cynthia   85, 86, 87, 88p

Nina – wooden boat   26, 76, 110, 116, 128, 129p, 130, 130p, 161, 162, 163, 233, 267, 274

Nipigon, Ontario   94, 252

Nipigon Straits   42, 213, 282

No.10 Lighthouse – see also Number 10 Island, and Shaganash Lighthouse   7, 26, 28, 42, 50, 78, 107p, 184, 196, 199, 245, 247, 248, 249p, 264, 264p, 269p, 271p, 291, 297, 305, 313, 314, 330, 332, 336

Nokomis – CCG ship   60, 118, 119p, 197

Nolast, Joelle   213p

Noman, Juzer   43

North Channel   42, 106, 184, 196, 245, 264

North Star – ship   52

Northern Focus Photography Club   33

Northern Lights   231, 232p, 319

Northern Ontario Heritage Fund   328

Northern Wilds magazine   288

Northland College   121

Northwest Heli-Tours and Adventures   85, 108

NorWest Community Health Centres   237, 237p

Number 10 Island – see also No.10 Lighthouse   8, 26, 27p, 28, 28p, 42, 43p, 54, 86, 106, 168, 182, 185, 245, 264, 267, 314

Nuttall, Lois   37, 38, 40, 50

– O –

OceanBridge - Direct Action   144, 146, 148, 153, 154p, 156, 157, 160, 161

Old Man's Beard (*Usnea florida*) – lichen   81, 252, 259, 265, 303

Oldale, Rick   245, 247, 248, 249p

Olson, Jon   130

Ongaro, John   33, 189

Ontario Historical Society (OHS)   7, 78, 79, 79p, 80

Ontario History Press   2, 3

Ontario Parks   179, 238, 260, 287

Ontario Superior Country   331

Ornge Air Ambulance   218, 324, 325p, 332

INDEX

Otterman, Helen 162

Ouellette, Aleia 175, 180

outhouses 26, 42, 88, 138, 253, 255, 262, 270, 271p, 273, 286, 314, 332

Outward Bound – *see Voyageur Outward Bound School*

Oxford School, Woodstock, Ontario 207p, 244, 245p

– P –

Painting Superior program 250, 251, 279, 313, 315, 318, 320, 321, 323p, 331, 332

Palermo-White, Lucy 243p

Palko, Gail 231

Parks Canada 26, 74, 81, 97, 129, 168, 186, 199, 204, 205p, 236, 250, 251, 254, 256, 260, 279, 283, 287, 303, 307, 313, 315, 318, 320, 321, 323p, 332

Passage Island 44, 184, 204, 223, 298

Passos, Josue 19

Paterson, Alexander 15

Paterson Foundation 72, 85, 97, 236

Paterson Sauna 106, 290, 320

Paterson ships 14, 257

Paterson Steamship Company 14, 290

Pays Plat, Ontario 36

Peggy's Point Lighthouse, Nova Scotia 233, 246, 300

Pendziwol, Jean 66, 77, 108, 123, 215, 216, 219

Perry Bay 280

people-mover 303, 304p, 305, 306, 307, 314

Perzan, Rachel 222p

Petersen, Arthur and Peggy 44, 45p

Pettigrew, Carl 189

Pie Island 42, 59, 144, 152, 195p, 221, 328

Pilon, April 237p

Piper, William 194

Pipes and Drums of Thunder Bay 217

Por phyry Reef 14p, 48, 190, 195

Porphyry beer 275, 283, 288

Porphyry boathouse 17, 198, 296p

Porphyry Harbour 19, 39p, 42, 51p, 52, 52p, 55, 82p, 91, 94p, 95, 111p, 113p, 128, 129p, 173, 213p, 232p, 290, 299p, 302, 304, 329p

Porphyry poem 106

Porphyry swamp 92, 93, 181, 216

Port Arthur 14, 119, 276, 302

Port of Thunder 254

Portelance, Bonnie and David 243p

Post family 15, 186

Postenka, Hilda 243p

Poulin, Cindy 124p

Pratt, Bea and Jerald 114

Primavesi, Lisa 124p

Prince Arthur Hotel 44, 162, 296, 299

Prince Arthur's Landing 48, 75, 248

Prince of Wales 48

Pringle Bay 56

Psenicnik, Keanu 226p

Puff the dog 40, 41p

Pulkki, Kristina 275p

– Q, R –

Queen Elizabeth II, death 233

Queen Elizabeth cake 281

Queen's coronation 281

Radbourne, Betty 243p

Radforth, Ian 79p

Ranta, Lissi 29, 30p, 43p, front cover photo (c)
  Justin 123, 124p

Rasmussen, Peter and Peter 145p
RCMP – see Royal Canadian Mounted Police
Read, Emily 216, 219, 220p
Red Chairs, Parks Canada 32, 283
Reinikka, Marsha 83
Renco's Foods 118
Rescue – ship 48
rift system – see mid-continental rift
Ringham, Arlo, Bill and Nancy 281, 281p
Robertson, Maureen 233, 234p, 235
Robin Hood flour 13, 14
Rooney, Paul 243, 243p
Rosenthal, Julie 204, 205c 206, 247p
Ross, Annie 204, 205p, 213p, 225, 226p, 238, 244
    Donald – lightkeeper 21, 23, 58
Rossport, Ontario 36, 145, 184, 252, 303
Royal Canadian Mounted Police (RCMP) 93, 169
Rum Bottle Bay 118, 135, 268

– S –

Sail Superior 72, 105, 199, 244, 276, 278p, 286, 298, 302, 304, 332
Salo, Jenn 185
S.A.N.D. Adventures – see Such A Nice Day Adventures
Sandford, Christine and Chuck 121, 222
Santarossa, Anne 243p
Sardine wood stove 305
Sargent family 93
Sault Ste. Marie, Ontario 245, 297
sauna 8, 72, 73p, 74, 76, 77, 81, 84p, 85, 89, 91, 93, 97, 105, 106, 114, 116, 128, 131, 166, 173, 182, 229, 231, 236, 253, 259, 269p, 290, 297, 305, 317, 320, 328
Saunders family 78

Save Ontario Shipwrecks (SOS) 54, 55, 57, 73, 88
Save Our Lighthouses 3
Savinainen-Mountain, Kaija 93, 95
Saxifraga 265
Sayed, Hafi 205p
Scarcello, Bob 248
Schritmeyer, Jim 107p
Schroede, Cathy 243p
Schulz, Wayne 174p
Science North 250, 287
Scotiadoc – ship 135, 135p, 197, 248
Scotland 48
Scott van Teeffelen Band – see also van Teeffelen, Scott 153, 155, 156p, 187, 190, 192, 209, 217, 260, 321
Sea Doo 100
Sea Lion rock 224
sea-glass 52, 57, 135, 142, 153, 154p, 179, 207, 207p, 211, 226p, 244, 250, 257, 271, 278p, 280, 283
Seguin, Marc 2, 3c, 28, 168c, 235
    Marjorie 2
Shaganash Channel 28
Shaganash Island 264
Shaganash Lighthhouse – see also No.10 Lighthouse 7, 26, 27p, 28, 28p, 42, 43p, 50, 78, 86, 106, 168p, 184, 196, 245, 248, 264, 264p, 267, 271, 291, 314, 332, 336
Shaminitou 252
Shaw, Graeme 158p
shipwrecks 59, 88, 135, 245, 247, 248, 249p, 295, 309
Shron, Rorik 182, 183p, 188
Sibley, Alexander 151
Sibley Peninsula 151, 188, 235, 321
Siciliano, Todd 148, 149p
Silver Islet 10, 53, 57, 85, 93, 130, 131, 146, 150, 151, 153, 155, 157, 166, 167, 198, 202, 219, 223, 224, 252, 293, 328

INDEX

Silver Islet Campers Association 8, 200, 292

Silver Islet General Store 150, 171, 194, 200, 202, 294p,

Silver Islet Harbour Association 8, 131, 171, 173, 194, 200, 238, 260, 292

Silver Islet Mine 151, 151p, 197, 219, 256, 257, 309

Silver Islet Mining Company 151

Silver Islet Yacht Club 8, 64, 65, 73, 95, 106, 119p, 125, 292

Sinclair, Michelle 258

Singh brothers, Amrik, Sartaj and Xammy 85, 86p

Singh, Gangandeep 174p

Sirkka Creagh Memorial Fund 35

Sleeping Giant 10, 11, 12, 15, 32, 42, 57, 63p, 65p, 85, 87, 91, 107, 110, 116, 124, 128, 137, 140, 144, 152, 200p, 206, 211, 221, 249, 259, 270, 276, 312, 321, 324, 326, 328, 336

Sleeping Giant Provincial Park 65, 148, 153, 270, 287

Sloan, Matthew 63, 68

Smart, Penelope 227

Smith, David 243p

Solmes, helen 110, 112, 114

St. Andrews – ship 247

St. Claire, Andrew 243, 243p

St. John, Karen 309

Starlink 295

Starr, Jan 182

Strong Seniors Fitness Group 181p

Such A Nice Day (S.A.N.D.) Adventures 89, 146, 184, 286, 314, 316p

Sukhoverkhova, Anna 174p

Suki the cat 275p

Sulston, Paula 182, 183p, 188

SUNORA (SUperior NOrth-shore RegattA) 12, 34, 35, 37p, 58, 60, 90, 91, 112, 146, 184, 199, 221, 260, 263, 317, 332

Superior Collegiate and Vocational Institute 86

Superior Rocket – Zodiac 72, 79, 81, 82p, 83, 91, 105, 114, 134, 144, 146, 162, 278, 314

Superior Shores Gaming Association 121, 199

SVDcompany 248

Swatton, captain 244

Szymaniak, Sarah 121

– T –

Tator, Aaron 275p

Tbaycation contest 162

Tee Harbour 65, 162

Terrace Bay, Ontario 330

Theano – ship 59, 235, 246, 309

Thompson Island 162

Thordoc – ship 13, 14, 14p, 105, 184, 197, 257

Thunder Bay, city – see also Thunder Bay water body 1, 2, 8, 14, 36, 48, 66, 75, 100, 118, 119, 131p, 135, 137, 144, 150, 153, 181, 242, 263, 290, 299

Thunder Bay Coast Guard Base (SAR) 59, 118, 238

Thunder Bay Community Foundation 238

Thunder Bay Hiking Association 180, 242, 243, 286, 292, 295, 297, 300

Thunder Bay Main Lighthouse kiosk 210, 220, 248

Thunder Bay Main lighthouse (on the breakwater) 336

Thunder Bay Marina 134, 304, 321

Thunder Bay Museum 48, 59, 133, 194, 283, 287, 288, 308, 333

Thunder Bay, Pipes and Drums 217

Thunder Bay, Port 76, 217, 254

Thunder Bay Railway Historical Society 248

Thunder Bay Raptor Rescue 185

Thunder Bay Salmon Association 85

Thunder Bay, Tourism – see Tourism Thunder Bay

Thunder Bay Trails Associatiion 332

Thunder Bay, Transportation Museum – see Lakehead Transportation Museum Society, and Transportation Museum of Thunder Bay

Thunder Bay Tug Services 253, 287

Thunder Bay, water body – see also Thunder Bay city 50, 59, 85, 129, 135, 137, 155, 196, 223, 233, 246, 258

Thunder Bay Yacht Club 11, 12, 13p, 17, 26, 33, 35, 39, 41, 53, 65, 68, 72, 73, 76, 97, 106, 112, 130, 146, 162, 199, 206, 215, 219, 221, 233, 238, 243, 247, 251, 263, 279, 283, 286, 288, 291, 321, 332

Thunder Cape 14

Thunder Oak cheese 232

Tourism Ontario 13

Tourism Thunder Bay 162, 229, 238

TransCanada Trail 17, 51, 64, 66, 68, 242, 296, 297

Transportation Museum of Thunder Bay – see also Lakehead Transportation Museum Society 217, 246, 248, 250, 287

Trist, Darcy and Thomas 305

Trowbridge beer 291, 308, 332

Trowbridge, Charles 151, 309

Trowbridge Island 42, 44, 59, 76, 97, 107, 120p, 135p, 235, 235p, 246, 260p, 279, 299, 300, 309, 319, 330, 336

Trowbridge Island Lighthouse 7, 30, 42, 50, 59, 65, 76, 77p, 78, 85, 86p, 87, 106, 135, 150, 167, 184, 194, 196, 199, 223, 233, 234p, 235, 235p, 247p, 248, 260p, 280, 288, 291, 294, 296, 299, 300, 301p, 302p, 307, 308, 310p, 311p, 317, 322, 332, 336

Tug o' the North 290, 291

Tulip Festival 130p

Turcsanyi, Sandor 105, 105p, 113p, 120, 120p

Turk, Lucy 186, 187p

Turner, Gerri 107, 136

Turpin family 58, 58p

Turtle Head 42, 144, 152, 195p, 221, 328

Two Harbors, Minnesota 298

Tyson, Sylvia 66, 225

– U, V –

Urquhart, Fred 123

Van Breda, Erin 158p

Van Dellen family 267
    Beth-Anna 118
    Hudson 269p

van Teeffelen, James 156p
    Scott 156p, 313, 320
    Tanner 156p

Vanderheide, Maya 105p, 109p, 113p, 117, 120, 120p

Vanderploeg, Bob 19

Vanderwees, Katrina 222p
    William 85, 112, 113, 154

Vantaa, Gerry and Marvin 274p

Vibert, Natalie 142, 143p

Viking Cruise Lines 202, 223, 231, 280

Viking Polaris – cruise ship 280

Voyageur Outward Bound School 15, 26, 40, 64, 68, 93, 94p, 250, 259, 286, 317, 318p, 332

– W, X, Y, Z –

Wabasse, Donny 2, 60, 63c, 65c, 67c, 75c, 77c, 82c, 94c, 101c, 105p, 109c, 111c, 112, 113c, 122, 125, 126c, 131, 132p, 159, 160c, 169, 171, 172c, 176, 178c, 190, 200c, 239p, 259, 281, 286

Wabinski, Kasper 174, 174p

Wade, Susan 2

Walberg, Barb 121
    Lena 118
    Lloyd 118

Walberg's store 118

Walkers Channel 30, 56, 95, 179, 252

Walleye magazine 288

Waxman, Adam 192, 193
    Al 192

Waytowich, Trevor   205

Welcome Island   304

Wells, David   74

Whalen, James   119
– see also *James Whalen*, ship

Whelan, Diane ("500 Days in the Wild")   64, 65p

White, Gerry   243p

white birch   179, 265

Wilcox, Bruce   281p

Williams, Heather   243p

Williamson, Jeff   243p

Wilson, Chris   62

Wisk Air Helicopters   15, 16p, 44

Wiskemann, Mark   15

Youth Rangers,
    Ministry of Natural Resources and Forestry   68
    Stewardship   57

Zatti, Raija   243p, 325

Zodiac RIB vessel   81

ONTARIO HISTORY
PRESS

www.ingramcontent.com/pod-product-compliance
Lightning Source LLC
Chambersburg PA
CBHW080322080526

44585CB00021B/2434